大学英语立体化网络化系列教材·拓展课程教材

美国短篇小说与电影
The American Short Story Through Film

马乃强 编

图书在版编目（CIP）数据

美国短篇小说与电影/马乃强编. —北京：北京大学出版社，2016.8
（大学英语立体化网络化系列教材. 拓展课程教材）
ISBN 978-7-301-27482-8

Ⅰ.①美… Ⅱ.①马… Ⅲ.①英语—阅读教学—高等学校—教材 ②短篇小说—文学欣赏—美国 ③电影评论—美国　Ⅳ.① H319.4:I ② H319.4:J

中国版本图书馆CIP数据核字（2016）第212866号

书　　名	美国短篇小说与电影
	MEIGUO DUANPIAN XIAOSHUO YU DIANYING
著作责任者	马乃强　编
责任编辑	黄瑞明
标准书号	ISBN 978-7-301-27482-8
出版发行	北京大学出版社
地　　址	北京市海淀区成府路205号　100871
网　　址	http://www.pup.cn　　新浪微博:@北京大学出版社
电子信箱	zpup@pup.cn
电　　话	邮购部 62752015　发行部 62750672　编辑部 62754382
印 刷 者	三河市博文印刷有限公司
经 销 者	新华书店
	787毫米×1092毫米　16开本　16.75印张　350千字
	2016年8月第1版　2016年8月第1次印刷
定　　价	49.00元

未经许可，不得以任何方式复制或抄袭本书之部分或全部内容。
版权所有，侵权必究
举报电话：010-62752024　电子信箱：fd@pup.pku.edu.cn
图书如有印装质量问题，请与出版部联系，电话：010-62756370

Introduction

The advances in Information Technology have greatly changed the practice of language teaching. We used to teach language with texts in print, and now multimedia, the integration of sound, text, graphics, and video, is enriching our instruction. Yet, the introduction of multimedia is not to help students learn how to liberate themselves from the printed texts. Rather, the broader goal is to cultivate systematic methods of inquiry, models of critique, and analytical ways of reading visual images and messages in both print and media texts. Media are the important teaching tool, but the current language teaching further requires teaching with as well as teaching about multimedia.

1. A Rationale for Teaching Literature in ELT

The teaching of language and literature is inseparable. There has been controversy on the place of literature in language teaching. The controversy, however, centers not on if literature should be used, but always on how it should be used. The opponents often argue about when and where to use literary works, but literature takes varied forms in ELT classroom, and its significance has never been ignored.

Literature has great cultural value. Besides language instruction, the students of English also require an orientation to the target culture. The world of literature provides abundant cultural insights and experiences for language students. When reading literature from the foreign culture, we would encounter different cultural barriers and problems. With their exposition and solution, we could develop the communication across cultures, and this will improve our cultural awareness.

Literature has important linguistic value. Literature in English could be called English at its best. There are rich resources of language in literary works, which are most fully and skillfully used. The literary language could help to elaborate vocabulary and syntax, grammar and context. It is also a teaching aid for all language skills, including listening and writing. And moreover, we, as students, could learn many communicative skills through various characters that English literature displays.

Literature also has much educational value. We integrate the study of literary work into teaching English, and this demands that English literature should contribute to language instruction. Literature actually does more than that. With the appreciation and enjoyment from literature, it refines our language skills, and further stimulates us toward more advanced discussion and knowledge. Learning from classic literary characters, we could even make our own personal growth.

Considering the linguistic level of college students, the exclusive use of literature in English language teaching is hard to achieve, and not necessary, either. Yet, English literature is an available and also valuable resource for our language instruction. J. F. Povey comments on the place of literature in classroom, "Literature gives evidence of the widest variety of syntax, the richest variations of vocabulary discrimination. It provides examples of the language employed at its most effective, subtle, and suggestive. As literature sets out the potential of the English language it serves as an encouragement, guide, target to the presently limited linguistic achievement of the foreign student."[1] Fully understanding the significance of literature in language arts, we could say that the integration of literature with English teaching is both feasible and inevitable.

2. A Rationale for Using Multimedia in ELT

Multimedia means the combined use of several mass media, especially for the purpose of education or entertainment. It integrates sound, text, graphics, and video, and interacting with computer technology, multimedia invades into almost every corner of our society. Apart from the entertaining function, multimedia still "provides continuous education throughout our life, offering a popular day and night school for the nation."[2] For many educators, multimedia is only for entertainment, not worth for serious study. However, we have to realize that the students nowadays are barraged with multimedia and technique advances. Facing this challenge, we are to provide students with media skills for today and tomorrow, and that forms a rationale for using multimedia in classroom, especially of language arts. English language teaching intends to improve students' potential, so it has no reason to refuse using multimedia.

With the development of information technology, the introduction of multimedia into curriculum expands the notion of school literacy, which used to be principally the ability to read printed texts. Following traditional communication skills, the students are likely to fall into rote memorization. We know that many students of English try to learn the language through only memorizing vocabulary list, but often in vain. Media education stimulates critical thinking and analytical reading of students, and therefore, the school literacy today should also include the critical reading of media texts. The media literacy could help students comprehend and communicate through both traditional and emerging skills of information exchange.

Actually, multimedia is not strange to English language teaching from the very beginning.

---

[1] Povey, J. F. "The Teaching of Literature in Advanced ESL Classes." In L. McIntosh & M. Celce-Murcia, Eds. *Teaching English as a Second or Foreign Language.* Rowley: Newbury House, 1979, pp. 162–186.

[2] Semali, Ladislaus M. *Literacy in Multimedia America: Integrating Media Education across the Curriculum.* New York: Falmer Press, 2000, p. 13.

Introduction

The audiovisual materials have long accompanied the teaching of English listening, such as tapes, videos, and in recent years, computer courseware. Yet, most teachers use media only as a teaching tool, namely as audiovisuals to illustrate instruction or even as entertainment to compensate students' hard work. This is far from satisfactory, and we should further teach about media as a source of information, messages and texts. Semali believes that the real expansion of school literacy will "require teaching with as well as teaching about television, computers, video, and film,"① and only in this way could the students really become media literate.

The introduction of multimedia into language classroom does not mean exclusion of texts in print. Like the place of literature in English language teaching, the exclusive use of multimedia materials is not practical, either. Since they both function well in enriching language instruction, we are to integrate literature and multimedia into teaching English. The students would acquire systematic knowledge about analytical reading and critical thinking from the printed texts and media texts, to be specific, from the short story and video film.

3. Teaching Short Story in ELT Classroom

English literature is an available and valuable resource for teaching the language, and now the problem is how to select and prepare literary works for classroom instruction. When teaching foreign literature, we mainly worry about the linguistic and cultural barriers between literary texts and students. Still, most teachers don't favor the abridged or simplified versions, because they simply have no place in literature anthology. The students do not have to understand everything they read, as the failure in some difficult structures usually does not prevent general comprehension. Thus, English language teaching demands literature in completeness. Literature is classified in genres, such as poetry, novel, play, essay, and short story, among which short story is the most approachable and satisfying literary form for College English teaching.

Short story is relatively brief. By the classic definition of Edgar Allan Poe, a short story must be short enough to be read at one sitting.② The contemporary short story most often refers to a work of fiction no longer than 20,000 words and no shorter than 1,000. So, short stories are short enough to maintain students' interest within class, although they also vary in length. The length fits well our teaching unit, and it makes the students' reading task and teachers' coverage both easier.

Short story is complete. Allan Poe defines that short story must have a unified plot about a single protagonist, and it must aim at producing a single effect within the complete work.③ Short

---

① Semali, Ladislaus M. *Literacy in Multimedia America: Integrating Media Education across the Curriculum*. New York: Falmer Press, 2000, p. 22.

② Poe, Edgar Allan. "Nathaniel Hawthorne." In G. R. Thompson, Ed. *The Selected Writings of Edgar Allan Poe*. New York: Norton, 2004, pp. 643–647.

③ Ibid.

story has a beginning to initiate the main action, a middle to presume what has gone before and require something to follow, and an ending to finish the plot. The simple beginning-middle-ending structure could illustrate completeness of literature. Actually, the structure of short story is more complicated, like this classic five-part scheme: "the first stage presents the conflict or problem to be solved; the second stage complicates that conflict; the third stage brings it to climax; the fourth explores the implications of choice at the climax; and the fifth presents the resolution."[①] Reading a short story, we could experience a complete literary piece rather than some key passages, chapters, or episodes of long works.

Short story is universal. It represents different English-speaking world, and it could further cross the limitation of age, sex, class and even nation. The universal themes of short story are to involve the readers rapidly, making an immediate impact and a single impression. Although outside the target culture, the students possibly have some similar experiences in life, and they could relate to the tales in front. Focused and memorable, short story serves as an essential part of the language and cultural experience available to the students of English.

These are the benefits of teaching short story, which grant this literary form a safe place in English language curriculum. The inclusion of short fiction does not expel the potential of poetry, novel or play, but comparing advantages (varied literary genres and writing characteristics) and disadvantages (poetry is often very abstract, while novel or play is too long), short story is still the most approachable and satisfying. The remaining question is how to integrate selected tales into English classroom. The teaching of short story requires the active participation of students, but the teachers' elaborate instruction is the same important.

When teaching short story, the focus must be on the text of tales. Considering the linguistic and cultural barriers facing the students, it is necessary to provide some background knowledge before approaching difficult vocabulary and allusion. Text notes could always help, but the information should be related enough not to distract attention or cause confusion. Additional cultural questions are to be cleared up whenever they arise. The preview in class could also work, if not costing much time. Before coming to class for discussion, students are supposed to have read the short story. If possible, it is better to read twice, first a normal reading for general comprehension, and then a fast reading for the story line and basic relationships among characters. One possible assignment is to make plot summaries as preparation for class discussion. This summary exercise, as simple as who's-doing-what-where, does not guarantee, but does encourage the basic understanding of tales.

Only when students are ready to talk could those discussion questions function well, which are prepared elaborately and cast carefully. For fruitful discussion, literary terms are probably an annoying holdback. They should be defined in familiar language, and it is very likely to find some appropriate examples from stories we are reading. Of course, we don't have to be so

---

① Dunning, Stephen. *Teaching Literature to Adolescents.* Glenview: Scott, Foreman and Company, 1968, p. 133.

ambitious as to teach all literary terms through one or two tales. Naturally, we are not satisfied with the plot summaries or literary terms, because "our ultimate aim is extension of students' skills as readers rather than consolidation of their skills as readers of simple narrative."[1] To extend beyond the narrative level, students should learn how to read between the lines, from concrete examples to abstract ideas.

Very often, classroom discussion will not yield a true consensus. Within the range of rationality, every reader could have his own interpretation of the story. When students achieve enough literary taste, they start to read out the voice, scene, image, and angle from the printed text. Now they come close to the role of screenwriter or film director. The comparative study of short story and film could expand students' vision and further inspire their desire for advanced discussion.

4. Using Film in ELT Classroom

Literature comes into being with the appearance of human beings, but film has a much shorter history, a little more than a century. "On December 28, 1895, the Lumière brothers held one of the first public showing of motion picture projected on a screen, at the Grand Café in Paris,"[2] and film critics usually agree that this date signifies the birth of movie industry. Yet, film is a medium of ever-increasing popularity, and nowadays it is attracting billions of audience every year. By and large people go to the movies for the same reason they read literature: to lose themselves in a good story. Only the nature of film is an artistic form of collaboration, and it tells a story by integrating language, costumes, makeup, music, sound effects, color, light, locations, and visual images. For many teachers, it seems that reading is considered a highbrow activity, while movies are for the mass. This preference for literature over film is not necessarily correct, for in the past century, film writers, directors, and actors have produced many profound and lasting works of no less artistic value. Besides, the movies illustrate the language spoken in diverse context by native speakers and provide richly detailed cultural information. Thus, we could contend that literature and film both have a deserved place in language teaching. As we ask our students to be active readers of literature, we also challenge them to become active viewers of film, so that they could achieve both verbal and visual literacy.

Most students have positive experience of watching film, and they will not refuse the appearance of movies in English class. We are not to show films, but to teach films, teaching with as well as teaching about film. After reading a literary work, we could give a movie version as an extension or comparison, since most film adaptation is an act of effective interpretation. Film viewing imparts pleasure and always generates fruitful discussion, but teaching film language would bring more benefits. Previously, when watching movies, we focus our attention on story

---

[1] Dunning, Stephen. *Teaching Literature to Adolescents*. Glenview: Scott, Foreman and Company, 1968, p. 20.
[2] Bordwell, David & Kristin Thompson. *Film Art: An Introduction* (7th edition). New York: McGraw-Hill, 2004, p. 466.

lines, plot conventions, and popular actors. If we favor some particular movie, we mainly like its plot or characters. This is a superficial viewing. Like fiction, film has plot, character, setting, theme, and point of view. Like play, film has actors, costumes, makeup, locations, and director. We could say that film shares a lot with literature on literary and dramatic aspects. But after all, film is another medium, and it has basic difference from printed texts. It relies on the visual image combined with spoken word, so movie has its own special language.

We are not familiar with the cinematic aspects of a film, but they are hard to skip when teaching about movies. The introduction of film language becomes necessary, and this includes technical terms that describe cinematography, sound, editing, and special visual effects. Similar to teaching literary terms, we are to define and give examples of various shots, editing techniques, and sound sources. This will facilitate our discussion and enrich our viewing. Teasley & Wilder state that studying film language could "make explicit the techniques for telling a story visually, heighten our appreciation for the art of film, and increase our awareness of how subtle cues can shade meaning."[1] We cannot agree more, and only with the mastery of film language could we begin to see and hear things that have been invisible and inaudible before.

The film adaptation of literary works has a long history, and novels, plays, and even poems have been adapted into movies. No matter how hard it tries, a film cannot exactly represent its literary source, mainly because of the difference between printed text and media text. The most we can expect of a film adaptation is that it is relatively faithful to the original work and still a good film. When adapting a novel or a play, we have to compress events and simplify characters to suit the running time and match the taste of common audience, so it is easy to invite criticism. Harrison cites Béla Balázs, one of the first film theorists in adaptations, who goes to the extreme and says, "One may perhaps make a good film out of a bad novel, but never out of a good one."[2] His word proves the criticism for novel adaptation, but it seems that short story is exempted from this problem. According to Alfred Hitchcock, a film bears a closer similarity to a short story, because "they both sustain one idea that culminates when the action has reached the highest point of dramatic curve."[3] With this reassurance, we could integrate short story and film into our English teaching curriculum.

5. Selecting Short Story and Film for ELT

Short story is printed text, and film is media text, but English language teaching benefits from the combined reading of both texts. Short stories exist to be read, to be experienced, and to be interpreted, while adaptations extend, enhance, and elaborate on their sources. Film scripts start the process of adaptation and interpret the original texts, translating the stories from one me-

---

[1] Teasley, Alan B. & Ann Wilder. *Reel Conversations: Reading Films with Young Adults.* Portsmouth: Boynton / Cook Publishers, 1997, p. 26.

[2] Harrison, Stephanie, ed. *Adaptations: From Short Story to Big Screen.* New York: Three Rivers Press, 2005, p. xv.

[3] Aquino, John. *Film in the Language Arts Class.* Washington, D.C.: National Education Association, 1977, p. 16.

dium into another. Yet, film scripts are still words on pages, and they need another step of interpretation. When shooting films, the scripts are transmuted into visual images by directors, actors, cinematographers, designers, and other film craftspeople. The writing of a script and the making of a film, therefore, both require unfolding the original story, and "in the end the film is here and the story is there and one hopes there is a fruitful interaction."[1] As active readers and positive viewers, we experience different interpretative approaches when reading the story in print and watching the story in film. This mutual collaboration could improve our verbal and visual literacy, and hence students become more media literate.

Talking about literature in English, the amount of short stories is immense. We have the task to keep in front of students a few stories to represent those many fine ones. The Americans are said to have invented the short story, which has thrived in this country from the moment of its literary independence. American writers are "the first to define the short story as a specific literary form, different from the novel or the long narrative poem not only in length but also in kind."[2] Most great American novelists, from Nathaniel Hawthorne and Henry James in the 19th century to Ernest Hemingway and William Faulkner in the 20th century, have written great short stories. Many other American writers, such as Edgar Allan Poe, Sherwood Anderson, and Katherine Anne Porter, have especially excelled in writing short story with its own rules and values. The flourishing American magazines have been featuring in publishing short stories. With the invasive development of radio, television, and film, they only fade out gradually in the second half of last century, but still far from disappearance. Recently, the successful film adaptation of the short story "Brokeback Mountain" proves its continuous popularity. This literary form demands the highest literary craft and still attracts many most talented writers. Thus, the heritage of American short story, reflecting the diversity of American experience, fully deserves our attention in the teaching of English language.

The amount of films adapted from short stories is the same huge. Carol Emmens' book *Short Stories on Film and Video* claims to include all the films produced between 1920 and 1984 that are based on the short stories by American authors or outstanding international authors well known in America. This book has approximately 1,375 entries. Surely many more movies have been adapted from short stories during the past thirty years. Some films have achieved more success than the original stories, such as Alfred Hitchcock's *Rear Window* (Cornell Woolrich's "It Had to Be Murder"), and Stanley Kubrick's *2001: A Space Odyssey* (Arthur Clarke's "The Sentinel"). Some others are successful on their own terms, even if receiving less acclaim than their sources, and here we have Robert Siodmak's *The Killers* (Ernest Hemingway's same title story) and Richard Brooks' *The Last Time I Saw Paris* (F. Scott Fitzgerald's "Babylon Revisited"). Still others have failed, not because they are unfaithful, but because they are not good films. (One obvious example is the recent version of *Scarlet Letter* starring Demi Moore, though it is

---

[1] Harrison, Stephanie, ed. *Adaptations: From Short Story to Big Screen*. New York: Three Rivers Press, 2005, p. xix.
[2] Skaggs, Calvin, ed. *The American Short Story*. New York: Dell Publishing, 1977, p. 11.

not based on a short story.) With American short story in our mind, we are to choose the corresponding and most appropriate movies for English language class.

The films adapted from short stories are not necessarily short, and the above-mentioned several movies all last about two hours. We have said that the potential use of novel or play in English teaching class is limited by its length, and the same problem confronts film using. With both story and film to discuss, it is not practical to spend two hours of class time only watching a movie. One solution is to use film clips to illustrate the whole movie, and many teachers have been doing this way, but this will definitely affect its completeness. Another approach is to choose short films. Many great short stories have been adapted into short films, such as Henry James' "The Real Thing," Charlotte Perkins Gilman's "The Yellow Wallpaper," and William Faulkner's "A Rose for Emily." The American Short Story series are among the best ever shot, and they have received much acclaim from critics and audience. Funded by National Endowment for the Humanities, Learning in Focus has been shooting this series from the late 1970s, which are shown on the influential American Public Broadcasting Service. It is a collection of some finest short stories covering a diverse range of topics by some of America's greatest authors such as Mark Twain, F. Scott Fitzgerald, Ernest Hemingway, and many others.

To illustrate the integration of literature and multimedia in ELT classroom, we are to give a sample of teaching short story through film. "Rappaccini's Daughter" (story: 1844; film: 1980), the most problematic but also the most characteristic of all of Hawthorne's tales, could provide us a model worksheet. The story explores two essential Hawthorne themes: the sin of interfering with another's soul and the futility of trying to tamper with nature, both relevant till today. Starring Kathleen Beller (the Academy Award nominee) and Kristopher Tabori, the film is written by Herbert Hartig and directed by Dezsö Magyar. Vividly reproducing its mysterious, ambiguous and symbolic world, the film adaptation is faithful to but not confined by Hawthorne's text. We read the story and watch the movie, enjoying both but not to decide which is better.

6. Model Worksheet for "Rappaccini's Daughter"

6.1 Preview
1. Introduce Nathaniel Hawthorne and his tales.
2. Point out linguistic barriers: Middle English usage and Italian words.

6.2 Plot Summary
1. Read the tale and sum up story plot: who's-doing-what-where pattern.
2. Think over discussion questions, and prepare for class discussion.

6.3 Story Discussion
1. Structure: Do you like and agree with the story's conclusion? If you were the author, how would you finish the tale?
2. Style: Do you think "Rappaccini's Daughter" is a gothic story, a feminist story, or an al-

legorical story? Please explain why.

3. Theme: How does Hawthorne explore the nature of good and evil in this story? What about the portraying of science?

4. Character: Is Beatrice an angelic figure, a seductive temptress, neither, something else? Analyze the relationships between Beatrice and three male characters, Giovanni, Doctor Rappaccini, and Professor Baglioni.

5. Symbol: Discuss and explain the symbolic meaning of the garden and the color purple. Can you find some other symbols in the story?

6. Setting: What effect does the post-medieval Italian setting have on the action and interpretation of the story?

6.4 Visual View

1. Sketch the garden image and the final scene of the story. What would compose the foreground and background? Please explain.

2. Watch the movie together and take notes for any interesting point.

6.5 Film Analysis

1. Introduce high angle shot and low angle shot with the sequence of Giovanni throwing the bouquet to Beatrice, from his window to her in the garden. Could you find some other shooting point of view, such as the reverse angle?

2. What do you think of the color, sound, and costume of the movie? Is it necessary to use a voiceover for Giovanni?

6.6 Integration of Story and Film

1. Does the film confirm or oppose against your impression from reading the story? Are you satisfied with the film?

2. Compare the different conclusions to the story and the film. Further talk about the addition (a servant to the landlady; the little restaurant; some friends of Giovanni) and omission (Professor Baglioni's final cry) when adapting a tale to film.

7. Beyond the Integration of Literature and Multimedia

The advances of information society demand more literate students, literate in both printed texts and media texts. The expansion of school literacy, therefore, extends the realm of our education and also challenges the traditional instruction. Teaching the English language with literature and multimedia is a possible tendency for future media education, and it could contribute a bit to cultivating the graduates of new ages. English, as a universal language, is not only a tool; neither is multimedia in our teaching practice. We are to master language skills, but we should not exclude the culture and literature of the target language. We teach the English language with the help of multimedia, and the teaching about media texts is equally necessary.

Up to today, the American Short Story series have released twenty-one films. Teachers of

the story-film courses could choose from, but of course not limited by this series. There are more and more choices with the flourishing of film and media industry. The collection *The American Short Story Through Film* here includes twelve filmed short stories, for one semester of College English teaching. With this book, we intend to teach the English language through the integration of both media. The teaching combines traditional fiction criticism and modern film study, and hence improves the students' cultural awareness, literary education, and school literacy. English language teaching benefits a lot from the development of information technology, and looking beyond, we would like to wait for its positive influence in every corner of our coming society.

Contents

Unit One Theme ··· **1**
   Chapter 1 Rappaccini's Daughter ································· 3
   Chapter 2 The Blue Hotel ·· 32

Unit Two Setting ··· **59**
   Chapter 3 Paul's Case ··· 61
   Chapter 4 Bernice Bobs Her Hair································· 85

Unit Three Point of View ·· **113**
   Chapter 5 I'm a Fool ·· 115
   Chapter 6 The Golden Honeymoon ···························· 130

Unit Four Character ·· **151**
   Chapter 7 Soldier's Home ··· 153
   Chapter 8 The Jilting of Granny Weatherall ················ 166

Unit Five Tone and Style ·· **181**
   Chapter 9 The Greatest Man in the World ·················· 183
   Chapter 10 Barn Burning ·· 197

Unit Six Symbol ··· **217**
   Chapter 11 Almos' a Man ··· 219
   Chapter 12 The Sky Is Gray ······································ 235

Appendix ··· **247**

References ·· **252**

Unit One
Theme

Chapter 1

Rappaccini's Daughter

Nathaniel Hawthorne

Author Introduction:

Nathaniel Hawthorne (1804—1864) was born in Salem, Massachusetts, into a prominent family who traced their lineage back to the Puritans. After graduating from Bowdoin College in 1825, Hawthorne returned to Salem to live a life of almost total seclusion for twelve years as he mastered his skills as a writer. Only when his first collections *Twice-Told Tales* (1837) made money did he feel secure enough to marry Sophia Peabody and settle in the Old Manse in Concord, Massachusetts. *The Scarlet Letter* (1850), his greatest novel of a woman taken into adultery, brought him recognition as a major literary figure, which was followed by three more novels, *The House of Seven Gables* (1851), a story tinged with nightmarish humor, *The Blithedale Romance* (1852), drawn from his short, disgruntled stay at a Utopian commune, Brook Farm, and *The Marble Faun* (1860), inspired by a short stay in Italy. In 1853 he was appointed consul to Liverpool by his college friend Franklin Pierce, who had become President of the United States. After four years of service in his post, Hawthorne traveled in England and Italy until his return to America in 1860. Much of his work is centered on New England and colored by romanticism, while the weight of his Puritan heritage, with its ethical biases and emphasis on sin, radically shaped his themes. His books of short stories are two volumes of *Twice-Told Tales* (1837 and 1842) and *Mosses from an Old Manse* (1846). Hawthorne wrote for children, too, retelling classic legends in *The Wonder Book* (1852) and *Tanglewood Tales* (1853).

Story Summary:

Young Giovanni comes to Padua to study. His apartment window overlooks a voluptuously beautiful garden which comforts him in his otherwise dismal surroundings and homesick state. The garden is cultivated by Dr. Rappaccini, a strange man of science who grows deadly plants for use in medicines. One day Giovanni sees Rappaccini's daughter tending the garden. Her bloom is as deep and vivid as the poisonous flowers in her care. But she has been nourished by the garden and her very breath and touch are deadly. Giovanni's love for her and fateful quest to free her begins. But he is unable to save his innocent mistress from her fate. His fears and mistrust ultimately destroy her.

Key Terms:
Allegory, Symbolism, Femme Fatale, Ethics, Feminism, Nineteenth Century Masculinity

Rappaccini's Daughter[1]

A young man, named Giovanni Guasconti, came, very long ago, from the more southern region of Italy, to pursue his studies at the University of Padua[2]. Giovanni, who had but a scanty supply of gold ducats[3] in his pocket, took lodgings in a high and gloomy chamber of an old edifice, which looked not unworthy to have been the palace of a Paduan noble, and which, in fact, exhibited over its entrance the armorial bearings of a family long since extinct. The young stranger, who was not unstudied in the great poem of his country, recollected that one of the ancestors of this family, and perhaps an occupant of this very mansion, had been pictured by Dante[4] as a partaker of the immortal agonies of his Inferno[5]. These reminiscences and associations, together with the tendency to heart-break natural to a young man for the first time out of his native sphere, caused Giovanni to sigh heavily, as he looked around the desolate and ill-furnished apartment.

"Holy Virgin, signor," cried old dame Lisabetta, who, won by the youth's remarkable beauty of person, was kindly endeavoring to give the chamber a habitable air, "what a sigh was that to come out of a young man's heart! Do you find this old mansion gloomy? For the love of heaven, then, put your head out of the window, and you will see as bright sunshine as you have left in Naples."

Guasconti mechanically did as the old woman advised, but could not quite agree with her that the Lombard[6] sunshine was as cheerful as that of southern Italy. Such as it was, however, it fell upon a garden beneath the window, and expended its fostering influences on a variety of

---

[1] First published in the *Democratic Review*, December 1844, then in *Mosses from an Old Manse*, 1846.
[2] City in northern Italy, near Venice.
[3] Italian coins.
[4] Italian poet, whose major work was *Divine Comedy*, an epic tale of the poet's journey through Hell, Purgatory, and Heaven.
[5] Hell in Dante's *Divine Comedy*. In *Inferno* 18:71, Dante observes an unnamed Paduan nobleman among those who have committed crimes against Nature.
[6] A member of a Germanic people that invaded northern Italy in the sixth century and established a kingdom in the Po River valley.

Unit One Theme
Chapter 1 Rappaccinni's Daughter

plants, which seemed to have been cultivated with exceeding care.

"Does this garden belong to the house?" asked Giovanni.

"Heaven forbid, signor!—unless it were fruitful of better pot-herbs than any that grow there now," answered old Lisabetta. "No; that garden is cultivated by the own hands of Signor Giacomo Rappaccini, the famous Doctor, who, I warrant him, has been heard of as far as Naples. It is said he distils these plants into medicines that are as potent as a charm. Oftentimes you may see the Signor Doctor at work, and perchance the Signora his daughter, too, gathering the strange flowers that grow in the garden."

The old woman had now done what she could for the aspect of the chamber, and, commending the young man to the protection of the saints, took her departure.

Giovanni still found no better occupation than to look down into the garden beneath his window. From its appearance, he judged it to be one of those botanic gardens, which were of earlier date in Padua than elsewhere in Italy, or in the world. Or, not improbably, it might once have been the pleasure-place of an opulent family; for there was the ruin of a marble fountain in the center, sculptured with rare art, but so woefully shattered that it was impossible to trace the original design from the chaos of remaining fragments. The water, however, continued to gush and sparkle into the sunbeams as cheerfully as ever. A little gurgling sound ascended to the young man's window, and made him feel as if a fountain were an immortal spirit, that sung its song unceasingly, and without heeding the vicissitudes[①] around it; while one century embodied it in marble, and another scattered the perishable garniture on the soil. All about the pool into which the water subsided, grew various plants, that seemed to require a plentiful supply of moisture for the nourishment of gigantic leaves, and, in some instances, flowers gorgeously magnificent. There was one shrub in particular, set in a marble vase in the midst of the pool, that bore a profusion of purple blossoms, each of which had the luster and richness of a gem; and the whole together made a show so resplendent that it seemed enough to illuminate the garden, even had there been no sunshine. Every portion of the soil was peopled with plants and herbs, which, if less beautiful, still bore tokens of assiduous care; as if all had their individual virtues, known to the scientific mind that fostered them. Some were placed in urns, rich with old carving, and others in common garden-pots; some crept serpent-like along the ground, or climbed on high, using whatever means of ascent was offered them. One plant had wreathed itself round a statue of Vertumnus[②], which was thus quite veiled and shrouded in a drapery of hanging foliage, so happily arranged that it might have served a sculptor for a study.

While Giovanni stood at the window, he heard a rustling behind a screen of leaves, and became aware that a person was at work in the garden. His figure soon emerged into view, and showed itself to be that of no common laborer, but a tall, emaciated, sallow, and sickly looking

---

① Changes.
② The Roman god of seasons. In Ovid's *Metamorphoses* 14, Vertumnus woos and wins the modest Pomona in her secluded garden.

man, dressed in a scholar's garb of black. He was beyond the middle term of life, with gray hair, a thin gray beard, and a face singularly marked with intellect and cultivation, but which could never, even in his more youthful days, have expressed much warmth of heart.

Nothing could exceed the intentness with which this scientific gardener examined every shrub which grew in his path; it seemed as if he was looking into their inmost nature, making observations in regard to their creative essence, and discovering why one leaf grew in this shape, and another in that, and wherefore such and such flowers differed among themselves in hue and perfume. Nevertheless, in spite of the deep intelligence on his part, there was no approach to intimacy between himself and these vegetable existences. On the contrary, he avoided their actual touch, or the direct inhaling of their odors, with a caution that impressed Giovanni most disagreeably; for the man's demeanor was that of one walking among malignant influences, such as savage beasts, or deadly snakes, or evil spirits, which, should he allow them one moment of license, would wreak upon him some terrible fatality. It was strangely frightful to the young man's imagination, to see this air of insecurity in a person cultivating a garden, that most simple and innocent of human toils, and which had been alike the joy and labor of the unfallen parents of the race.① Was this garden, then, the Eden of the present world?—and this man, with such a perception of harm in what his own hands caused to grow, was he the Adam?

The distrustful gardener, while plucking away the dead leaves or pruning the too luxuriant growth of the shrubs, defended his hands with a pair of thick gloves. Nor were these his only armor. When, in his walk through the garden, he came to the magnificent plant that hung its purple gems beside the marble fountain, he placed a kind of mask over his mouth and nostrils, as if all this beauty did but conceal a deadlier malice. But finding his task still too dangerous, he drew back, removed the mask, and called loudly, but in the infirm voice of a person affected with inward disease:

"Beatrice!—Beatrice!"

"Here am I, my father! What would you?" cried a rich and youthful voice from the window of the opposite house; a voice as rich as a tropical sunset, and which made Giovanni, though he knew not why, think of deep hues of purple or crimson, and of perfumes heavily delectable.— "Are you in the garden?"

"Yes, Beatrice," answered the gardener, "and I need your help."

Soon there emerged from under a sculptured portal the figure of a young girl, arrayed with as much richness of taste as the most splendid of the flowers, beautiful as the day, and with a bloom so deep and vivid that one shade more would have been too much. She looked redundant with life, health, and energy; all of which attributes were bound down and compressed, as it were, and girdled tensely, in their luxuriance, by her virgin zone②. Yet Giovanni's fancy must have grown morbid, while he looked down into the garden; for the impression which the fair

---

① Referring to Adam and Eve in the Garden of Eden.
② Her belt, the word "virgin" is used because Beatrice appears to be an unmarried girl.

Unit One Theme
Chapter 1 Rappaccinni's Daughter

stranger made upon him was as if here were another flower, the human sister of those vegetable ones, as beautiful as they—more beautiful than the richest of them—but still to be touched only with a glove, nor to be approached without a mask. As Beatrice came down the garden-path, it was observable that she handled and inhaled the odor of several of the plants, which her father had most sedulously① avoided.

"Here, Beatrice," said the latter, —"see how many needful offices require to be done to our chief treasure. Yet, shattered as I am, my life might pay the penalty of approaching it so closely as circumstances demand. Henceforth, I fear, this plant must be consigned to your sole charge."

"And gladly will I undertake it," cried again the rich tones of the young lady, as she bent towards the magnificent plant, and opened her arms as if to embrace it. "Yes, my sister, my splendor, it shall be Beatrice's task to nurse and serve thee; and thou shalt reward her with thy kisses and perfume breath, which to her is as the breath of life!"

Then, with all the tenderness in her manner that was so strikingly expressed in her words, she busied herself with such attentions as the plant seemed to require; and Giovanni, at his lofty window, rubbed his eyes, and almost doubted whether it were a girl tending her favorite flower, or one sister performing the duties of affection to another. The scene soon terminated. Whether Doctor Rappaccini had finished his labors in the garden, or that his watchful eye had caught the stranger's face, he now took his daughter's arm and retired. Night was already closing in; oppressive exhalations seemed to proceed from the plants, and steal upward past the open window; and Giovanni, closing the lattice, went to his couch, and dreamed of a rich flower and beautiful girl. Flower and maiden were different and yet the same, and fraught with some strange peril in either shape.

But there is an influence in the light of morning that tends to rectify whatever errors of fancy, or even of judgment, we may have incurred during the sun's decline, or among the shadows of the night, or in the less wholesome glow of moonshine. Giovanni's first movement on starting from sleep, was to throw open the window, and gaze down into the garden which his dreams had made so fertile of mysteries. He was surprised, and a little ashamed, to find how real and matter-of-fact an affair it proved to be, in the first rays of the sun, which gilded the dew-drops that hung upon leaf and blossom, and, while giving a brighter beauty to each rare flower, brought everything within the limits of ordinary experience. The young man rejoiced, that, in the heart of the barren city, he had the privilege of overlooking this spot of lovely and luxuriant vegetation. It would serve, he said to himself, as a symbolic language, to keep him in communion with Nature. Neither the sickly and thought-worn Doctor Giacomo Rappaccini, it is true, nor his brilliant daughter, were now visible; so that Giovanni could not determine how much of the singularity which he attributed to both, was due to their own qualities, and how much to his wonder-working fancy. But he was inclined to take a most rational view of the whole matter.

---

① With diligence and intent.

In the course of the day, he paid his respects to Signor Pietro Baglioni, Professor of Medicine in the University, a physician of eminent repute, to whom Giovanni had brought a letter of introduction. The Professor was an elderly personage, apparently of genial nature, and habits that might almost be called jovial; he kept the young man to dinner, and made himself very agreeable by the freedom and liveliness of his conversation, especially when warmed by a flask or two of Tuscan wine.① Giovanni, conceiving that men of science, inhabitants of the same city, must needs be on familiar terms with one another, took an opportunity to mention the name of Doctor Rappaccini. But the Professor did not respond with so much cordiality as he had anticipated.

"Ill would it become a teacher of the divine art of medicine," said Professor Pietro Baglioni, in answer to a question of Giovanni, "to withhold due and well-considered praise of a physician so eminently skilled as Rappaccini. But, on the other hand, I should answer it but scantily to my conscience, were I to permit a worthy youth like yourself, Signor Giovanni, the son of an ancient friend, to imbibe erroneous ideas respecting a man who might hereafter chance to hold your life and death in his hands. The truth is, our worshipful Doctor Rappaccini has as much science as any member of the faculty—with perhaps one single exception—in Padua, or all Italy. But there are certain grave objections to his professional character."

"And what are they?" asked the young man.

"Has my friend Giovanni any disease of body or heart, that he is so inquisitive about physicians?" said the Professor, with a smile. "But as for Rappaccini, it is said of him—and I, who know the man well, can answer for its truth—that he cares infinitely more for science than for mankind. His patients are interesting to him only as subjects for some new experiment. He would sacrifice human life, his own among the rest, or whatever else was dearest to him, for the sake of adding so much as a grain of mustard-seed to the great heap of his accumulated knowledge."

"Methinks he is an awful man, indeed," remarked Guasconti, mentally recalling the cold and purely intellectual aspect of Rappaccini. "And yet, worshipful Professor, is it not a noble spirit? Are there many men capable of so spiritual a love of science?"

"God forbid," answered the Professor, somewhat testily—"at least, unless they take sounder views of the healing art than those adopted by Rappaccini. It is his theory, that all medicinal virtues are comprised within those substances which we term vegetable poisons. These he cultivates with his own hands, and is said even to have produced new varieties of poison, more horribly deleterious② than Nature, without the assistance of this learned person, would ever have plagued the world withal. That the Signor Doctor does less mischief than might be expected, with such dangerous substances, is undeniable. Now and then, it must be owned, he has effected—or seemed to effect—a marvelous cure. But, to tell you my private mind, Signor Giovanni, he should receive little credit for such instances of success—they being probably the

---

① Tuscany is a province of Italy known for its wine.
② Harmful.

Unit One Theme
Chapter 1 Rappaccinni's Daughter

work of chance—but should be held strictly accountable for his failures, which may justly be considered his own work."

The youth might have taken Baglioni's opinions with many grains of allowance, had he known that there was a professional warfare of long continuance between him and Doctor Rappaccini, in which the latter was generally thought to have gained the advantage. If the reader be inclined to judge for himself, we refer him to certain black-letter tracts[①] on both sides, preserved in the medical department of the University of Padua.

"I know not, most learned Professor," returned Giovanni, after musing on what had been said of Rappaccini's exclusive zeal for science—"I know not how dearly this physician may love his art; but surely there is one object more dear to him. He has a daughter."

"Aha!" cried the Professor with a laugh. "So now our friend Giovanni's secret is out. You have heard of this daughter, whom all the young men in Padua are wild about, though not half a dozen have ever had the good hap to see her face. I know little of the Signora Beatrice, save that Rappaccini is said to have instructed her deeply in his science, and that, young and beautiful as fame reports her, she is already qualified to fill a professor's chair. Perchance her father destines her for mine! Other absurd rumors there be, not worth talking about, or listening to. So now, Signor Giovanni, drink off your glass of Lacryma[②]."

Guasconti returned to his lodgings somewhat heated with the wine he had quaffed, and which caused his brain to swim with strange fantasies in reference to Doctor Rappaccini and the beautiful Beatrice. On his way, happening to pass by a florist's, he bought a fresh bouquet of flowers.

Ascending to his chamber, he seated himself near the window, but within the shadow thrown by the depth of the wall, so that he could look down into the garden with little risk of being discovered. All beneath his eye was a solitude. The strange plants were basking in the sunshine, and now and then nodding gently to one another, as if in acknowledgment of sympathy and kindred. In the midst, by the shattered fountain, grew the magnificent shrub, with its purple gems clustering all over it; they glowed in the air, and gleamed back again out of the depths of the pool, which thus seemed to overflow with colored radiance from the rich reflection that was steeped in it. At first, as we have said, the garden was a solitude. Soon, however,—as Giovanni had half hoped, half feared, would be the case,—a figure appeared beneath the antique sculptured portal, and came down between the rows of plants, inhaling their various perfumes, as if she were one of those beings of old classic fable, that lived upon sweet odors. On again beholding Beatrice, the young man was even startled to perceive how much her beauty exceeded his recollection of it; so brilliant, so vivid in its character, that she glowed amid the sunlight, and, as Giovanni whispered to himself, positively illuminated the more shadowy intervals of the garden path. Her face being now more revealed than on the former occasion, he was struck by its expres-

---
① Ancient writings done by medieval scribes.
② An Italian wine, grown near Mount Vesuvius.

sion of simplicity and sweetness; qualities that had not entered into his idea of her character, and which made him ask anew, what manner of mortal she might be. Nor did he fail again to observe, or imagine, an analogy between the beautiful girl and the gorgeous shrub that hung its gem-like flowers over the fountain; a resemblance which Beatrice seemed to have indulged a fantastic humor in heightening, both by the arrangement of her dress and the selection of its hues.

Approaching the shrub, she threw open her arms, as with a passionate ardor, and drew its branches into an intimate embrace; so intimate, that her features were hidden in its leafy bosom, and her glistening ringlets all intermingled with the flowers.

"Give me thy breath, my sister," exclaimed Beatrice; "for I am faint with common air! And give me this flower of thine, which I separate with gentlest fingers from the stem, and place it close beside my heart."

With these words, the beautiful daughter of Rappaccini plucked one of the richest blossoms of the shrub, and was about to fasten it in her bosom. But now, unless Giovanni's draughts of wine had bewildered his senses, a singular incident occurred. A small orange colored reptile, of the lizard or chameleon species, chanced to be creeping along the path, just at the feet of Beatrice. It appeared to Giovanni—but, at the distance from which he gazed, he could scarcely have seen anything so minute — it appeared to him, however, that a drop or two of moisture from the broken stem of the flower descended upon the lizard's head. For an instant, the reptile contorted itself violently, and then lay motionless in the sunshine. Beatrice observed this remarkable phenomenon, and crossed herself, sadly, but without surprise; nor did she therefore hesitate to arrange the fatal flower in her bosom. There it blushed, and almost glimmered with the dazzling effect of a precious stone, adding to her dress and aspect the one appropriate charm, which nothing else in the world could have supplied. But Giovanni, out of the shadow of his window, bent forward and shrank back, and murmured and trembled.

"Am I awake? Have I my senses?" said he to himself. "What is this being?—beautiful, shall I call her?—or inexpressibly terrible?"

Beatrice now strayed carelessly through the garden, approaching closer beneath Giovanni's window, so that he was compelled to thrust his head quite out of its concealment, in order to gratify the intense and painful curiosity which she excited. At this moment, there came a beautiful insect over the garden wall; it had perhaps wandered through the city and found no flowers nor verdure[①] among those antique haunts of men, until the heavy perfumes of Doctor Rappaccini's shrubs had lured it from afar. Without alighting on the flowers, this winged brightness seemed to be attracted by Beatrice, and lingered in the air and fluttered about her head. Now here it could not be but that Giovanni Guasconti's eyes deceived him. Be that as it might, he fancied that while Beatrice was gazing at the insect with childish delight, it grew faint and fell at her feet;— its bright wings shivered; it was dead—from no cause that he could discern, unless it were the at-

---

① The lush greenness of flourishing vegetation.

Unit One Theme
Chapter 1 Rappaccinni's Daughter

mosphere of her breath. Again Beatrice crossed herself and sighed heavily, as she bent over the dead insect.

An impulsive movement of Giovanni drew her eyes to the window. There she beheld the beautiful head of the young man—rather a Grecian than an Italian head, with fair, regular features, and a glistening of gold among his ringlets—gazing down upon her like a being that hovered in mid-air. Scarcely knowing what he did, Giovanni threw down the bouquet which he had hitherto held in his hand.

"Signora," said he, "there are pure and healthful flowers. Wear them for the sake of Giovanni Guasconti!"

"Thanks, Signor," replied Beatrice, with her rich voice that came forth as it were like a gush of music; and with a mirthful expression half childish and half woman-like. "I accept your gift, and would fain recompense it with this precious purple flower; but if I toss it into the air, it will not reach you. So Signor Guasconti must even content himself with my thanks."

She lifted the bouquet from the ground, and then as if inwardly ashamed at having stepped aside from her maidenly reserve to respond to a stranger's greeting, passed swiftly homeward through the garden. But, few as the moments were, it seemed to Giovanni when she was on the point of vanishing beneath the sculptured portal, that his beautiful bouquet was already beginning to wither in her grasp. It was an idle thought; there could be no possibility of distinguishing a faded flower from a fresh one, at so great a distance.

For many days after this incident, the young man avoided the window that looked into Doctor Rappaccini's garden, as if something ugly and monstrous would have blasted his eye-sight, had he been betrayed into a glance. He felt conscious of having put himself, to a certain extent, within the influence of an unintelligible power, by the communication which he had opened with Beatrice. The wisest course would have been, if his heart were in any real danger, to quit his lodgings and Padua itself, at once; the next wiser, to have accustomed himself, as far as possible, to the familiar and day-light view of Beatrice; thus bringing her rigidly and systematically within the limits of ordinary experience. Least of all, while avoiding her sight, should Giovanni have remained so near this extraordinary being, that the proximity and possibility even of intercourse, should give a kind of substance and reality to the wild vagaries① which his imagination ran riot continually in producing. Guasconti had not a deep heart—or at all events, its depths were not sounded now—but he had a quick fancy, and an ardent southern temperament, which rose every instant to a higher fever-pitch. Whether or no Beatrice possessed those terrible attributes—that fatal breath—the affinity with those so beautiful and deadly flowers—which were indicated by what Giovanni had witnessed, she had at least instilled a fierce and subtle poison into his system. It was not love, although her rich beauty was a madness to him; nor horror, even while he fancied her spirit to be imbued with the same baneful essence that seemed to pervade her physical

---

① Extravagant or erratic notion or action.

frame; but a wild offspring of both love and horror that had each parent in it, and burned like one and shivered like the other. Giovanni knew not what to dread; still less did he know what to hope; yet hope and dread kept a continual warfare in his breast, alternately vanquishing one another and starting up afresh to renew the contest. Blessed are all simple emotions, be they dark or bright! It is the lurid intermixture of the two that produces the illuminating blaze of the infernal regions.

Sometimes he endeavored to assuage the fever of his spirit by a rapid walk through the streets of Padua, or beyond its gates; his footsteps kept time with the throbbings of his brain, so that the walk was apt to accelerate itself to a race. One day, he found himself arrested; his arm was seized by a portly personage who had turned back on recognizing the young man, and expended much breath in overtaking him.

"Signor Giovanni!—stay, my young friend!"—cried he. "Have you forgotten me? That might well be the case, if I were as much altered as yourself."

It was Baglioni, whom Giovanni had avoided, ever since their first meeting, from a doubt that the Professor's sagacity would look too deeply into his secrets. Endeavoring to recover himself, he stared forth wildly from his inner world into the outer one, and spoke like a man in a dream.

"Yes; I am Giovanni Guasconti. You are Professor Pietro Baglioni. Now let me pass!"

"Not yet—not yet, Signor Giovanni Guasconti," said the Professor, smiling, but at the same time scrutinizing the youth with an earnest glance. "What, did I grow up side by side with your father, and shall his son pass me like a stranger, in these old streets of Padua? Stand still, Signor Giovanni; for we must have a word or two before we part."

"Speedily, then, most worshipful Professor, speedily!" said Giovanni, with feverish impatience. "Does not your worship see that I am in haste?"

Now, while he was speaking, there came a man in black along the street, stooping and moving feebly, like a person in inferior health. His face was all overspread with a most sickly and sallow hue, but yet so pervaded with an expression of piercing and active intellect, that an observer might easily have overlooked the merely physical attributes, and have seen only this wonderful energy. As he passed, this person exchanged a cold and distant salutation with Baglioni, but fixed his eyes upon Giovanni with an intentness that seemed to bring out whatever was within him worthy of notice. Nevertheless, there was a peculiar quietness in the look, as if taking merely a speculative, not a human interest, in the young man.

"It is Doctor Rappaccini!" whispered the Professor, when the stranger had passed.—"Has he ever seen your face before?"

"Not that I know," answered Giovanni, starting at the name.

"He *has* seen you!—he must have seen you!" said Baglioni, hastily. "For some purpose or other, this man of science is making a study of you. I know that look of his! It is the same that coldly illuminates his face, as he bends over a bird, a mouse, or a butterfly, which, in pursuance

Unit One Theme
Chapter 1 Rappaccinni's Daughter

of some experiment, he has killed by the perfume of a flower;—a look as deep as Nature itself, but without Nature's warmth of love. Signor Giovanni, I will stake my life upon it, you are the subject of one of Rappaccini's experiments!"

"Will you make a fool of me?" cried Giovanni, passionately. "*That*, Signor Professor, were an untoward experiment."

"Patience, patience!" replied the imperturbable① Professor. "I tell thee, my poor Giovanni, that Rappaccini has a scientific interest in thee. Thou hast fallen into fearful hands! And the Signora Beatrice? What part does she act in this mystery?"

But Guasconti, finding Baglioni's pertinacity intolerable, here broke away, and was gone before the Professor could again seize his arm. He looked after the young man intently, and shook his head.

"This must not be," said Baglioni to himself. "The youth is the son of my old friend, and shall not come to any harm from which the arcana② of medical science can preserve him. Besides, it is too insufferable an impertinence in Rappaccini thus to snatch the lad out of my own hands, as I may say, and make use of him for his infernal experiments. This daughter of his! It shall be looked to. Perchance, most learned Rappaccini, I may foil you where you little dream of it!"

Meanwhile, Giovanni had pursued a circuitous route, and at length found himself at the door of his lodgings. As he crossed the threshold, he was met by old Lisabetta, who smirked and smiled, and was evidently desirous to attract his attention; vainly, however, as the ebullition③ of his feelings had momentarily subsided into a cold and dull vacuity④. He turned his eyes full upon the withered face that was puckering itself into a smile, but seemed to behold it not. The old dame, therefore, laid her grasp upon his cloak.

"Signor!—Signor!" whispered she, still with a smile over the whole breadth of her visage, so that it looked not unlike a grotesque carving in wood, darkened by centuries—"Listen, Signor! There is a private entrance into the garden!"

"What do you say?" exclaimed Giovanni, turning quickly about, as if an inanimate thing should start into feverish life.—"A private entrance into Doctor Rappaccini's garden!"

"Hush! hush!—not so loud!" whispered Lisabetta, putting her hand over his mouth. "Yes; into the worshipful Doctor's garden, where you may see all his fine shrubbery. Many a young man in Padua would give gold to be admitted among those flowers."

Giovanni put a piece of gold into her hand.

"Show me the way," said he.

A surmise, probably excited by his conversation with Baglioni, crossed his mind, that this

---

① Calm and even-tempered.
② Elixirs.
③ Enthusiasm; liveliness.
④ Emptiness.

interposition of old Lisabetta might perchance be connected with the intrigue, whatever were its nature, in which the Professor seemed to suppose that Doctor Rappaccini was involving him. But such a suspicion, though it disturbed Giovanni, was inadequate to restrain him. The instant he was aware of the possibility of approaching Beatrice, it seemed an absolute necessity of his existence to do so. It mattered not whether she were angel or demon; he was irrevocably within her sphere, and must obey the law that whirled him onward, in ever lessening circles, towards a result which he did not attempt to foreshadow. And yet, strange to say, there came across him a sudden doubt, whether this intense interest on his part were not delusory[1]—whether it were really of so deep and positive a nature as to justify him in now thrusting himself into an incalculable position—whether it were not merely the fantasy of a young man's brain, only slightly, or not at all, connected with his heart!

He paused—hesitated—turned half about—but again went on. His withered guide led him along several obscure passages, and finally undid a door, through which, as it was opened, there came the sight and sound of rustling leaves, with the broken sunshine glimmering among them. Giovanni stepped forth, and forcing himself through the entanglement of a shrub that wreathed its tendrils over the hidden entrance, he stood beneath his own window, in the open area of Doctor Rappaccini's garden.

How often is it the case, that, when impossibilities have come to pass, and dreams have condensed their misty substance into tangible realities, we find ourselves calm, and even coldly self-possessed, amid circumstances which it would have been a delirium of joy or agony to anticipate! Fate delights to thwart us thus. Passion will choose his own time to rush upon the scene, and lingers sluggishly behind, when an appropriate adjustment of events would seem to summon his appearance. So was it now with Giovanni. Day after day, his pulses had throbbed with feverish blood, at the improbable idea of an interview with Beatrice, and of standing with her, face to face, in this very garden, basking in the oriental sunshine of her beauty, and snatching from her full gaze the mystery which he deemed the riddle of his own existence. But now there was a singular and untimely equanimity[2] within his breast. He threw a glance around the garden to discover if Beatrice or her father were present, and perceiving that he was alone, began a critical observation of the plants.

The aspect of one and all of them dissatisfied him; their gorgeousness seemed fierce, passionate, and even unnatural. There was hardly an individual shrub which a wanderer, straying by himself through a forest, would not have been startled to find growing wild, as if an unearthly face had glared at him out of the thicket. Several, also, would have shocked a delicate instinct by an appearance of artificialness, indicating that there had been such commixture, and, as it were, adultery of various vegetable species, that the production was no longer of God's making, but the monstrous offspring of man's depraved fancy, glowing with only an evil mockery of beauty.

---

[1] Deceptive; artificial.
[2] Calmness; serenity.

Unit One Theme
Chapter 1 Rappaccinni's Daughter

They were probably the result of experiment, which, in one or two cases, had succeeded in mingling plants individually lovely into a compound possessing the questionable and ominous character that distinguished the whole growth of the garden. In fine, Giovanni recognized but two or three plants in the collection, and those of a kind that he well knew to be poisonous. While busy with these contemplations, he heard the rustling of a silken garment, and turning, beheld Beatrice emerging from beneath the sculptured portal.

Giovanni had not considered with himself what should be his deportment; whether he should apologize for his intrusion into the garden, or assume that he was there with the privity, at least, if not by the desire, of Doctor Rappaccini or his daughter. But Beatrice's manner placed him at his ease, though leaving him still in doubt by what agency he had gained admittance. She came lightly along the path, and met him near the broken fountain. There was surprise in her face, but brightened by a simple and kind expression of pleasure.

"You are a connoisseur in flowers, Signor," said Beatrice with a smile, alluding to the bouquet which he had flung her from the window. "It is no marvel, therefore, if the sight of my father's rare collection has tempted you to take a nearer view. If he were here, he could tell you many strange and interesting facts as to the nature and habits of these shrubs, for he has spent a life-time in such studies, and this garden is his world."

"And yourself, lady"—observed Giovanni—"if fame says true—you, likewise, are deeply skilled in the virtues indicated by these rich blossoms, and these spicy perfumes. Would you deign① to be my instructress, I should prove an apter scholar than under Signor Rappaccini himself."

"Are there such idle rumors?" asked Beatrice, with the music of a pleasant laugh. "Do people say that I am skilled in my father's science of plants? What a jest is there! No; though I have grown up among these flowers, I know no more of them than their hues and perfume; and sometimes, methinks I would fain rid myself of even that small knowledge. There are many flowers here, and those not the least brilliant, that shock and offend me, when they meet my eye. But, pray, Signor, do not believe these stories about my science. Believe nothing of me save what you see with your own eyes."

"And must I believe all that I have seen with my own eyes?" asked Giovanni pointedly, while the recollection of former scenes made him shrink. "No, Signora, you demand too little of me. Bid me believe nothing, save what comes from your own lips."

It would appear that Beatrice understood him. There came a deep flush to her cheek; but she looked full into Giovanni's eyes, and responded to his gaze of uneasy suspicion with a queen-like haughtiness.

"I do so bid you, Signor!" she replied. "Forget whatever you may have fancied in regard to me. If true to the outward senses, still it may be false in its essence. But the words of Beatrice

---

① To condescend to give or grant; stoop.

Rappaccini's lips are true from the heart outward. Those you may believe!"

A fervor glowed in her whole aspect, and beamed upon Giovanni's consciousness like the light of truth itself. But while she spoke, there was a fragrance in the atmosphere around her rich and delightful, though evanescent[①], yet which the young man, from an indefinable reluctance, scarcely dared to draw into his lungs. It might be the odor of the flowers. Could it be Beatrice's breath, which thus embalmed her words with a strange richness, as if by steeping them in her heart? A faintness passed like a shadow over Giovanni, and flitted away; he seemed to gaze through the beautiful girl's eyes into her transparent soul, and felt no more doubt or fear.

The tinge of passion that had colored Beatrice's manner vanished; she became gay, and appeared to derive a pure delight from her communion with the youth, not unlike what the maiden of a lonely island might have felt, conversing with a voyager from the civilized world. Evidently her experience of life had been confined within the limits of that garden. She talked now about matters as simple as the day-light or summer-clouds, and now asked questions in reference to the city, or Giovanni's distant home, his friends, his mother, and his sisters; questions indicating such seclusion, and such lack of familiarity with modes and forms, that Giovanni responded as if to an infant. Her spirit gushed out before him like a fresh rill, that was just catching its first glimpse of the sunlight, and wondering, at the reflections of earth and sky which were flung into its bosom. There came thoughts, too, from a deep source, and fantasies of a gem-like brilliancy, as if diamonds and rubies sparkled upward among the bubbles of the fountain. Ever and anon, there gleamed across the young man's mind a sense of wonder, that he should be walking side by side with the being who had so wrought upon his imagination—whom he had idealized in such hues of terror—in whom he had positively witnessed such manifestations of dreadful attributes—that he should be conversing with Beatrice like a brother, and should find her so human and so maiden-like. But such reflections were only momentary; the effect of her character was too real, not to make itself familiar at once.

In this free intercourse, they had strayed through the garden, and now, after many turns among its avenues, were come to the shattered fountain, beside which grew the magnificent shrub with its treasury of glowing blossoms. A fragrance was diffused from it, which Giovanni recognized as identical with that which he had attributed to Beatrice's breath, but incomparably more powerful. As her eyes fell upon it, Giovanni beheld her press her hand to her bosom, as if her heart were throbbing suddenly and painfully.

"For the first time in my life," murmured she, addressing the shrub, "I had forgotten thee!"

"I remember, Signora," said Giovanni, "that you once promised to reward me with one of these living gems for the bouquet, which I had the happy boldness to fling to your feet. Permit me now to pluck it as a memorial of this interview."

He made a step towards the shrub, with extended hand. But Beatrice darted forward, utter-

---

① Vanishing.

Unit One Theme
Chapter 1 Rappaccinni's Daughter

ing a shriek that went through his heart like a dagger. She caught his hand, and drew it back with the whole force of her slender figure. Giovanni felt her touch thrilling through his fibers.

"Touch it not!" exclaimed she, in a voice of agony. "Not for thy life! It is fatal!"

Then, hiding her face, she fled from him, and vanished beneath the sculptured portal. As Giovanni followed her with his eyes, he beheld the emaciated figure and pale intelligence of Doctor Rappaccini, who had been watching the scene, he knew not how long, within the shadow of the entrance.

No sooner was Guasconti alone in his chamber, than the image of Beatrice came back to his passionate musings, invested with all the witchery that had been gathering around it ever since his first glimpse of her, and now likewise imbued with a tender warmth of girlish womanhood. She was human: her nature was endowed with all gentle and feminine qualities; she was worthiest to be worshipped; she was capable, surely, on her part, of the height and heroism of love. Those tokens, which he had hitherto considered as proofs of a frightful peculiarity in her physical and moral system, were now either forgotten, or, by the subtle sophistry① of passion, transmuted into a golden crown of enchantment, rendering Beatrice the more admirable, by so much as she was the more unique. Whatever had looked ugly, was now beautiful; or, if incapable of such a change, it stole away and hid itself among those shapeless half-ideas, which throng the dim region beyond the daylight of our perfect consciousness. Thus did Giovanni spend the night, nor fell asleep, until the dawn had begun to awake the slumbering flowers in Doctor Rappaccini's garden, whither his dreams doubtless led him. Up rose the sun in his due season, and flinging his beams upon the young man's eyelids, awoke him to a sense of pain. When thoroughly aroused, he became sensible of a burning and tingling agony in his hand—in his right hand—the very hand which Beatrice had grasped in her own, when he was on the point of plucking one of the gem-like flowers. On the back of that hand there was now a purple print, like that of four small fingers, and the likeness of a slender thumb upon his wrist.

Oh, how stubbornly does love—or even that cunning semblance of love which flourishes in the imagination, but strikes no depth of root into the heart—how stubbornly does it hold its faith, until the moment come, when it is doomed to vanish into thin mist! Giovanni wrapt a handkerchief about his hand, and wondered what evil thing had stung him, and soon forgot his pain in a reverie of Beatrice.

After the first interview, a second was in the inevitable course of what we call fate. A third; a fourth; and a meeting with Beatrice in the garden was no longer an incident in Giovanni's daily life, but the whole space in which he might be said to live; for the anticipation and memory of that ecstatic hour made up the remainder. Nor was it otherwise with the daughter of Rappaccini. She watched for the youth's appearance, and flew to his side with confidence as unreserved as if they had been playmates from early infancy—as if they were such playmates still. If, by any un-

---

① Plausible but fallacious argumentation.

wonted chance, he failed to come at the appointed moment, she stood beneath the window, and sent up the rich sweetness of her tones to float around him in his chamber, and echo and reverberate throughout his heart—"Giovanni! Giovanni! Why tarriest thou? Come down!" And down he hastened into that Eden of poisonous flowers.

But, with all this intimate familiarity, there was still a reserve in Beatrice's demeanor, so rigidly and invariably sustained, that the idea of infringing① it scarcely occurred to his imagination. By all appreciable signs, they loved; they had looked love, with eyes that conveyed the holy secret from the depths of one soul into the depths of the other, as if it were too sacred to be whispered by the way; they had even spoken love, in those gushes of passion when their spirits darted forth in articulated breath, like tongues of long-hidden flame; and yet there had been no seal of lips, no clasp of hands, nor any slightest caress, such as love claims and hallows. He had never touched one of the gleaming ringlets of her hair; her garment—so marked was the physical barrier between them—had never been waved against him by a breeze. On the few occasions when Giovanni had seemed tempted to overstep the limit, Beatrice grew so sad, so stern, and withal wore such a look of desolate separation, shuddering at itself, that not a spoken word was requisite to repel him. At such times, he was startled at the horrible suspicions that rose, monster-like, out of the caverns of his heart, and stared him in the face; his love grew thin and faint as the morning-mist; his doubts alone had substance. But when Beatrice's face brightened again, after the momentary shadow, she was transformed at once from the mysterious, questionable being, whom he had watched with so much awe and horror; she was now the beautiful and unsophisticated girl, whom he felt that his spirit knew with a certainty beyond all other knowledge.

A considerable time had now passed since Giovanni's last meeting with Baglioni. One morning, however, he was disagreeably surprised by a visit from the Professor, whom he had scarcely thought of for whole weeks, and would willingly have forgotten still longer. Given up, as he had long been, to a pervading excitement, he could tolerate no companions, except upon condition of their perfect sympathy with his present state of feeling. Such sympathy was not to be expected from Professor Baglioni.

The visitor chatted carelessly, for a few moments, about the gossip of the city and the University, and then took up another topic.

"I have been reading an old classic author lately," said he, "and met with a story② that strangely interested me. Possibly you may remember it. It is of an Indian prince, who sent a beautiful woman as a present to Alexander the Great. She was as lovely as the dawn, and gorgeous as the sunset; but what especially distinguished her was a certain rich perfume in her breath—richer than a garden of Persian roses. Alexander, as was natural to a youthful conqueror, fell in love at

---

① Violating.
② Hawthorne met with the story in Sir Thomas Browne's *Vulgar Errors* (1646), an "old classic" for New England readers.

Unit One Theme
Chapter 1 Rappaccinni's Daughter

first sight with this magnificent stranger. But a certain sage physician, happening to be present, discovered a terrible secret in regard to her."

"And what was that?" asked Giovanni, turning his eyes downward to avoid those of the Professor.

"That this lovely woman," continued Baglioni, with emphasis, "had been nourished with poisons from her birth upward, until her whole nature was so imbued with them, that she herself had become the deadliest poison in existence. Poison was her element of life. With that rich perfume of her breath, she blasted the very air. Her love would have been poison!—her embrace death! Is not this a marvelous tale?"

"A childish fable," answered Giovanni, nervously starting from his chair. "I marvel how your worship finds time to read such nonsense, among your graver studies."

"By the bye," said the Professor, looking uneasily about him, "what singular fragrance is this in your apartment? Is it the perfume of your gloves? It is faint, but delicious, and yet, after all, by no means agreeable. Were I to breathe it long, methinks it would make me ill. It is like the breath of a flower—but I see no flowers in the chamber."

"Nor are there any," replied Giovanni, who had turned pale as the Professor spoke; "nor, I think, is there any fragrance, except in your worship's imagination. Odors, being a sort of element combined of the sensual and the spiritual, are apt to deceive us in this manner. The recollection of a perfume—the bare idea of it—may easily be mistaken for a present reality."

"Aye; but my sober imagination does not often play such tricks," said Baglioni; "and were I to fancy any kind of odor, it would be that of some vile apothecary drug, wherewith my fingers are likely enough to be imbued. Our worshipful friend Rappaccini, as I have heard, tinctures his medicaments with odors richer than those of Araby[①]. Doubtless, likewise, the fair and learned Signora Beatrice would minister to her patients with draughts as sweet as a maiden's breath. But woe to him that sips them!"

Giovanni's face evinced many contending emotions. The tone in which the Professor alluded to the pure and lovely daughter of Rappaccini was a torture to his soul; and yet, the intimation of a view of her character, opposite to his own, gave instantaneous distinctness to a thousand dim suspicions, which now grinned at him like so many demons. But he strove hard to quell them, and to respond to Baglioni with a true lover's perfect faith.

"Signor Professor," said he, "you were my father's friend—perchance, too, it is your purpose to act a friendly part towards his son. I would fain feel nothing towards you save respect and deference. But I pray you to observe, Signor, that there is one subject on which we must not speak. You know not the Signora Beatrice. You cannot, therefore, estimate the wrong—the blasphemy, I may even say—that is offered to her character by a light or injurious word."

"Giovanni!—my poor Giovanni!" answered the Professor, with a calm expression of pity,

---

① Arabia.

"I know this wretched girl far better than yourself. You shall hear the truth in respect to the poisoner Rappaccini, and his poisonous daughter. Yes; poisonous as she is beautiful! Listen; for even should you do violence to my gray hairs, it shall not silence me. That old fable of the Indian woman has become a truth, by the deep and deadly science of Rappaccini, and in the person of the lovely Beatrice!"

Giovanni groaned and hid his face.

"Her father," continued Baglioni, "was not restrained by natural affection from offering up his child, in this horrible manner, as the victim of his insane zeal for science. For—let us do him justice—he is as true a man of science as ever distilled his own heart in an alembic①. What, then, will be your fate? Beyond a doubt, you are selected as the material of some new experiment. Perhaps the result is to be death—perhaps a fate more awful still! Rappaccini, with what he calls the interest of science before his eyes, will hesitate at nothing."

"It is a dream!" muttered Giovanni to himself, "surely it is a dream!"

"But," resumed the Professor, "be of good cheer, son of my friend! It is not yet too late for the rescue. Possibly, we may even succeed in bringing back this miserable child within the limits of ordinary nature, from which her father's madness has estranged her. Behold this little silver vase! It was wrought by the hands of the renowned Benvenuto Cellini②, and is well worthy to be a love-gift to the fairest dame in Italy. But its contents are invaluable. One little sip of this antidote would have rendered the most virulent poisons of the Borgias③ innocuous. Doubt not that it will be as efficacious against those of Rappaccini. Bestow the vase, and the precious liquid within it, on your Beatrice, and hopefully await the result."

Baglioni laid a small, exquisitely wrought silver phial on the table, and withdrew, leaving what he had said to produce its effect upon the young man's mind.

"We will thwart Rappaccini yet!" thought he, chuckling to himself, as he descended the stairs. "But, let us confess the truth of him, he is a wonderful man!—a wonderful man indeed! A vile empiric, however, in his practice, and therefore not to be tolerated by those who respect the good old rules of the medical profession!"

Throughout Giovanni's whole acquaintance with Beatrice, he had occasionally, as we have said, been haunted by dark surmises as to her character. Yet, so thoroughly had she made herself felt by him as a simple, natural, most affectionate and guileless creature, that the image now held up by Professor Baglioni, looked as strange and incredible, as if it were not in accordance with his own original conception. True, there were ugly recollections connected with his first glimpses of the beautiful girl; he could not quite forget the bouquet that withered in her grasp, and the insect that perished amid the sunny air, by no ostensible agency save the fragrance of her breath. These incidents, however, dissolving in the pure light of her character, had no longer the

---

① Device for distilling. In other words, Rappaccini's heart was in his work.
② Benvenuto Cellini (1500—1571), Italian sculptor and metalworker.
③ Infamous Italian family supposed to have poisoned their enemies.

Unit One   Theme
Chapter 1 Rappaccinni's Daughter

efficacy of facts, but were acknowledged as mistaken fantasies, by whatever testimony of the senses they might appear to be substantiated. There is something truer and more real, than what we can see with the eyes, and touch with the finger. On such better evidence, had Giovanni founded his confidence in Beatrice, though rather by the necessary force of her high attributes, than by any deep and generous faith on his part. But, now, his spirit was incapable of sustaining itself at the height to which the early enthusiasm of passion had exalted it; he fell down, groveling among earthly doubts, and defiled therewith the pure whiteness of Beatrice's image. Not that he gave her up; he did but distrust. He resolved to institute some decisive test that should satisfy him, once for all, whether there were those dreadful peculiarities in her physical nature, which could not be supposed to exist without some corresponding monstrosity[①] of soul. His eyes, gazing down afar, might have deceived him as to the lizard, the insect, and the flowers. But if he could witness, at the distance of a few paces, the sudden blight of one fresh and healthful flower in Beatrice's hand, there would be room for no further question. With this idea, he hastened to the florist's, and purchased a bouquet that was still gemmed with the morning dew-drops.

It was now the customary hour of his daily interview with Beatrice. Before descending into the garden, Giovanni failed not to look at his figure in the mirror; a vanity to be expected in a beautiful young man, yet, as displaying itself at that troubled and feverish moment, the token of a certain shallowness of feeling and insincerity of character. He did gaze, however, and said to himself, that his features had never before possessed so rich a grace, nor his eyes such vivacity, nor his cheeks so warm a hue of superabundant life.

"At least," thought he, "her poison has not yet insinuated itself into my system. I am no flower to perish in her grasp!"

With that thought, he turned his eyes on the bouquet, which he had never once laid aside from his hand. A thrill of indefinable horror shot through his frame, on perceiving that those dewy flowers were already beginning to droop; they wore the aspect of things that had been fresh and lovely, yesterday. Giovanni grew white as marble, and stood motionless before the mirror, staring at his own reflection there, as at the likeness of something frightful. He remembered Baglioni's remark about the fragrance that seemed to pervade the chamber. It must have been the poison in his breath! Then he shuddered—shuddered at himself! Recovering from his stupor[②], he began to watch, with curious eye, a spider that was busily at work, hanging its web from the antique cornice of the apartment, crossing and re-crossing the artful system of interwoven lines, as vigorous and active a spider as ever dangled from an old ceiling. Giovanni bent towards the insect, and emitted a deep, long breath. The spider suddenly ceased its toil; the web vibrated with a tremor originating in the body of the small artizan. Again Giovanni sent forth a breath, deeper, longer, and imbued with a venomous feeling out of his heart; he knew not whether he

---

① Being abnormal.
② Mental numbness, resulting from shock.

were wicked or only desperate. The spider made a convulsive gripe with his limbs, and hung dead across the window.

"Accursed! Accursed!" muttered Giovanni, addressing himself. "Hast thou grown so poisonous, that this deadly insect perishes by thy breath?"

At that moment, a rich, sweet voice came floating up from the garden: "Giovanni! Giovanni! It is past the hour! Why tarriest thou! Come down!"

"Yes," muttered Giovanni again. "She is the only being whom my breath may not slay! Would that it might!"

He rushed down, and in an instant, was standing before the bright and loving eyes of Beatrice. A moment ago, his wrath and despair had been so fierce that he could have desired nothing so much as to wither her by a glance. But, with her actual presence, there came influences which had too real an existence to be at once shaken off; recollections of the delicate and benign power of her feminine nature, which had so often enveloped him in a religious calm; recollections of many a holy and passionate outgush of her heart, when the pure fountain had been unsealed from its depths, and made visible in its transparency to his mental eye; recollections which, had Giovanni known how to estimate them, would have assured him that all this ugly mystery was but an earthly illusion, and that, whatever mist of evil might seem to have gathered over her, the real Beatrice was a heavenly angel. Incapable as he was of such high faith, still her presence had not utterly lost its magic. Giovanni's rage was quelled into an aspect of sullen insensibility. Beatrice, with a quick spiritual sense, immediately felt that there was a gulf of blackness between them, which neither he nor she could pass. They walked on together, sad and silent, and came thus to the marble fountain, and to its pool of water on the ground, in the midst of which grew the shrub that bore gem-like blossoms. Giovanni was affrighted at the eager enjoyment—the appetite, as it were—with which he found himself inhaling the fragrance of the flowers.

"Beatrice," asked he abruptly, "whence came this shrub?"

"My father created it," answered she, with simplicity.

"Created it! created it!" repeated Giovanni. "What mean you, Beatrice?"

"He is a man fearfully acquainted with the secrets of nature," replied Beatrice; "and, at the hour when I first drew breath, this plant sprang from the soil, the offspring of his science, of his intellect, while I was but his earthly child. Approach it not!" continued she, observing with terror that Giovanni was drawing nearer to the shrub. "It has qualities that you little dream of. But I, dearest Giovanni—I grew up and blossomed with the plant, and was nourished with its breath. It was my sister, and I loved it with a human affection: for—alas! hast thou not suspected it? there was an awful doom."

Here Giovanni frowned so darkly upon her that Beatrice paused and trembled. But her faith in his tenderness reassured her, and made her blush that she had doubted for an instant.

"There was an awful doom," she continued,—"the effect of my father's fatal love of science — which estranged me from all society of my kind. Until Heaven sent thee, dearest

Unit One Theme
Chapter 1 Rappaccini's Daughter

Giovanni, Oh! how lonely was thy poor Beatrice!"

"Was it a hard doom?" asked Giovanni, fixing his eyes upon her.

"Only of late have I known how hard it was," answered she tenderly. "Oh, yes; but my heart was torpid①, and therefore quiet."

Giovanni's rage broke forth from his sullen gloom like a lightning-flash out of a dark cloud.

"Accursed one!" cried he, with venomous scorn and anger. "And finding thy solitude wearisome, thou hast severed me, likewise, from all the warmth of life, and enticed me into thy region of unspeakable horror!"

"Giovanni!" exclaimed Beatrice, turning her large bright eyes upon his face. The force of his words had not found its way into her mind; she was merely thunder-struck.

"Yes, poisonous thing!" repeated Giovanni, beside himself with passion. "Thou hast done it! Thou hast blasted me! Thou hast filled my veins with poison! Thou hast made me as hateful, as ugly, as loathsome and deadly a creature as thyself—a world's wonder of hideous monstrosity! Now—if our breath be happily as fatal to ourselves as to all others—let us join our lips in one kiss of unutterable hatred, and so die!"

"What has befallen me?" murmured Beatrice, with a low moan out of her heart. "Holy Virgin pity me, a poor heartbroken child!"

"Thou! Dost thou pray?" cried Giovanni, still with the same fiendish scorn. "Thy very prayers, as they come from thy lips, taint the atmosphere with death. Yes, yes; let us pray! Let us to church, and dip our fingers in the holy water at the portal! They that come after us will perish as by a pestilence②. Let us sign crosses in the air! It will be scattering curses abroad in the likeness of holy symbols!"

"Giovanni," said Beatrice calmly, for her grief was beyond passion, "Why dost thou join thyself with me thus in those terrible words? I, it is true, am the horrible thing thou namest me. But thou!—what hast thou to do, save with one other shudder at my hideous misery, to go forth out of the garden and mingle with thy race, and forget that there ever crawled on earth such a monster as poor Beatrice?"

"Dost thou pretend ignorance?" asked Giovanni, scowling upon her. "Behold! This power have I gained from the pure daughter of Rappaccini!"

There was a swarm of summer-insects flitting through the air, in search of the food promised by the flower-odors of the fatal garden. They circled round Giovanni's head, and were evidently attracted towards him by the same influence which had drawn them, for an instant, within the sphere of several of the shrubs. He sent forth a breath among them, and smiled bitterly at Beatrice, as at least a score of the insects fell dead upon the ground.

"I see it! I see it!" shrieked Beatrice. "It is my father's fatal science? No, no, Giovanni; it was not I! Never, never! I dreamed only to love thee, and be with thee a little time, and so to let

---

① Slow-moving; sluggish.
② Epidemic; plague.

thee pass away, leaving but thine image in mine heart. For, Giovanni—believe it—though my body be nourished with poison, my spirit is God's creature, and craves love as its daily food. But my father!—he has united us in this fearful sympathy. Yes; spurn me!—tread upon me!—kill me! Oh, what is death, after such words as thine? But it was not I! Not for a world of bliss would I have done it!"

Giovanni's passion had exhausted itself in its outburst from his lips. There now came across him a sense, mournful, and not without tenderness, of the intimate and peculiar relationship between Beatrice and himself. They stood, as it were, in an utter solitude, which would be made none the less solitary by the densest throng of human life. Ought not, then, the desert of humanity around them to press this insulated pair closer together? If they should be cruel to one another, who was there to be kind to them? Besides, thought Giovanni, might there not still be a hope of his returning within the limits of ordinary nature, and leading Beatrice—the redeemed Beatrice—by the hand? Oh, weak, and selfish, and unworthy spirit, that could dream of an earthly union and earthly happiness as possible, after such deep love had been so bitterly wronged as was Beatrice's love by Giovanni's blighting words! No, no; there could be no such hope. She must pass heavily, with that broken heart, across the borders of Time—she must bathe her hurts in some fount of Paradise, and forget her grief in the light of immortality—and *there* be well!

But Giovanni did not know it.

"Dear Beatrice," said he, approaching her, while she shrank away, as always at his approach, but now with a different impulse—"dearest Beatrice, our fate is not yet so desperate. Behold! There is a medicine, potent, as a wise physician has assured me, and almost divine in its efficacy①. It is composed of ingredients the most opposite to those by which thy awful father has brought this calamity upon thee and me. It is distilled of blessed herbs. Shall we not quaff it together, and thus be purified from evil?"

"Give it me!" said Beatrice, extending her hand to receive the little silver phial which Giovanni took from his bosom. She added, with a peculiar emphasis: "I will drink—but do thou await the result."

She put Baglioni's antidote to her lips; and, at the same moment, the figure of Rappaccini emerged from the portal, and came slowly towards the marble fountain. As he drew near, the pale man of science seemed to gaze with a triumphant expression at the beautiful youth and maiden, as might an artist who should spend his life in achieving a picture or a group of statuary, and finally be satisfied with his success. He paused—his bent form grew erect with conscious power, he spread out his hand over them, in the attitude of a father imploring a blessing upon his children. But those were the same hands that had thrown poison into the stream of their lives! Giovanni trembled. Beatrice shuddered very nervously, and pressed her hand upon her heart.

---

① Effectiveness.

Unit One Theme

Chapter 1 Rappaccinni's Daughter

"My daughter," said Rappaccini, "thou art no longer lonely in the world! Pluck one of those precious gems from thy sister shrub, and bid thy bridegroom wear it in his bosom. It will not harm him now! My science, and the sympathy between thee and him, have so wrought within his system, that he now stands apart from common men, as thou dost, daughter of my pride and triumph, from ordinary women. Pass on, then, through the world, most dear to one another, and dreadful to all besides!"

"My father," said Beatrice, feebly—and still, as she spoke, she kept her hand upon her heart—"wherefore didst thou inflict this miserable doom upon thy child?"

"Miserable!" exclaimed Rappaccini. "What mean you, foolish girl? Dost thou deem it misery to be endowed with marvelous gifts, against which no power nor strength could avail an enemy? Misery, to be able to quell the mightiest with a breath? Misery, to be as terrible as thou art beautiful? Wouldst thou, then, have preferred the condition of a weak woman, exposed to all evil, and capable of none?"

"I would fain have been loved, not feared," murmured Beatrice, sinking down upon the ground.—"But now it matters not; I am going, father, where the evil, which thou hast striven to mingle with my being, will pass away like a dream—like the fragrance of these poisonous flowers, which will no longer taint my breath among the flowers of Eden. Farewell, Giovanni! Thy words of hatred are like lead within my heart—but they, too, will fall away as I ascend. Oh, was there not, from the first, more poison in thy nature than in mine?"

To Beatrice—so radically had her earthly part been wrought upon by Rappaccini's skill—as poison had been life, so the powerful antidote was death. And thus the poor victim of man's ingenuity and of thwarted nature, and of the fatality that attends all such efforts of perverted wisdom, perished there, at the feet of her father and Giovanni. Just at that moment, Professor Pietro Baglioni looked forth from the window, and called loudly, in a tone of triumph mixed with horror, to the thunder-stricken man of science:

"Rappaccini! Rappaccini! And is *this* the upshot① of your experiment?"

Film Comment:

Nathaniel Hawthorne's *Rappaccini's Daughter*: 57 minutes, color
Starring: Kathleen Beller & Kristopher Tabori
Screenplay by: Herbert Hartig
Directed by: Dezso Magyar

Set in 18th-century Italy, "Rappaccini's Daughter" is the tale of a young scholar named Giovanni (Kristopher Tabori) who falls in love with a beautiful, yet forbidden, girl who tends her father's poison garden.

---

① The final result.

However, the strange and unearthly beauty of Beatrice (Kathleen Beller) masks a terrifying curse which Giovanni must tragically discover. Her father, the mysterious Dr. Rappaccini, has made her the subject of a diabolical experiment. In Giovanni's attempt to free Beatrice from the control of her father and to escape the poisonous effect she begins to have on him, he unwittingly destroys her.

From the short story of master American novelist Nathaniel Hawthorne, two quintessential Hawthorne themes are explored: the sins of interfering with another's soul and the futility of trying to tamper with nature.

Film Scenes:

Scene 1: The poison garden
Scene 2: The forbidden daughter
Scene 3: The meeting
Scene 4: Fever or poison?
Scene 5: Confrontation
Scene 6: The kiss

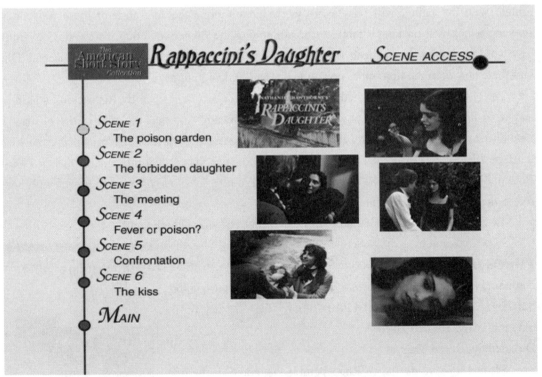

Script Excerpts:

Once upon a time...young Giovanni Guasconti comes from Naples to the city of Padua to pursue his education. Taking lodging in an old mansion, he discovers outside his window a beautiful garden. When he sees there a lovely young girl and her father, he is mystified by their be-

Unit One　Theme
Chapter 1　Rappaccinni's Daughter

havior and demeanor—nor can he find out much about them from his landlady or her servant. When he contacts his father's old friend, Professor Baglioni, the learned man explains that the garden is the property of a rather obsessive scientist, Dr. Rappaccini; and that the girl, Rappaccini's daughter, Beatrice, has never been seen outside the garden. Returning to his room, Giovanni goes to his window, and the following scenes begin.

Exterior. Rappaccini's garden. Late afternoon.

Wearing a gown the color of amethyst, Beatrice makes her way through the dappled sun and shade along the flagstone path, the Camera never leaving her. There is a girlishness about her that we did not see before; alone and thinking herself unobserved, she executes a little skipping step. She hums to herself, reaching out to touch favorite blossoms as she passes. When she comes to the plant with the amethyst flowers, she suddenly and unexpectedly kneels, throws open her arms with passionate ardor, and draws its branches into an intimate embrace, leaning her head against a cluster of blossoms.

Beatrice (*to the plant, her voice at Long Shot distance*): Give me your breath, my sister, for I am faint with common air... And give me this blossom to wear beside my heart.

(*She gently separates one of the clusters from the shrub, and arranges it in her bosom, where it seems to take on all at once added life and luster.*)

Cut to: Inferior. Giovanni's room. Late afternoon.

Giovanni moves his hand across his eyes as if to clear his vision.

Cut to: Exterior. Rappaccini's garden. Late afternoon.

Beatrice now strays through the garden, almost dancing as she moves. She looks up and smiles. We see a butterfly flitting about. Entranced, she extends her hand to it. It circles about her; then to her childlike delight, it lights on her wrist. Delicately, she brings it toward his lips, as if to kiss it. It flutters agitatedly, and drops from her wrist. Beatrice's face falls.

Cut to: Interior. Giovanni's room. Late afternoon.

Giovanni watching, fixated, uneasiness mingling with his curiosity.

Cut to: Exterior. Rappaccini's garden. Close-Up. Beatrice's frock on the flagged walk. Late afternoon.

The dead butterfly at her feet. Camera tilts up Beatrice to Medium Close-Up. She gazes down forlornly, but without surprise. Slowly, she crosses herself.

Cut to: Exterior. Giovanni's window. Giovanni. Late afternoon.

Horrified. Drawing back as if in revulsion, Giovanni overturns the vase on his windowsill.

Cut to: Exterior. Rappacci's garden. High angle shot. Late afternoon.

At the sound, Beatrice looks up and sees Giovanni (the Camera).

Cut to: Exterior. Giovanni's window. Low angle shot. Giovanni. Late afternoon.

Giovanni, as seen for the first time by Beatrice. A handsome, romantic-looking youth, embarrassed at being discovered.

Giovanni (*with a shamefaced grin*): Good evening, Signora.

Cut to: Exterior. Giovanni's window. Medium Close–Up. Giovanni. Late afternoon.

Giovanni (*scarcely knowing what he's saying*): Signora...these pure flowers deserve a better fate than a scholar's musty room. Will you wear them, too, for the sake of Giovanni Guasconti?

He removes the bouquet from the vase and throws it down to Beatrice.

Cut to: Exterior. Rappaccini's garden. Beatrice. Late afternoon.

Stooping to pick up the bouquet that has landed at her feet, she rises, and with a little curtsey:

Beatrice (*smiling shyly*): Grazie, Signor. I would return your gift in kind, with this flower of *mine*, but I could never toss it high enough to reach you. So Signor...Guasconti—?

Cut to: Exterior. Giovanni's window. Late afternoon.

Giovanni nods smiling.

Cut to: Exterior. Rappaccini's garden. Beatrice. Late afternoon.

Beatrice (*as before*):...you must content yourself with my thanks.

(*As she bows to withdraw.*)

Cut to: Exterior. Giovanni's window. Late afternoon.

Giovanni smiles back at her. Suddenly his eyes widen.

Cut to: Exterior. Rappaccini's garden. High angle shot. Beatrice. Late afternoon.

Looking down. Camera tilts down to see the bouquet she is holding. *Are the flowers shriveling in her grasp?* Tilt up to her face, as she moves away quickly toward the house, the Camera following.

Cut to: Exterior. Giovanni's window. Low angle shot. Late afternoon.

Staring.

Cut to: Interior. Giovanni's room. Late afternoon.

Giovanni turns from the window, trying to understand what he has just seen—or *imagined* he's seen...

Slow fade out.

Dissolve to:

Interior. Giovanni's room. Night.

Giovanni with a notebook in the light of an oil lamp, not far from the open window. He looks toward it, as he writes. Giovanni lays down his pen, turns decisively toward the window, and closes the shutters. He picks up a book and begins to read, but his thoughts remain on the window. He hears "Beatrice's Theme" played on the spinet, then looks up from the book, defeated, and shuts the book. After a moment he opens the book again, but he looks up as we...

Dissolve to:

Interior. Giovanni's room. A different angle. Morning.

Unit One　Theme
Chapter 1　Rappaccinni's Daughter

Giovanni beside the window, looking out from such an angle that he could not be observed from outside. In the room behind him, Emma clears away his breakfast tray, watching him with an ambiguous curiosity.

Dissolve to:

Interior. Giovanni's room. Another angle. Late afternoon.

Giovanni at the window. Outside it's raining. In the garden all the plants stand out more sharply defined, their leaves darkened and highlighted by the rain.

Dissolve to:

Interior. Giovanni's room. A different angle. Night.

Giovanni at this writing table, the shutters closed. Now showing signs of nervous strain, he moves toward the window and throws back the shutters.

Cut to:

Exterior. Giovanni's window. Reverse angle. Night.

The night-darkened pensione, Giovanni in his lighted window, thrown into silhouette by the oil lamp behind him. A slow 270 Pan across and down reveals Dr. Rappaccini in the shadow of his doorway, watching Giovanni's room with interest. Over this we hear:

Baglioni (OS, *calling*): Giovanni Guasconti!

Cut to:

Exterior. A street near the university. Late afternoon.

In the foreground, Giovanni, carrying schoolbooks, stopped by the shout, turns. The portly Professor Baglioni comes puffing toward the camera from across the street.

Baglioni (*laughing at his own winded state*): I said to myself: "What! Did I grow up side by side with the father? And shall the son pass me like a stranger?"

He smiles, but his eyes subject Giovanni to a penetrating scrutiny.

Giovanni (*laughs*): I ask your pardon, Professor. I was lost in thought.

Baglioni: I *am* relieved. I thought perhaps you had forgotten me.

Medium close-up. Giovanni.

As he appears to Baglioni: A bit haggard and distracted. He tries to laugh and take his leave but Baglioni puts a restraining hand upon his arm.

Baglioni: Our meeting is a most happy coincidence. I was on my way to see you. I received this morning a letter from your father, saying he has had very little word of you since you left Naples.

Giovanni (*laughs*): You are my conscience, I meant to write. I shall do so this very night.

He starts to go again, but Baglioni is still holding his arm.

Baglioni: And so shall I, and tell him that I saw you and you are well—but tell me, *are* you well, my boy?

Giovanni (*laughs*): Quite well.

Medium close-up. Baglioni.

Eyeing him judiciously.

Baglioni: I am glad to hear it. And yet···it seems to me, that pallor,....the slight...neglect in dress, this impatience to be going you-know-not-where....Were you my patient, I should say you were *far* from well—

Two shot. Giovanni and Baglioni.

Giovanni, irked.

Giovanni: Yes, but, you see, I am not your patient. And so, professor...

(*He interrupts himself as his attention is suddenly riveted elsewhere.*)

Camera Pans Sweepingly from them to the head of the street, to see the stooped, feeble-looking figure of Rappaccini making his way toward us (Giovanni and Baglioni). Pull back to a wider shot, including all three men. Rappaccini fixes a cold-eyed nod on Baglioni. Baglioni replies with a tight little smile and an ironic slight bow. Upon Giovanni, the old man bestows a nod of thoughtful appraisal, then moves on.

Two shot. Giovanni and Baglioni.

Baglioni turns to Giovanni.

Baglioni: Rappaccini! Since last we met you have made his acquaintance?

Giovanni: No.

Baglioni: Yet he nodded to you as if he knew you.

Giovanni (*as if caught with some guilty secret*): Once or twice he may have seen me...at the window.

Baglioni: And nothing more?

Giovanni: No—though on one occasion I exchanged a few words with the signorina.

Baglioni: The daughter! How stupid of me! (*He turns to the bewildered Giovanni.*) My boy, your life is in grave danger! You must quit your lodgings at once.

Giovanni (*incredulously*): What?!

Baglioni: Your lodgings and, if need be, Padua itself.

Giovanni (*masking his annoyance*): Professor, I really must bid you good day.

He starts to go.

Baglioni (*seizing his arm*): I will not let you go until I have exacted a promise: that come what may you will avoid the beautiful Beatrice as though she were the...the forbidden fruit itself.

Giovanni (*quietly*): Signor Professor: You were my father's friend, and I want to show you every respect and deference. So I ask you—please—to let me pass. (*With a wry smile.*) As it happens, you can lay your fears to rest—the signorina has been avoiding *me*.

Baglioni looks at him, not knowing what to make of this unexpected information. Now Giovanni gently but firmly peels Baglioni's hand off his arm.

Giovanni (*continuing*): And *now*, sir, may I bid you good day?

Baglioni inclines his head in his slight ironic bow. And Giovanni goes off up the street.

Baglioni looks after him.

    Baglioni (*to himself, musingly*): Well, now, my fine young Giovanni Guasconti, we shall see...Rappaccini shall not snatch you from me.

Discussion Questions:

1. How does Giovanni meet Beatrice and fall in love with her? Is she a suitable lover?
2. As a scientist, Dr. Rappaccini has made his daughter the subject of a diabolical experiment. What kind of sacrifice is this?
3. Dr. Rappaccini's garden is the whole world for young Beatrice. What does this garden image imply?
4. Giovanni attempts to free Beatrice from her father's control and experiment. What does his good intention bring to her?
5. What are the relations between science and nature in the story? How dangerous is it to tamper with nature?

Further Reading and Watching:

    "Young Goodman Brown"

Chapter 2

The Blue Hotel

Stephen Crane

Author Introduction:

Stephen Crane (1871—1900) was born in Newark, New Jersey, the last and fourteenth child of a Methodist minister. After schooling at Lafayette College and Syracuse University, he worked in New York as a freelance journalist. In 1893 he published at his own expense the novel *Maggie: A Girl of the Streets*, a pioneering work of American literary Naturalism. Without having any battle experience, Crane brought out his famous short novel about the Civil War, *The Red Badge of Courage* (1895), which in theme and technique foreshadows the war novels of the twentieth century. In his brief and energetic life he published fourteen books while acting out, in his personal adventures, the legend of the writer as soldier of fortune. On his way to Cuba for the first time he picked up a mistress at the Hotel de Dream in Jacksonville, Florida—a woman who accompanied him when he went on to Greece as a war correspondent. Malicious gossip about his private life subsequently drove him from America to England, where he settled in 1897 and made friends with leading English writers such as Joseph Conrad and H. G. Wells. Hounded by creditors and afflicted by tuberculosis, he died in Germany at the age of 28. In Crane, the contradictions and tensions present in many writers seem to be intensified, and his common themes involve fear, spiritual crises and social isolation. His short stories were collected in *The Open Boat and Other Tales of Adventure* (1898), *The Monster and Other Stories* (1899), and *Wounds in the Rain* (1900). His complete works in prose and verse were published in 1925-1926.

Story Summary:

A century ago, a foreigner (a Swede) travels to a Nebraska hotel, his mind filled with the romantic violence of Western dime novels. He soon finds his expectations fulfilled,

Unit One Theme

Chapter 2 The Blue Hotel

confronting a disturbing fate whose mysterious cause ultimately seems to elude us. Being accused of cheating at cards, the young man must defend his personal identity, his father must give up some protection of his son, and the Swede must prove his worth. The tensions created by this scenario come to a head, when the two have to fight to prove they are worthy of the reputations of the West. After the battle is decided, the final duel with fear proves to be the most significant of them all.

Key Terms:
Naturalism, Dime Novel, Impressionist, Realism, Community, Outsider

The Blue Hotel[①]

I

The Palace Hotel at Fort Romper was painted a light blue, a shade that is on the legs of a kind of heron, causing the bird to declare its position against any background. The Palace Hotel, then, was always screaming and howling in a way that made the dazzling winter landscape of Nebraska seem only a gray swampish hush. It stood alone on the prairie, and when the snow was falling the town two hundred yards away was not visible. But when the traveler alighted at the railway station he was obliged to pass the Palace Hotel before he could come upon the company of low clapboard houses which composed Fort Romper, and it was not to be thought that any traveler could pass the Palace Hotel without looking at it. Pat Scully, the proprietor, had proved himself a master of strategy when he chose his paints. It is true that on clear days, when the great trans-continental expresses, long lines of swaying Pullmans[②], swept through Fort Romper, passengers were overcome at the sight, and the cult that knows the brown-reds and the subdivisions of the dark greens of the East expressed shame, pity, horror, in a laugh. But to the citizens of this prairie town and to the people who would naturally stop there, Pat Scully had performed a feat. With this opulence and splendor, these creeds, classes, egotisms, that streamed through Romper on the rails day after day, they had no color in common.

As if the displayed delights of such a blue hotel were not sufficiently enticing, it was Scully's habit to go every morning and evening to meet the leisurely trains that stopped at Romper and work his seductions upon any man that he might see wavering, gripsack[③] in hand.

One morning, when a snow-crusted engine dragged its long string of freight cars and its one passenger coach to the station, Scully performed the marvel of catching three men. One was a shaky and quick-eyed Swede, with a great shining cheap valise; one was a tall bronzed cowboy,

---

① First published in two installments in *Collier's Weekly* for November 26 and December 3, 1898, then in *The Monster and Other Stories* (1899).
② Railroad cars with sleeping accommodations.
③ Suitcase.

who was on his way to a ranch near the Dakota line; one was a little silent man from the East, who didn't look it, and didn't announce it. Scully practically made them prisoners. He was so nimble and merry and kindly that each probably felt it would be the height of brutality to try to escape. They trudged off over the creaking board sidewalks in the wake of the eager little Irishman. He wore a heavy fur cap squeezed tightly down on his head. It caused his two red ears to stick out stiffly, as if they were made of tin.

At last, Scully, elaborately, with boisterous hospitality, conducted them through the portals of the blue hotel. The room which they entered was small. It seemed to be merely a proper temple for an enormous stove, which, in the center, was humming with godlike violence. At various points on its surface the iron had become luminous and glowed yellow from the heat. Beside the stove Scully's son Johnnie was playing High-Five① with an old farmer who had whiskers both gray and sandy. They were quarrelling. Frequently the old farmer turned his face towards a box of sawdust—colored brown from tobacco juice—that was behind the stove, and spat with an air of great impatience and irritation. With a loud flourish of words Scully destroyed the game of cards, and bustled his son up-stairs with part of the baggage of the new guests. He himself conducted them to three basins of the coldest water in the world. The cowboy and the Easterner burnished themselves fiery-red with this water, until it seemed to be some kind of a metal polish. The Swede, however, merely dipped his fingers gingerly and with trepidation. It was notable that throughout this series of small ceremonies the three travelers were made to feel that Scully was very benevolent. He was conferring great favors upon them. He handed the towel from one to the other with an air of philanthropic impulse.

Afterwards they went to the first room, and, sitting about the stove, listened to Scully's officious clamor at his daughters, who were preparing the mid-day meal. They reflected in the silence of experienced men who tread carefully amid new people. Nevertheless, the old farmer, stationary, invincible in his chair near the warmest part of the stove, turned his face from the sawdust box frequently and addressed a glowing commonplace to the strangers. Usually he was answered in short but adequate sentences by either the cowboy or the Easterner. The Swede said nothing. He seemed to be occupied in making furtive estimates of each man in the room. One might have thought that he had the sense of silly suspicion which comes to guilt. He resembled a badly frightened man.

Later, at dinner, he spoke a little, addressing his conversation entirely to Scully. He volunteered that he had come from New York, where for ten years he had worked as a tailor. These facts seemed to strike Scully as fascinating, and afterwards he volunteered that he had lived at Romper for fourteen years. The Swede asked about the crops and the price of labor. He seemed barely to listen to Scully's extended replies. His eyes continued to rove from man to man.

Finally, with a laugh and a wink, he said that some of these Western communities were very

---

① Cinch, a card game.

dangerous; and after his statement he straightened his legs under the table, tilted his head, and laughed again, loudly. It was plain that the demonstration had no meaning to the others. They looked at him wondering and in silence.

II

As the men trooped heavily back into the front-room, the two little windows presented views of a turmoiling sea of snow. The huge arms of the wind were making attempts—mighty, circular, futile—to embrace the flakes as they sped. A gate-post like a still man with a blanched face stood aghast amid this profligate fury. In a hearty voice Scully announced the presence of a blizzard. The guests of the blue hotel, lighting their pipes, assented with grunts of lazy masculine contentment. No island of the sea could be exempt in the degree of this little room with its humming stove. Johnnie, son of Scully, in a tone which defined his opinion of his ability as a card-player, challenged the old farmer of both gray and sandy whiskers to a game of High-Five. The farmer agreed with a contemptuous and bitter scoff. They sat close to the stove, and squared their knees under a wide board. The cowboy and the Easterner watched the game with interest. The Swede remained near the window, aloof, but with a countenance that showed signs of an inexplicable excitement.

The play of Johnnie and the gray-beard was suddenly ended by another quarrel. The old man arose while casting a look of heated scorn at his adversary. He slowly buttoned his coat, and then stalked with fabulous dignity from the room. In the discreet silence of all other men the Swede laughed. His laughter rang somehow childish. Men by this time had begun to look at him askance, as if they wished to inquire what ailed him.

A new game was formed jocosely. The cowboy volunteered to become the partner of Johnnie, and they all then turned to ask the Swede to throw in his lot with the little Easterner. He asked some questions about the game, and, learning that it wore many names, and that he had played it when it was under an alias, he accepted the invitation. He strode towards the men nervously, as if he expected to be assaulted. Finally, seated, he gazed from face to face and laughed shrilly. This laugh was so strange that the Easterner looked up quickly, the cowboy sat intent and with his mouth open, and Johnnie paused, holding the cards with still fingers.

Afterwards there was a short silence. Then Johnnie said, "Well, let's get at it. Come on now!" They pulled their chairs forward until their knees were bunched under the board. They began to play, and their interest in the game caused the others to forget the manner of the Swede.

The cowboy was a board-whacker. Each time that he held superior cards he whanged them, one by one, with exceeding force, down upon the improvised table, and took the tricks with a glowing air of prowess and pride that sent thrills of indignation into the hearts of his opponents. A game with a board-whacker in it is sure to become intense. The countenances of the Easterner and the Swede were miserable whenever the cowboy thundered down his aces and kings, while Johnnie, his eyes gleaming with joy, chuckled and chuckled.

Because of the absorbing play none considered the strange ways of the Swede. They paid strict heed to the game. Finally, during a lull caused by a new deal, the Swede suddenly addressed Johnnie: "I suppose there have been a good many men killed in this room." The jaws of the others dropped and they looked at him.

"What in hell are you talking about?" said Johnnie.

The Swede laughed again his blatant laugh, full of a kind of false courage and defiance. "Oh, you know what I mean all right," he answered.

"I'm a liar if I do!" Johnnie protested. The card was halted, and the men stared at the Swede. Johnnie evidently felt that as the son of the proprietor he should make a direct inquiry. "Now, what might you be drivin' at, mister?" he asked. The Swede winked at him. It was a wink full of cunning. His fingers shook on the edge of the board. "Oh, maybe you think I have been to nowheres. Maybe you think I'm a tenderfoot?"

"I don't know nothin' about you," answered Johnnie, "and I don't give a damn where you've been. All I got to say is that I don't know what you're driving at. There hain't never been nobody killed in this room."

The cowboy, who had been steadily gazing at the Swede, then spoke: "What's wrong with you, mister?"

Apparently it seemed to the Swede that he was formidably menaced. He shivered and turned white near the corners of his mouth. He sent an appealing glance in the direction of the little Easterner. During these moments he did not forget to wear his air of advanced pot-valor[①]. "They say they don't know what I mean," he remarked mockingly to the Easterner.

The latter answered after prolonged and cautious reflection. "I don't understand you," he said, impassively.

The Swede made a movement then which announced that he thought he had encountered treachery from the only quarter where he had expected sympathy, if not help. "Oh, I see you are all against me. I see—"

The cowboy was in a state of deep stupefaction. "Say," he cried, as he tumbled the deck violently down upon the board "—say, what are you gittin' at, hey?"

The Swede sprang up with the celerity of a man escaping from a snake on the floor. "I don't want to fight!" he shouted. "I don't want to fight!"

The cowboy stretched his long legs indolently and deliberately. His hands were in his pockets. He spat into the sawdust box. "Well, who the hell thought you did?" he inquired.

The Swede backed rapidly towards a corner of the room. His hands were out protectingly in front of his chest, but he was making an obvious struggle to control his fright. "Gentlemen," he quavered, "I suppose I am going to be killed before I can leave this house! I suppose I am going to be killed before I can leave this house!" In his eyes was the dying-swan look. Through the

---

① Drunken bravado.

windows could be seen the snow turning blue in the shadow of dusk. The wind tore at the house and some loose thing beat regularly against the clap-boards like a spirit tapping.

A door opened, and Scully himself entered. He paused in surprise as he noted the tragic attitude of the Swede. Then he said, "What's the matter here?"

The Swede answered him swiftly and eagerly: "These men are going to kill me."

"Kill you!" ejaculated Scully. "Kill you! What are you talkin'?"

The Swede made the gesture of a martyr.

Scully wheeled sternly upon his son. "What is this, Johnnie?"

The lad had grown sullen. "Damned if I know," he answered. "I can't make no sense to it." He began to shuffle the cards, fluttering them together with an angry snap. "He says a good many men have been killed in this room, or something like that. And he says he's goin' to be killed here too. I don't know what ails him. He's crazy, I shouldn't wonder."

Scully then looked for explanation to the cowboy, but the cowboy simply shrugged his shoulders.

"Kill you?" said Scully again to the Swede. "Kill you? Man, you're off your nut."

"Oh, I know," burst out the Swede. "I know what will happen. Yes, I'm crazy—yes. Yes, of course, I'm crazy—yes. But I know one thing—" There was a sort of sweat of misery and terror upon his face. "I know I won't get out of here alive."

The cowboy drew a deep breath, as if his mind was passing into the last stages of dissolution. "Well, I'm dog-goned," he whispered to himself.

Scully wheeled suddenly and faced his son. "You've been troublin' this man!"

Johnnie's voice was loud with its burden of grievance. "Why, good Gawd, I ain't done nothin' to 'im."

The Swede broke in. "Gentlemen, do not disturb yourselves. I will leave this house. I will go away because"—he accused them dramatically with his glance—"because I do not want to be killed."

Scully was furious with his son. "Will you tell me what is the matter, you young divil? What's the matter, anyhow? Speak out!"

"Blame it!" cried Johnnie in despair, "don't I tell you I don't know. He—he says we want to kill him, and that's all I know. I can't tell what ails him."

The Swede continued to repeat: "Never mind, Mr. Scully; never mind. I will leave this house. I will go away, because I do not wish to be killed. Yes, of course, I am crazy—yes. But I know one thing! I will go away. I will leave this house. Never mind, Mr. Scully; never mind. I will go away."

"You will not go 'way," said Scully. "You will not go 'way until I hear the reason of this business. If anybody has troubled you I will take care of him. This is my house. You are under my roof, and I will not allow any peaceable man to be troubled here." He cast a terrible eye upon Johnnie, the cowboy, and the Easterner.

"Never mind, Mr. Scully; never mind. I will go away. I do not wish to be killed." The Swede moved towards the door, which opened upon the stairs. It was evidently his intention to go at once for his baggage.

"No, no," shouted Scully peremptorily; but the white-faced man slid by him and disappeared. "Now," said Scully severely, "what does this mane?"

Johnnie and the cowboy cried together: "Why, we didn't do nothin' to 'im!"

Scully's eyes were cold. "No," he said, "you didn't?"

Johnnie swore a deep oath. "Why this is the wildest loon I ever see. We didn't do nothin' at all. We were jest sittin' here playin' cards, and he—"

The father suddenly spoke to the Easterner. "Mr. Blanc," he asked, "what has these boys been doin'?"

The Easterner reflected again. "I didn't see anything wrong at all," he said at last, slowly.

Scully began to howl. "But what does it mane?" He stared ferociously at his son. "I have a mind to lather you for this, me boy."

Johnnie was frantic. "Well, what have I done?" he bawled at his father.

III

"I think you are tongue-tied," said Scully finally to his son, the cowboy, and the Easterner; and at the end of this scornful sentence he left the room.

Up-stairs the Swede was swiftly fastening the straps of his great valise. Once his back happened to be half turned towards the door, and, hearing a noise there, he wheeled and sprang up, uttering a loud cry. Scully's wrinkled visage showed grimly in the light of the small lamp he carried. This yellow effulgence, streaming upward, colored only his prominent features, and left his eyes, for instance, in mysterious shadow. He resembled a murderer.

"Man! man!" he exclaimed, "have you gone daffy?"

"Oh, no! Oh, no!" rejoined the other. "There are people in this world who know pretty nearly as much as you do—understand?"

For a moment they stood gazing at each other. Upon the Swede's deathly pale cheeks were two spots brightly crimson and sharply edged, as if they had been carefully painted. Scully placed the light on the table and sat himself on the edge of the bed. He spoke ruminatively. "By cracky, I never heard of such a thing in my life. It's a complete muddle. I can't, for the soul of me, think how you ever got this idea into your head." Presently he lifted his eyes and asked: "And did you sure think they were going to kill you?"

The Swede scanned the old man as if he wished to see into his mind. "I did," he said at last. He obviously suspected that this answer might precipitate an outbreak. As he pulled on a strap his whole arm shook, the elbow wavering like a bit of paper.

Scully banged his hand impressively on the foot-board of the bed. "Why, man, we're goin' to have a line of ilictric street-cars in this town next spring."

Unit One　Theme
Chapter 2　The Blue Hotel

"'A line of electric street-cars,'" repeated the Swede, stupidly.

"And," said Scully, "there's a new railroad goin' to be built down from Broken Arm to here. Not to mintion the four churches and the smashin' big brick school-house. Then there's the big factory, too. Why, in two years Romper'll be a *metropolis*."

Having finished the preparation of his baggage, the Swede straightened himself. "Mr. Scully," he said, with sudden hardihood, "how much do I owe you?"

"You don't owe me anythin'," said the old man, angrily.

"Yes, I do," retorted the Swede. He took seventy-five cents from his pocket and tendered it to Scully; but the latter snapped his fingers in disdainful refusal. However, it happened that they both stood gazing in a strange fashion at three silver pieces on the Swede's open palm.

"I'll not take your money," said Scully at last. "Not after what's been goin' on here." Then a plan seemed to strike him. "Here," he cried, picking up his lamp and moving towards the door. "Here! Come with me a minute."

"No," said the Swede, in overwhelming alarm.

"Yes," urged the old man. "Come on! I want you to come and see a picter—just across the hall—in my room."

The Swede must have concluded that his hour was come. His jaw dropped and his teeth showed like a dead man's. He ultimately followed Scully across the corridor, but he had the step of one hung in chains.

Scully flashed the light high on the wall of his own chamber. There was revealed a ridiculous photograph of a little girl. She was leaning against a balustrade of gorgeous decoration, and the formidable bang to her hair was prominent. The figure was as graceful as an upright sled-stake, and, withal, it was of the hue of lead. "There," said Scully, tenderly, "that's the picter of my little girl that died. Her name was Carrie. She had the purtiest hair you ever saw! I was that fond of her, she—"

Turning then, he saw that the Swede was not contemplating the picture at all, but, instead, was keeping keen watch on the gloom in the rear.

"Look, man!" cried Scully, heartily. "That's the picter of my little gal that died. Her name was Carrie. And then here's the picter of my oldest boy, Michael. He's a lawyer in Lincoln, an' doin' well. I gave that boy a grand eddycation, and I'm glad for it now. He's a fine boy. Look at 'im now. Ain't he bold as blazes, him there in Lincoln, an honored an' respected gintleman. An honored an' respected gintleman," concluded Scully with a flourish. And, so saying, he smote the Swede jovially on the back.

The Swede faintly smiled.

"Now," said the old man, "there's only one more thing." He dropped suddenly to the floor and thrust his head beneath the bed. The Swede could hear his muffled voice. "I'd keep it under me piller if it wasn't for that boy Johnnie. Then there's the old woman—Where is it now? I never put it twice in the same place. Ah, now come out with you!"

Presently he backed clumsily from under the bed, dragging with him an old coat rolled into a bundle. "I've fetched him," he muttered. Kneeling on the floor, he unrolled the coat and extracted from its heart a large yellow-brown whiskey bottle.

His first maneuver was to hold the bottle up to the light. Reassured, apparently, that nobody had been tampering with it, he thrust it with a generous movement towards the Swede.

The weak-kneed Swede was about to eagerly clutch this element of strength, but he suddenly jerked his hand away and cast a look of horror upon Scully.

"Drink," said the old man affectionately. He had risen to his feet, and now stood facing the Swede.

There was a silence. Then again Scully said: "Drink!"

The Swede laughed wildly. He grabbed the bottle, put it to his mouth, and as his lips curled absurdly around the opening and his throat worked, he kept his glance, burning with hatred, upon the old man's face.

IV

After the departure of Scully the three men, with the card-board still upon their knees, preserved for a long time an astounded silence. Then Johnnie said: "That's the dod-dangest Swede I ever see."

"He ain't no Swede," said the cowboy, scornfully.

"Well, what is he then?" cried Johnnie. "What is he then?"

"It's my opinion," replied the cowboy deliberately, "he's some kind of a Dutchman." It was a venerable custom of the country to entitle as Swedes all light-haired men who spoke with a heavy tongue. In consequence the idea of the cowboy was not without its daring. "Yes, sir," he repeated. "It's my opinion this feller is some kind of a Dutchman."

"Well, he says he's a Swede, anyhow," muttered Johnnie, sulkily. He turned to the Easterner: "What do you think, Mr. Blanc?"

"Oh, I don't know," replied the Easterner.

"Well, what do you think makes him act that way?" asked the cowboy.

"Why, he's frightened." The Easterner knocked his pipe against a rim of the stove. "He's clear frightened out of his boots."

"What at?" cried Johnnie and cowboy together.

The Easterner reflected over his answer.

"What at?" cried the others again.

"Oh, I don't know, but it seems to me this man has been reading dime-novels, and he thinks he's right out in the middle of it—the shootin' and stabbin' and all."

"But," said the cowboy, deeply scandalized, "this ain't Wyoming, ner none of them places. This is Nebrasker."

"Yes," added Johnnie, "an' why don't he wait till he gits *out West*?"

The travelled Easterner laughed. "It isn't different there even—not in these days. But he thinks he's right in the middle of hell."

Johnnie and the cowboy mused long.

"It's awful funny," remarked Johnnie at last.

"Yes," said the cowboy. "This is a queer game. I hope we don't git snowed in, because then we'd have to stand this here man bein' around with us all the time. That wouldn't be no good."

"I wish pop would throw him out," said Johnnie.

Presently they heard a loud stamping on the stairs, accompanied by ringing jokes in the voice of old Scully, and laughter, evidently from the Swede. The men around the stove stared vacantly at each other. "Gosh!" said the cowboy. The door flew open, and old Scully, flushed and anecdotal, came into the room. He was jabbering at the Swede, who followed him, laughing bravely. It was the entry of two roisterers from a banquet-hall.

"Come now," said Scully sharply to the three seated men, "move up and give us a chance at the stove." The cowboy and the Easterner obediently sidled their chairs to make room for the new-comers. Johnnie, however, simply arranged himself in a more indolent attitude, and then remained motionless.

"Come! Git over, there," said Scully.

"Plenty of room on the other side of the stove," said Johnnie.

"Do you think we want to sit in the draught?" roared the father.

But the Swede here interposed with a grandeur of confidence. "No, no. Let the boy sit where he likes," he cried in a bullying voice to the father.

"All right! All right!" said Scully, deferentially. The cowboy and the Easterner exchanged glances of wonder.

The five chairs were formed in a crescent about one side of the stove. The Swede began to talk; he talked arrogantly, profanely, angrily. Johnnie, the cowboy, and the Easterner maintained a morose silence, while old Scully appeared to be receptive and eager, breaking in constantly with sympathetic ejaculations.

Finally the Swede announced that he was thirsty. He moved in his chair, and said that he would go for a drink of water.

"I'll git it for you," cried Scully at once.

"No," said the Swede, contemptuously. "I'll get it for myself." He arose and stalked with the air of an owner off into the executive parts of the hotel.

As soon as the Swede was out of hearing Scully sprang to his feet and whispered intensely to the others: "Up-stairs he thought I was tryin' to poison 'im."

"Say," said Johnnie, "this makes me sick. Why don't you throw 'im out in the snow?"

"Why, he's all right now," declared Scully. "It was only that he was from the East, and he thought this was a tough place. That's all. He's all right now."

The cowboy looked with admiration upon the Easterner. "You were straight," he said. "You were on to that there Dutchman."

"Well," said Johnnie to his father, "he may be all right now, but I don't see it. Other time he was scared, but now he's too fresh."

Scully's speech was always a combination of Irish brogue and idiom, Western twang and idiom, and scraps of curiously formal diction taken from the story-books and newspapers. He now hurled a strange mass of language at the head of his son. "What do I keep? What do I keep? What do I keep?" he demanded, in a voice of thunder. He slapped his knee impressively, to indicate that he himself was going to make reply, and that all should heed. "I keep a hotel," he shouted. "A hotel, do you mind? A guest under my roof has sacred privileges. He is to be intimidated by none. Not one word shall he hear that would prejudice him in favor of goin' away. I'll not have it. There's no place in this here town where they can say they iver took in a guest of mine because he was afraid to stay here." He wheeled suddenly upon the cowboy and the Easterner. "Am I right?"

"Yes, Mr. Scully," said the cowboy, "I think you're right."

"Yes, Mr. Scully," said the Easterner, "I think you're right."

V

At six-o'clock supper, the Swede fizzed like a fire-wheel. He sometimes seemed on the point of bursting into riotous song, and in all his madness he was encouraged by old Scully. The Easterner was incased in reserve; the cowboy sat in wide-mouthed amazement, forgetting to eat, while Johnnie wrathily demolished great plates of food. The daughters of the house, when they were obliged to replenish the biscuits, approached as warily as Indians, and, having succeeded in their purpose, fled with ill-concealed trepidation. The Swede domineered the whole feast, and he gave it the appearance of a cruel bacchanal. He seemed to have grown suddenly taller; he gazed, brutally disdainful, into every face. His voice rang through the room. Once when he jabbed out harpoon-fashion with his fork to pinion a biscuit, the weapon nearly impaled the hand of the Easterner which had been stretched quietly out for the same biscuit.

After supper, as the men filed towards the other room, the Swede smote Scully ruthlessly on the shoulder. "Well, old boy, that was a good, square meal." Johnnie looked hopefully at his father; he knew that shoulder was tender from an old fall; and, indeed, it appeared for a moment as if Scully was going to flame out over the matter, but in the end he smiled a sickly smile and remained silent. The others understood from his manner that he was admitting his responsibility for the Swede's new view-point.

Johnnie, however, addressed his parent in an aside. "Why don't you license somebody to kick you down-stairs?" Scully scowled darkly by way of reply.

When they were gathered about the stove, the Swede insisted on another game of High Five. Scully gently deprecated the plan at first, but the Swede turned a wolfish glare upon him.

Unit One Theme
Chapter 2 The Blue Hotel

The old man subsided, and the Swede canvassed the others. In his tone there was always a great threat. The cowboy and the Easterner both remarked indifferently that they would play. Scully said that he would presently have to go to meet the 6.58 train, and so the Swede turned menacingly upon Johnnie. For a moment their glances crossed like blades, and then Johnnie smiled and said, "Yes, I'll play."

They formed a square, with the little board on their knees. The Easterner and the Swede were again partners. As the play went on, it was noticeable that the cowboy was not board-whacking as usual. Meanwhile, Scully, near the lamp, had put on his spectacles and, with an appearance curiously like an old priest, was reading a newspaper. In time he went out to meet the 6.58 train, and, despite his precautions, a gust of polar wind whirled into the room as he opened the door. Besides scattering the cards, it dulled the players to the marrow. The Swede cursed frightfully. When Scully returned, his entrance disturbed a cosey and friendly scene. The Swede again cursed. But presently they were once more intent, their heads bent forward and their hands moving swiftly. The Swede had adopted the fashion of board-whacking.

Scully took up his paper and for a long time remained immersed in matters which were extraordinarily remote from him. The lamp burned badly, and once he stopped to adjust the wick. The newspaper, as he turned from page to page, rustled with a slow and comfortable sound. Then suddenly he heard three terrible words: "You are cheatin'!"

Such scenes often prove that there can be little of dramatic import in environment. Any room can present a tragic front; any room can be comic. This little den was now hideous as a torture-chamber. The new faces of the men themselves had changed it upon the instant. The Swede held a huge fist in front of Johnnie's face, while the latter looked steadily over it into the blazing orbs of his accuser. The Easterner had grown pallid; the cowboy's jaw had dropped in that expression of bovine amazement which was one of his important mannerisms. After the three words, the first sound in the room was made by Scully's paper as it floated forgotten to his feet. His spectacles had also fallen from his nose, but by a clutch he had saved them in air. His hand, grasping the spectacles, now remained poised awkwardly and near his shoulder. He stared at the card-players.

Probably the silence was while a second elapsed. Then, if the floor had been suddenly twitched out from under the men they could not have moved quicker. The five had projected themselves headlong towards a common point. It happened that Johnnie, in rising to hurl himself upon the Swede, had stumbled slightly because of his curiously instinctive care for the cards and the board. The loss of the moment allowed time for the arrival of Scully, and also allowed the cowboy time to give the Swede a great push which sent him staggering back. The men found tongue together, and hoarse shouts of rage, appeal, or fear burst from every throat. The cowboy pushed and jostled feverishly at the Swede, and the Easterner and Scully clung wildly to Johnnie; but, through the smoky air, above the swaying bodies of the peace-compellers, the eyes of the two warriors ever sought each other in glances of challenge that were at once hot and steely.

Of course the board had been overturned, and now the whole company of cards was scattered over the floor, where the boots of the men trampled the fat and painted kings and queens as they gazed with their silly eyes at the war that was waging above them.

Scully's voice was dominating the yells. "Stop now? Stop, I say! Stop, now—"

Johnnie, as he struggled to burst through the rank formed by Scully and the Easterner, was crying, "Well, he says I cheated! He says I cheated! I won't allow no man to say I cheated! If he says I cheated, he's a—!"

The cowboy was telling the Swede, "Quit, now! Quit, d'ye hear—"

The screams of the Swede never ceased: "He did cheat! I saw him! I saw him—"

As for the Easterner, he was importuning in a voice that was not heeded: "Wait a moment, can't you? Oh, wait a moment. What's the good of a fight over a game of cards? Wait a moment—"

In this tumult no complete sentences were clear. "Cheat"—"Quit"—"He says"—these fragments pierced the uproar and rang out sharply. It was remarkable that, whereas Scully undoubtedly made the most noise, he was the least heard of any of the riotous band.

Then suddenly there was a great cessation. It was as if each man had paused for breath; and although the room was still lighted with the anger of men, it could be seen that there was no danger of immediate conflict, and at once Johnnie, shouldering his way forward, almost succeeded in confronting the Swede. "What did you say I cheated for? What did you say I cheated for? I don't cheat, and I won't let no man say I do!"

The Swede said, "I saw you! I saw you!"

"Well," cried Johnnie, "I'll fight any man what says I cheat!"

"No, you won't," said the cowboy. "Not here."

"Ah, be still, can't you?" said Scully, coming between them.

The quiet was sufficient to allow the Easterner's voice to be heard. He was repeating, "Oh, wait a moment, can't you? What's the good of a fight over a game of cards? Wait a moment!"

Johnnie, his red face appearing above his father's shoulder, hailed the Swede again. "Did you say I cheated?"

The Swede showed his teeth. "Yes."

"Then," said Johnnie, "we must fight."

"Yes, fight," roared the Swede. He was like a demoniac. "Yes, fight! I'll show you what kind of a man I am! I'll show you who you want to fight! Maybe you think I can't fight! Maybe you think I can't! I'll show you, you skin[①], you card-sharp! Yes, you cheated! You cheated! You cheated!"

"Well, let's go at it, then, mister," said Johnnie, coolly.

The cowboy's brow was beaded with sweat from his efforts in intercepting all sorts of

---

① Cheat (colloquial).

raids. He turned in despair to Scully. "What are you goin' to do now?"

A change had come over the Celtic visage of the old man. He now seemed all eagerness; his eyes glowed.

"We'll let them fight," he answered, stalwartly. "I can't put up with it any longer. I've stood this damned Swede till I'm sick. We'll let them fight."

VI

The men prepared to go out-of-doors. The Easterner was so nervous that he had great difficulty in getting his arms into the sleeves of his new leather coat. As the cowboy drew his fur cap down over his ears his hands trembled. In fact, Johnnie and old Scully were the only ones who displayed no agitation. These preliminaries were conducted without words.

Scully threw open the door. "Well, come on," he said. Instantly a terrific wind caused the flame of the lamp to struggle at its wick, while a puff of black smoke sprang from the chimney-top. The stove was in mid-current of the blast, and its voice swelled to equal the roar of the storm. Some of the scarred and bedabbled cards were caught up from the floor and dashed helplessly against the farther wall. The men lowered their heads and plunged into the tempest as into a sea.

No snow was falling, but great whirls and clouds of flakes, swept up from the ground by the frantic winds, were streaming southward with the speed of bullets. The covered land was blue with the sheen of an unearthly satin, and there was no other hue save where, at the low, black railway station—which seemed incredibly distant—one light gleamed like a tiny jewel. As the men floundered into a thigh deep drift, it was known that the Swede was bawling out something. Scully went to him, put a hand on his shoulder and projected an ear. "What's that you say?" he shouted.

"I say," bawled the Swede again, "I won't stand much show against this gang. I know you'll all pitch on me."

Scully smote him reproachfully on the arm. "Tut, man!" he yelled. The wind tore the words from Scully's lips and scattered them far alee.

"You are all a gang of—" boomed the Swede, but the storm also seized the remainder of this sentence.

Immediately turning their backs upon the wind, the men had swung around a corner to the sheltered side of the hotel. It was the function of the little house to preserve here, amid this great devastation of snow, an irregular V-shape of heavily incrusted grass, which crackled beneath the feet. One could imagine the great drifts piled against the windward side. When the party reached the comparative peace of this spot it was found that the Swede was still bellowing.

"Oh, I know what kind of a thing this is! I know you'll all pitch on me. I can't lick you all!"

Scully turned upon him panther fashion. "You'll not have to whip all of us. You'll have to whip my son Johnnie. An' the man what troubles you durin' that time will have me to dale with."

The arrangements were swiftly made. The two men faced each other, obedient to the harsh commands of Scully, whose face, in the subtly luminous gloom, could be seen set in the austere impersonal lines that are pictured on the countenances of the Roman veterans. The Easterner's teeth were chattering, and he was hopping up and down like a mechanical toy. The cowboy stood rock-like.

The contestants had not stripped off any clothing. Each was in his ordinary attire. Their fists were up, and they eyed each other in a calm that had the elements of leonine cruelty in it.

During this pause, the Easterner's mind, like a film, took lasting impressions of three men—the iron-nerved master of the ceremony; the Swede, pale, motionless, terrible; and Johnnie, serene yet ferocious, brutish yet heroic. The entire prelude had in it a tragedy greater than the tragedy of action, and this aspect was accentuated by the long, mellow cry of the blizzard, as it sped the tumbling and wailing flakes into the black abyss of the south.

"Now!" said Scully.

The two combatants leaped forward and crashed together like bullocks. There was heard the cushioned sound of blows, and of a curse squeezing out from between the tight teeth of one.

As for the spectators, the Easterner's pent-up breath exploded from him with a pop of relief, absolute relief from the tension of the preliminaries. The cowboy bounded into the air with a yowl. Scully was immovable as from supreme amazement and fear at the fury of the fight which he himself had permitted and arranged.

For a time the encounter in the darkness was such a perplexity of flying arms that it presented no more detail than would a swiftly revolving wheel. Occasionally a face, as if illumined by a flash of light, would shine out, ghastly and marked with pink spots. A moment later, the men might have been known as shadows, if it were not for the involuntary utterance of oaths that came from them in whispers.

Suddenly a holocaust of warlike desire caught the cowboy, and he bolted forward with the speed of a broncho. "Go it, Johnnie! Go it! Kill him! Kill him!"

Scully confronted him. "Kape back," he said; and by his glance the cowboy could tell that this man was Johnnie's father.

To the Easterner there was a monotony of unchangeable fighting that was an abomination. This confused mingling was eternal to his sense, which was concentrated in a longing for the end, the priceless end. Once the fighters lurched near him, and as he scrambled hastily backward he heard them breathe like men on the rack.

"Kill him, Johnnie! Kill him! Kill him! Kill him!" The cowboy's face was contorted like one of those agony masks in museums.

"Keep still," said Scully, icily.

Then there was a sudden loud grunt, incomplete, cut short, and Johnnie's body swung away from the Swede and fell with sickening heaviness to the grass. The cowboy was barely in time to prevent the mad Swede from flinging himself upon his prone adversary. "No, you don't," said the cowboy, interposing an arm. "Wait a second."

Scully was at his son's side. "Johnnie! Johnnie, me boy!" His voice had a quality of melancholy tenderness. "Johnnie! Can you go on with it?" He looked anxiously down into the bloody, pulpy face of his son.

There was a moment of silence, and then Johnnie answered in his ordinary voice, "Yes, I—it—yes."

Assisted by his father he struggled to his feet. "Wait a bit now till you git your wind," said the old man.

A few paces away the cowboy was lecturing the Swede. "No, you don't! Wait a second!"

The Easterner was plucking at Scully's sleeve. "Oh, this is enough," he pleaded. "This is enough! Let it go as it stands. This is enough!"

"Bill," said Scully, "git out of the road." The cowboy stepped aside. "Now." The combatants were actuated by a new caution as they advanced towards collision. They glared at each other, and then the Swede aimed a lightning blow that carried with it his entire weight. Johnnie was evidently half stupid from weakness, but he miraculously dodged, and his fist sent the over-balanced Swede sprawling.

The cowboy, Scully, and the Easterner burst into a cheer that was like a chorus of triumphant soldiery, but before its conclusion the Swede had scuffled agilely to his feet and come in berserk abandon at his foe. There was another perplexity of flying arms, and Johnnie's body again swung away and fell, even as a bundle might fall from a roof. The Swede instantly staggered to a little wind-waved tree and leaned upon it, breathing like an engine, while his savage and flame-lit eyes roamed from face to face as the men bent over Johnnie. There was a splendor of isolation in his situation at this time which the Easterner felt once when, lifting his eyes from the man on the ground, he beheld that mysterious and lonely figure, waiting.

"Are you any good yet, Johnnie?" asked Scully in a broken voice.

The son gasped and opened his eyes languidly. After a moment he answered, "No—I ain't—any good—any—more." Then, from shame and bodily ill he began to weep, the tears furrowing down through the blood-stains on his face. "He was too—too—too heavy for me."

Scully straightened and addressed the waiting figure. "Stranger," he said, evenly, "it's all up with our side." Then his voice changed into that vibrant huskiness which is commonly the tone of the most simple and deadly announcements. "Johnnie is whipped."

Without replying, the victor moved off on the route to the front door of the hotel.

The cowboy was formulating new and un-spellable blasphemies. The Easterner was startled to find that they were out in a wind that seemed to come direct from the shadowed arctic floes. He heard again the wail of the snow as it was flung to its grave in the south. He knew now that all this time the cold had been sinking into him deeper and deeper, and he wondered that he had not perished. He felt indifferent to the condition of the vanquished man.

"Johnnie, can you walk?" asked Scully.

"Did I hurt—hurt him any?" asked the son.

"Can you walk, boy? Can you walk?"

Johnnie's voice was suddenly strong. There was a robust impatience in it. "I asked you whether I hurt him any!"

"Yes, yes, Johnnie," answered the cowboy, consolingly; "he's hurt a good deal."

They raised him from the ground, and as soon as he was on his feet he went tottering off, rebuffing all attempts at assistance. When the party rounded the corner they were fairly blinded by the pelting of the snow. It burned their faces like fire. The cowboy carried Johnnie through the drift to the door. As they entered some cards again rose from the floor and beat against the wall.

The Easterner rushed to the stove. He was so profoundly chilled that he almost dared to embrace the glowing iron. The Swede was not in the room. Johnnie sank into a chair, and, folding his arms on his knees, buried his face in them. Scully, warming one foot and then the other at a rim of the stove, muttered to himself with Celtic mournfulness. The cowboy had removed his fur cap, and with a dazed and rueful air he was running one hand through his tousled locks. From overhead they could hear the creaking of boards, as the Swede tramped here and there in his room.

The sad quiet was broken by the sudden flinging open of a door that led towards the kitchen. It was instantly followed by an inrush of women. They precipitated themselves upon Johnnie amid a chorus of lamentation. Before they carried their prey off to the kitchen, there to be bathed and harangued with that mixture of sympathy and abuse which is a feat of their sex, the mother straightened herself and fixed old Scully with an eye of stern reproach. "Shame be upon you, Patrick Scully!" she cried. "Your own son, too. Shame be upon you!"

"There, now! Be quiet, now!" said the old man, weakly.

"Shame be upon you, Patrick Scully!" The girls, rallying to this slogan, sniffed disdainfully in the direction of those trembling accomplices, the cowboy and the Easterner. Presently they bore Johnnie away, and left the three men to dismal reflection.

VII

"I'd like to fight this here Dutchman myself," said the cowboy, breaking a long silence.

Scully wagged his head sadly. "No, that wouldn't do. It wouldn't be right. It wouldn't be right."

"Well, why wouldn't it?" argued the cowboy. "I don't see no harm in it."

"No," answered Scully, with mournful heroism. "It wouldn't be right. It was Johnnie's fight, and now we mustn't whip the man just because he whipped Johnnie."

"Yes, that's true enough," said the cowboy; "but—he better not get fresh with me, because I couldn't stand no more of it."

"You'll not say a word to him," commanded Scully, and even then they heard the tread of the Swede on the stairs. His entrance was made theatric. He swept the door back with a bang and swaggered to the middle of the room. No one looked at him. "Well," he cried, insolently, at Scully, "I s'pose you'll tell me now how much I owe you?"

The old man remained stolid. "You don't owe me nothin'."

"Huh!" said the Swede, "huh! Don't owe 'im nothin'."

The cowboy addressed the Swede. "Stranger, I don't see how you come to be so gay around here."

Old Scully was instantly alert. "Stop!" he shouted, holding his hand forth, fingers upward. "Bill, you shut up!"

The cowboy spat carelessly into the sawdust box. "I didn't say a word, did I?" he asked.

"Mr. Scully," called the Swede, "how much do I owe you?" It was seen that he was attired for departure, and that he had his valise in his hand.

"You don't owe me nothin'," repeated Scully in his same imperturbable way.

"Huh!" said the Swede. "I guess you're right. I guess if it was any way at all, you'd owe me somethin'. That's what I guess." He turned to the cowboy. "'Kill him! Kill him! Kill him!'" he mimicked, and then guffawed victoriously. "'Kill him!'" He was convulsed with ironical humor.

But he might have been jeering the dead. The three men were immovable and silent, staring with glassy eyes at the stove.

The Swede opened the door and passed into the storm, giving one derisive glance backward at the still group.

As soon as the door was closed, Scully and the cowboy leaped to their feet and began to curse. They trampled to and fro, waving their arms and smashing into the air with their fists. "Oh, but that was a hard minute!" wailed Scully. "That was a hard minute! Him there leerin' and scoffin'! One bang at his nose was worth forty dollars to me that minute! How did you stand it, Bill?"

"How did I stand it?" cried the cowboy in a quivering voice. "How did I stand it? Oh!"

The old man burst into sudden brogue. "I'd loike to take that Swade," he wailed, "and hould 'im down on a shtone flure and bate 'im to a jelly wid a shtick!"

The cowboy groaned in sympathy. "I'd like to git him by the neck and ha-ammer him"—he brought his hand down on a chair with a noise like a pistol-shot—"hammer that there Dutchman until he couldn't tell himself from a dead coyote!"

"I'd bate 'im until he—"

"I'd show *him* some things—"

And then together they raised a yearning, fanatic cry—"Oh-o-oh! if we only could—"

"Yes!"

"Yes!"

"And then I'd—"

"O-o-oh!"

VIII

The Swede, tightly gripping his valise, tacked across the face of the storm as if he carried sails. He was following a line of little naked, gasping trees, which he knew must mark the way of the road. His face, fresh from the pounding of Johnnie's fists, felt more pleasure than pain in the wind and the driving snow. A number of square shapes loomed upon him finally, and he knew them as the houses of the main body of the town. He found a street and made travel along it, leaning heavily upon the wind whenever, at a corner, a terrific blast caught him.

He might have been in a deserted village. We picture the world as thick with conquering and elate humanity, but here, with the bugles of the tempest pealing, it was hard to imagine a peopled earth. One viewed the existence of man then as a marvel, and conceded a glamour of wonder to these lice which were caused to cling to a whirling, fire-smote, ice-locked, disease-stricken, space-lost bulb. The conceit of man was explained by this storm to be the very engine of life. One was a coxcomb not to die in it. However, the Swede found a saloon.

In front of it an indomitable red light was burning, and the snow-flakes were made blood-color as they flew through the circumscribed territory of the lamp's shining. The Swede pushed open the door of the saloon and entered. A sanded expanse was before him, and at the end of it four men sat about a table drinking. Down one side of the room extended a radiant bar, and its guardian was leaning upon his elbows listening to the talk of the men at the table. The Swede dropped his valise upon the floor, and, smiling fraternally upon the barkeeper, said, "Gimme some whiskey, will you?" The man placed a bottle, a whiskey-glass, and a glass of ice-thick water upon the bar. The Swede poured himself an abnormal portion of whiskey and drank it in three gulps. "Pretty bad night," remarked the bartender, indifferently. He was making the pretension of blindness which is usually a distinction of his class; but it could have been seen that he was furtively studying the half-erased blood-stains on the face of the Swede. "Bad night," he said again.

"Oh, it's good enough for me," replied the Swede, hardily, as he poured himself some more whiskey. The barkeeper took his coin and maneuvered it through its reception by the highly nickelled cash-machine. A bell rang; a card labelled "20 cts." had appeared.

"No," continued the Swede, "this isn't too bad weather. It's good enough for me."

"So?" murmured the barkeeper, languidly.

The copious drams made the Swede's eyes swim, and he breathed a trifle heavier. "Yes, I like this weather. I like it. It suits me." It was apparently his design to impart a deep significance to these words.

"So?" murmured the bartender again. He turned to gaze dreamily at the scroll-like birds and bird-like scrolls which had been drawn with soap upon the mirrors back of the bar.

Unit One Theme
Chapter 2 The Blue Hotel

"Well, I guess I'll take another drink," said the Swede, presently. "Have something?"

"No, thanks; I'm not drinkin'," answered the bartender. Afterwards he asked, "How did you hurt your face?"

The Swede immediately began to boast loudly. "Why, in a fight. I thumped the soul out of a man down here at Scully's hotel."

The interest of the four men at the table was at last aroused.

"Who was it?" said one.

"Johnnie Scully," blustered the Swede. "Son of the man what runs it. He will be pretty near dead for some weeks, I can tell you. I made a nice thing of him, I did. He couldn't get up. They carried him in the house. Have a drink?"

Instantly the men in some subtle way incased themselves in reserve. "No, thanks," said one. The group was of curious formation. Two were prominent local business men; one was the district-attorney; and one was a professional gambler of the kind known as "square"①. But a scrutiny of the group would not have enabled an observer to pick the gambler from the men of more reputable pursuits. He was, in fact, a man so delicate in manner, when among people of fair class, and so judicious in his choice of victims, that in the strictly masculine part of the town's life he had come to be explicitly trusted and admired. People called him a thoroughbred. The fear and contempt with which his craft was regarded was undoubtedly the reason that his quiet dignity shone conspicuous above the quiet dignity of men who might be merely hatters, billiard markers②, or grocery-clerks. Beyond an occasional unwary traveler, who came by rail, this gambler was supposed to prey solely upon reckless and senile farmers, who, when flush with good crops, drove into town in all the pride and confidence of an absolutely invulnerable stupidity. Hearing at times in circuitous fashion of the despoilment of such a farmer, the important men of Romper invariably laughed in contempt of the victim, and, if they thought of the wolf at all, it was with a kind of pride at the knowledge that he would never dare think of attacking their wisdom and courage. Besides, it was popular that this gambler had a real wife and two real children in a neat cottage in a suburb, where he led an exemplary home life; and when any one even suggested a discrepancy in his character, the crowd immediately vociferated descriptions of this virtuous family circle. Then men who led exemplary home lives, and men who did not lead exemplary home lives, all subsided in a bunch, remarking that there was nothing more to be said.

However, when a restriction was placed upon him—as, for instance, when a strong clique of members of the new Pollywog Club refused to permit him, even as a spectator, to appear in the rooms of the organization—the candor and gentleness with which he accepted the judgment disarmed many of his foes and made his friends more desperately partisan. He invariably distinguished between himself and a respectable Romper man so quickly and frankly that his manner actually appeared to be a continual broadcast compliment.

---

① Honest.
② Scorekeepers at billiards matches.

And one must not forget to declare the fundamental fact of his entire position in Romper. It is irrefutable that in all affairs outside of his business, in all matters that occur eternally and commonly between man and man, this thieving card-player was so generous, so just, so moral, that, in a contest, he could have put to flight the consciences of nine-tenths of the citizens of Romper.

And so it happened that he was seated in this saloon with the two prominent local merchants and the district attorney.

The Swede continued to drink raw whiskey, meanwhile babbling at the barkeeper and trying to induce him to indulge in potations. "Come on. Have a drink. Come on. What—no? Well, have a little one, then. By gawd, I've whipped a man to-night, and I want to celebrate. I whipped him good, too. Gentlemen," the Swede cried to the men at the table, "have a drink?"

"Ssh!" said the barkeeper.

The group at the table, although furtively attentive, had been pretending to be deep in talk, but now a man lifted his eyes towards the Swede and said, shortly, "Thanks. We don't want any more."

At this reply the Swede ruffled out his chest like a rooster. "Well," he exploded, "it seems I can't get anybody to drink with me in this town. Seems so, don't it? Well!"

"Ssh!" said the barkeeper.

"Say," snarled the Swede, "don't you try to shut me up. I won't have it. I'm a gentleman, and I want people to drink with me. And I want 'em to drink with me now. *Now*—do you understand?" He rapped the bar with his knuckles.

Years of experience had calloused the bartender. He merely grew sulky. "I hear you," he answered.

"Well," cried the Swede, "listen hard then. See those men over there? Well, they're going to drink with me, and don't you forget it. Now you watch."

"Hi!" yelled the barkeeper, "this won't do!"

"Why won't it?" demanded the Swede. He stalked over to the table, and by chance laid his hand upon the shoulder of the gambler. "How about this?" he asked, wrathfully. "I asked you to drink with me."

The gambler simply twisted his head and spoke over his shoulder. "My friend, I don't know you."

"Oh, hell!" answered the Swede, "come and have a drink."

"Now, my boy," advised the gambler, kindly, "take your hand off my shoulder and go 'way and mind your own business." He was a little, slim man, and it seemed strange to hear him use this tone of heroic patronage to the burly Swede. The other men at the table said nothing.

"What! You won't drink with me, you little dude? I'll make you then! I'll make you!" The Swede had grasped the gambler frenziedly at the throat, and was dragging him from his chair. The other men sprang up. The barkeeper dashed around the corner of his bar. There was a great tumult, and then was seen a long blade in the hand of the gambler. It shot forward, and a human body, this citadel of virtue, wisdom, power, was pierced as easily as if it had been a melon. The Swede fell with a cry of supreme astonishment.

The prominent merchants and the district attorney must have at once tumbled out of the place backward. The bartender found himself hanging limply to the arm of a chair and gazing into the eyes of a murderer.

"Henry," said the latter, as he wiped his knife on one of the towels that hung beneath the bar-rail, "you tell 'em where to find me. I'll be home, waiting for 'em." Then he vanished. A moment afterwards the barkeeper was in the street dinning through the storm for help, and, moreover, companionship.

The corpse of the Swede, alone in the saloon, had its eyes fixed upon a dreadful legend that dwelt atop of the cash-machine: "This registers the amount of your purchase."

IX

Months later, the cowboy was frying pork over the stove of a little ranch near the Dakota line, when there was a quick thud of hoofs outside, and presently the Easterner entered with the letters and the papers.

"Well," said the Easterner at once, "the chap that killed the Swede has got three years. Wasn't much, was it?"

"He has? Three years?" The cowboy poised his pan of pork, while he ruminated upon the news. "Three years. That ain't much."

"No. It was a light sentence," replied the Easterner as he unbuckled his spurs. "Seems there was a good deal of sympathy for him in Romper."

"If the bartender had been any good," observed the cowboy, thoughtfully, "he would have gone in and cracked that there Dutchman on the head with a bottle in the beginnin' of it and stopped all this here murderin'."

"Yes, a thousand things might have happened," said the Easterner, tartly.

The cowboy returned his pan of pork to the fire, but his philosophy continued. "It's funny, ain't it? If he hadn't said Johnnie was cheatin' he'd be alive this minute. He was an awful fool. Game played for fun, too. Not for money. I believe he was crazy."

"I feel sorry for that gambler," said the Easterner.

"Oh, so do I," said the cowboy. "He don't deserve none of it for killin' who he did."

"The Swede might not have been killed if everything had been square."

"Might not have been killed?" exclaimed the cowboy. "Everythin' square? Why, when he said that Johnnie was cheatin' and acted like such a jackass? And then in the saloon he fairly walked up to git hurt?" With these arguments the cowboy browbeat the Easterner and reduced him to rage.

"You're a fool!" cried the Easterner, viciously. "You're a bigger jackass than the Swede by a million majority. Now let me tell you one thing. Let me tell you something. Listen! Johnnie *was* cheating!"

"'Johnnie,'" said the cowboy, blankly. There was a minute of silence, and then he said, robustly, "Why, no. The game was only for fun."

"Fun or not," said the Easterner, "Johnnie was cheating. I saw him. I know it. I saw him. And I refused to stand up and be a man. I let the Swede fight it out alone. And you—you were simply puffing around the place and wanting to fight. And then old Scully himself! We are all in it! This poor gambler isn't even a noun. He is kind of an adverb. Every sin is the result of a collaboration. We, five of us, have collaborated in the murder of this Swede. Usually there are from a dozen to forty women really involved in every murder, but in this case it seems to be only five men—you, I, Johnnie, old Scully, and that fool of an unfortunate gambler came merely as a culmination, the apex of a human movement, and gets all the punishment."

The cowboy, injured and rebellious, cried out blindly into this fog of mysterious theory: "Well, I didn't do anything, did I?"

Film Comment:

Stephen Crane's *The Blue Hotel*: 55 minutes, color

Starring: David Warner & James Keach

Screenplay by: Harry M. Petrakis

Directed by: Jan Kadar

Nebraska in the 1880s...bleak, lonely, and far from what you'd expect the Wild West to be. But for a naïve Swedish immigrant, the frontier parlor of "The Blue Hotel" represents the quintessential western fantasy.

No one can convince the Swede that his dime-store notions about the West are foolish. He sees murderous intentions all around him...and in his terror he turns everyone against him.

Inevitably the Swede attracts tragedy. However, who is responsible? The negative Swede? Or the cliquish hotel guests? Academy Award-winner Jan Kadar ("The Shop on Main Street") directs this timely story of how society punishes outsiders for being different.

Film Scenes:

Scene 1: The Blue Hotel
Scene 2: A card game
Scene 3: Crazy Swede
Scene 4: Deadly game
Scene 5: The stranger
Scene 6: The truth

Unit One　Theme

Chapter 2　The Blue Hotel

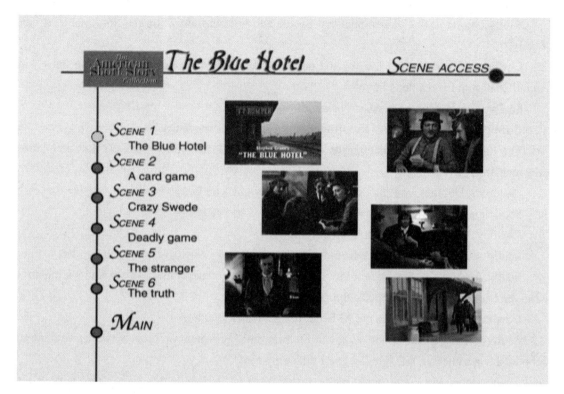

Script Excerpts:

A wild-eyed Swede arrives at a Nebraska hotel, along with other guests, and expresses what seems an irrational fear of being murdered. Scully, the proprietor, persuades him to remain. After drinking too much, the Swede provokes a card game and accuses Johnnie, the proprietor's son, of cheating. In the ritualized fight in the snow which follows, Johnnie is soundly beaten by the Swede. As the men return to the lobby, the climactic scene begins.

Interior. Lobby.

As the men enter the lobby, Scully and the Cowboy still dragging Johnnie between them, Scully motions toward the door leading to the other part of the house. They carry him through the door while the Easterner walks toward the fire glowing in the stove, removing his coat. From the other room can be heard the shrill, concerned voices of Scully's daughters.

Scully (*shouting*): He's all right! Just beaten up a little. You wash him and get him to bed!

Girl's Voice (*off-camera*): Shame on you, Pa! Letting this happen to Johnnie!

The second girl's voice joins the tirade against Scully. In a moment Scully and the Cowboy emerge from the door, Scully moving angrily toward the stove, muttering to himself with Celtic mournfulness. The Cowboy removes his hat and jacked and ruefully runs his fingers through his hair. Overhead they can hear the groaning of the boards as the Swede tamps back and forth in his room.

Scully shakes his fist at the ceiling.

Scully (*waiting*): I'd like to take that Swede and hold him down on the floor and beat 'im to jelly!

Cowboy: I'd like to git him by the neck and ham-mer that damned Dutchman until you couldn't tell him from a dead boyote!

Scully: That's what he needs! A beating!

Cowboy: By God, I think I'll ham-mer him when he comes down.

The Easterner has been listening to them and now he speaks quietly, for the first time since they reentered the hotel.

Easterner: No, that wouldn't do. It wouldn't be right, you know.

Scully and the Cowboy stare at him.

Cowboy: Why in hell wouldn't it be right?

Scully shakes his head in a sudden, mournful revelation.

Scully: He's right, Bill. It wouldn't be right or fair. It was Johnnie's fight and we mustn't whip the man because he whipped Johnnie.

Cowboy: That may be true but he better not get cheeky with me!

Scully (*sternly*): You'll not say a word to him, nor lay a hand on him. Whatever he done to Johnnie, he is a guest in this hotel, a guest under my roof.

Their discussion is interrupted by the heavy tread of the Swede descending the stairs. He is attired for departure, his valise in his hand. A certain swagger in his walk suggests he might have revisited the bottle of Bombay gin under Scully's bed.

Swede (*loudly*): I'm getting out of here now, going to check into a real hotel up the street. How much do I owe you?

Scully (*somberly*): You don't owe me nothing.

Swede (*mockingly*): Huh! Huh! You don't owe me nothing!

Cowboy (*making a mighty effort to control his temper*): Stranger, I don't see how come you're so damn cheeky...

Scully: Bill, you shut up!

The Cowboy spits into the sawdust box in disgust and turns away.

Swede (*harshly*): Scully, I asked how much I owe you?

Scully: I told you you don't owe me nothing.

Swede (*chortling*): Huh! I guess you're right. I guess you owe me something for teaching your boy a lesson he won't forget. That's what I guess. (*Turning toward the Cowboy he begins to mimic his voice.*) Kill him! Kill him! Kill him! Kill him! (*He is convulsed with derisive delight.*)

As the Swede, still laughing loudly, moves toward the door, it bursts open and a small, slender figure of a man in a coat with a fine fur collar enters the lobby. A gust of wind sweeps in around his legs, scattering the cards that litter the table, flickering the flame of the lamps. The man turns, pushing with all his strength to close the door against the wind. With a grunt the

Unit One　Theme

Chapter 2　The Blue Hotel

Swede reaches out his hand and arm and slams the door closed. The stranger nods to him in thanks and turns back to the lobby. He draws the fur cap off his head. He is a pale-faced, slender man with a certain grave dignity in his bearings.

　　Stranger: Good evening, gentleman. They told me at the stable I might get a room here. (*Motions toward the stove.*) That looks inviting. A bad night out there.

　　Scully: Warm yourself, stranger. We'll be glad to put you up when you're ready to sleep.

　　Swede (*delighted at another witness to his triumph*): This isn't bad weather! It's good weather for me!

　　The Stranger looks calmly at the Swede and doesn't answer. He removes his greatcoat, shaking off the snowflakes on the iron planking of the floor around the stove. He is neatly and precisely attired in the frock-coat and west of the professional gambler.

　　Swede (*heartily*): Yes, I like this weather. I like it fine! (*Winks at the Stranger.*) Want to know why it's been great weather for me?

　　The Stranger stands warming the back of his legs at the stove, looking at the Swede, not saying a word.

　　Swede: I had a fight here earlier tonight. I beat the living soul out of a man right here.

　　Scully mutters under his breath and the Cowboy shakes his head. The Easterner stares from one to the other, then looks back at the Swede.

　　Swede: Johnnie Scully! Son of this man here. (*Motions to Scully.*) He will be near dead for some weeks, I can tell you. I made a mess of him. They had to carry him into the house. (*Finishes with a boastful and raucous laugh.*)

　　The Cowboy lets out a low groan and Scully rubs his cheek in a might effort to rein in his temper.

　　Through the Swede's boasting the Stranger has been watching him silently. Now he deliberately turns his back on the Swede, extending his manicured and delicate hands toward the stove.

　　Swede (*offended*): Mister, I told you what I done to a man here tonight and it ain't polite to turn your back on a man who's talking to you. Hear?

　　Scully: You were just leaving. Why don't you keep going and let us alone? You done enough trouble here tonight.

　　Cowboy: By God, if he don't leave...

　　The Swede casts a look of contempt at Scully and the Cowboy and marches defiantly toward the Stranger at the stove. He places his big hand on the slender, frock-coated shoulder of the Stranger.

　　Swede: I told you it ain't polite to turn your back on a man who is talking to you...

　　Stranger (*quietly*): Now, my friend, take your hand off my shoulder.

　　Swede (*shouting*): Turn around and look at me when I'm talking to...

　　He clutches the Stranger's shoulder harder and begins to jerk him around. Scully and the

Cowboy move rapidly toward them, but not quickly enough. The Stranger completes turning around under his own power, moving with a sudden, catlike swiftness. For an instant the lamplight glistens on the long, slim blade of a knife that has sprung into his hand. He faces the Swede, who looms over him, and thrusts the knife upward, piercing the Swede's chest over his heart as easily as if he were slicing into a melon. A shattered shock sweeps the Swede's face; he opens his mouth to utter a shriek; a short, shrill whistle of breath is all that emerges. He plunges forward taking the table adjoining the stove down with him, landing with a thunderous thump, sprawled on the floor at the Stranger's feet.

For a stunned, disbelieving moment the men in the room stand transfixed. The Easterner covers his eyes with his hands. Scully tries to speak and mumbles only a few unintelligible words. The Cowboy walks slowly to the stove and stands staring down at the body.

Stranger (*quietly*): If there is a sheriff or marshal in this town, you can call him. I'll be waiting for him right here. You are all witnesses that this man was abusing me....

He turns back to the stove and calmly resumes warming his hands. Camera pans the faces of each of the men in the room and then settles on the dead face of the Swede.

Discussion Questions:

1. What is the source of the Swede's fear? To what extent does it spring from a distorted view of reality and his own preconceived ideas?
2. Is Scully acting from good motives in trying to keep peace in his hotel? Does the purity or impurity of his motives have anything to do with the outcome of the action?
3. Is Johnnie a victim or an aggressor? What does the story as a whole say about innocence and guilt?
4. How does the natural setting reinforce the theme and meaning of the story? What other kind of imagery does Crane employ?
5. What does Crane mean at the end of the story when he has the Easterner say that "Every sin is the result of a collaboration"? How are all five of the major characters implicated in the Swede's death?

Further Reading and Watching:
"The Open Boat"

Unit Two

Setting

Chapter 3

Paul's Case

Willa Cather

Author Introduction:

Willa Cather (1873—1947) was born of Anglo-Irish parents in Back Creek Valley, Virginia. At ten she moved with her family to Red Cloud, Nebraska, where she grew up, exploring the prairies on horseback and making friends with the immigrant farmers of the area. After graduating from the University of Nebraska, Cather lived in Pittsburgh for ten years, where the short story "Paul's Case" opens, working first as a journalist and then as a high-school teacher of English and Latin. At the age of 33, she moved to New York City, and held editorial positions for the popular magazine *McClure's* there, but her poetry and fiction looked to the Midwest and Southwest for their subject matters and to the depths of the American past for their values. She never married. The last part of her life was spent in New York, with occasional European travels that never swayed her from nostalgia or the conservatism of her views. Once she declared that the world had "broken apart" about 1922; unmistakably she preferred the manners, styles, and virtues that prevailed before that date. Incidentally she was awarded the Pulitzer Prize that year for *One of Ours* (1922), a novel set during the First World War. With remarkable skill, Cather might tell a story from a man's point of view, but her favorite characters are likely to be women of strong will who triumph over obstacles. Among her novels are *My Antonia* (1918), *A Lost Lady* (1923), *The Professor's House* (1925), and *Death Comes for the Archbishop* (1927). *Not under Forty* (1936) contains many of her essays. Her collections of short stories are *Youth and the Bright Medusa* (1920), *Obscure Destinies* (1932), and *The Old Beauty and Others* (1948).

Story Summary:

Paul was born into a respectable neighborhood in turn-of-the-century Pittsburgh. He comes to hate its "ugliness and commonness." His defiant manner, red buttonhole carnation and "hysterical brilliant" blue eyes infuriate his teachers. But Paul simply lives for the hours after school when he works as an usher in a concert hall. He loses himself in the majesty of the arts. Finally, his widower father takes him out of school and puts him to work at a job that won't "heat his brain..." Paul retaliates by stealing money and flees to New York. He just wants to float on waves of beauty. Briefly he lives in luxury and illusion—until reality comes crashing down.

Key Terms:
Adolescence, Rebellion, Family Relationships, Symbolic Power, Romance, Suicide

Paul's Case[①]

A Study in Temperament

It was Paul's afternoon to appear before the faculty of the Pittsburgh High School to account for his various misdemeanors. He had been suspended a week ago, and his father had called at the Principal's office and confessed his perplexity about his son. Paul entered the faculty room suave and smiling. His clothes were a trifle outgrown, and the tan velvet on the collar of his open overcoat was frayed and worn; but for all that there was something of the dandy[②] about him, and he wore an opal pin in his neatly knotted black four-in-hand[③], and a red carnation in his buttonhole. This latter adornment the faculty somehow felt was not properly significant of the contrite spirit befitting a boy under the ban of suspension.

Paul was tall for his age and very thin, with high, cramped shoulders and a narrow chest. His eyes were remarkable for a certain hysterical brilliancy, and he continually used them in a conscious, theatrical sort of way, peculiarly offensive in a boy. The pupils were abnormally large, as though he were addicted to belladonna[④], but there was a glassy glitter about them which that drug does not produce.

When questioned by the Principal as to why he was there Paul stated, politely enough, that he wanted to come back to school. This was a lie, but Paul was quite accustomed to lying; found it, indeed, indispensable for overcoming friction. His teachers were asked to state their respective charges against him, which they did with such a rancor and aggrievedness as evinced that this was not a usual case. Disorder and impertinence were among the offenses named, yet each of his instructors felt that it was scarcely possible to put into words the real cause of the trouble,

---

① First published in *McClure's Magazine*, 25 (May 1905), later collected in *The Troll Garden* (1905), and reprinted in *Youth and the Bright Medusa* (1920).
② A man who is too careful about his dress and appearance.
③ A long necktie tied in a slipknot with the ends hanging.
④ A poisonous plant whose leaves yield a medicine for stomach aches; taking it, however, dilates the eyes.

Unit Two Setting
Chapter 3 Paul's Case

which lay in a sort of hysterically defiant manner of the boy's; in the contempt which they all knew he felt for them, and which he seemingly made not the least effort to conceal. Once, when he had been making a synopsis of a paragraph at the blackboard, his English teacher had stepped to his side and attempted to guide his hand. Paul had started back with a shudder and thrust his hands violently behind him. The astonished woman could scarcely have been more hurt and embarrassed had he struck at her. The insult was so involuntary and definitely personal as to be unforgettable. In one way and another he had made all his teachers, men and women alike, conscious of the same feeling of physical aversion. In one class he habitually sat with his hand shading his eyes; in another he always looked out of the window during the recitation; in another he made a running commentary on the lecture, with humorous intention.

His teachers felt this afternoon that his whole attitude was symbolized by his shrug and his flippantly red carnation flower, and they fell upon him without mercy, his English teacher leading the pack. He stood through it smiling, his pale lips parted over his white teeth. (His lips were continually twitching, and he had a habit of raising his eyebrows that was contemptuous and irritating to the last degree.) Older boys than Paul had broken down and shed tears under that baptism of fire, but his set smile did not once desert him, and his only sign of discomfort was the nervous trembling of the fingers that toyed with the buttons of his overcoat, and an occasional jerking of the other hand that held his hat. Paul was always smiling, always glancing about him, seeming to feel that people might be watching him and trying to detect something. This conscious expression, since it was as far as possible from boyish mirthfulness, was usually attributed to insolence or "smartness."

As the inquisition proceeded one of his instructors repeated an impertinent remark of the boy's, and the Principal asked him whether he thought that a courteous speech to have made a woman. Paul shrugged his shoulders slightly and his eyebrows twitched.

"I don't know," he replied. "I didn't mean to be polite or impolite, either. I guess it's a sort of way I have of saying things regardless."

The Principal, who was a sympathetic man, asked him whether he didn't think that a way it would be well to get rid of. Paul grinned and said he guessed so. When he was told that he could go he bowed gracefully and went out. His bow was but a repetition of the scandalous red carnation.

His teachers were in despair, and his drawing master[①] voiced the feeling of them all when he declared there was something about the boy which none of them understood. He added: "I don't really believe that smile of his comes altogether from insolence; there's something sort of haunted about it. The boy is not strong, for one thing. I happen to know that he was born in Colorado, only a few months before his mother died out there of a long illness. There is something wrong about the fellow."

---

① Art teacher.

The drawing master had come to realize that, in looking at Paul, one saw only his white teeth and the forced animation of his eyes. One warm afternoon the boy had gone to sleep at his drawing board, and his master had noted with amazement what a white, blue-veined face it was; drawn and wrinkled like an old man's about the eyes, the lips twitching even in his sleep, and stiff with a nervous tension that drew them back from his teeth.

His teachers left the building dissatisfied and unhappy; humiliated to have felt so vindictive toward a mere boy, to have uttered this feeling in cutting terms, and to have set each other on, as it were, in the gruesome game of intemperate reproach. Some of them remembered having seen a miserable street cat set at bay by a ring of tormentors.

As for Paul, he ran down the hill whistling the "Soldiers' Chorus" from *Faust*[①], looking wildly behind him now and then to see whether some of his teachers were not there to writhe under his lightheartedness. As it was now late in the afternoon and Paul was on duty that evening as usher at Carnegie Hall[②], he decided that he would not go home to supper. When he reached the concert hall the doors were not yet open and, as it was chilly outside, he decided to go up into the picture gallery—always deserted at this hour—where there were some of Raffelli's[③] gay studies of Paris streets and an airy blue Venetian scene or two that always exhilarated him. He was delighted to find no one in the gallery but the old guard, who sat in one corner, a newspaper on his knee, a black patch over one eye and the other closed. Paul possessed himself of the peace and walked confidently up and down, whistling under his breath. After a while he sat down before a blue Rico[④] and lost himself. When he bethought him to look at his watch, it was after seven o'clock, and he rose with a start and ran downstairs, making a face at Augustus[⑤], peering out from the cast room, and an evil gesture at the Venus de Milo[⑥] as he passed her on the stairway.

When Paul reached the ushers' dressing room half a dozen boys were there already, and he began excitedly to tumble into his uniform. It was one of the few that at all approached fitting, and Paul thought it very becoming—though he knew that the tight, straight coat accentuated his narrow chest, about which he was exceedingly sensitive. He was always considerably excited while he dressed, twanging all over to the tuning of the strings and the preliminary flourishes of the horns in the music room; but tonight he seemed quite beside himself, and he teased and plagued the boys until, telling him that he was crazy, they put him down on the floor and sat on him.

Somewhat calmed by his suppression, Paul dashed out to the front of the house to seat the early comers. He was a model usher; gracious and smiling he ran up and down the aisles; nothing was too much trouble for him; he carried messages and brought programs as though it were

---

① An opera by French composer Charles Gounod (1818—1893).
② A Pittsburg music hall named for Andrew Carnegie (1835—1919), famous industrialist and philanthropist.
③ Jean-Francois Raffaelli (1850—1924), French painter, sculptor, and etcher.
④ Andreas Rico (1500—1550), Cretan-Italian painter.
⑤ First emperor of Rome (27 B.C.—A.D.14) and grand-nephew of Julius Caesar.
⑥ A famous Greek statue; the original is in the Louvre, Paris.

Unit Two Setting
Chapter 3 Paul's Case

his greatest pleasure in life, and all the people in his section thought him a charming boy, feeling that he remembered and admired them. As the house filled, he grew more and more vivacious and animated, and the color came to his cheeks and lips. It was very much as though this were a great reception and Paul were the host. Just as the musicians came out to take their places, his English teacher arrived with checks for the seats which a prominent manufacturer had taken for the season. She betrayed some embarrassment when she handed Paul the tickets, and a *hauteur*① which subsequently made her feel very foolish. Paul was startled for a moment, and had the feeling of wanting to put her out; what business had she here among all these fine people and gay colors? He looked her over and decided that she was not appropriately dressed and must be a fool to sit downstairs in such togs. The tickets had probably been sent her out of kindness, he reflected as he put down a seat for her, and she had about as much right to sit there as he had.

When the symphony began Paul sank into one of the rear seats with a long sigh of relief, and lost himself as he had done before the Rico. It was not that symphonies, as such, meant anything in particular to Paul, but the first sigh of the instruments seemed to free some hilarious and potent spirit within him; something that struggled there like the genie in the bottle found by the Arab fisherman.② He felt a sudden zest of life; the lights danced before his eyes and the concert hall blazed into unimaginable splendor. When the soprano soloist came on Paul forgot even the nastiness of his teacher's being there and gave himself up to the peculiar stimulus such personages always had for him. The soloist chanced to be a German woman, by no means in her first youth, and the mother of many children; but she wore an elaborate gown and a tiara, and above all she had that indefinable air of achievement, that world-shine upon her, which, in Paul's eyes, made her a veritable queen of Romance.

After a concert was over Paul was always irritable and wretched until he got to sleep, and tonight he was even more than usually restless. He had the feeling of not being able to let down, of its being impossible to give up this delicious excitement which was the only thing that could be called living at all. During the last number he withdrew and, after hastily changing his clothes in the dressing room, slipped out to the side door where the soprano's carriage stood. Here he began pacing rapidly up and down the walk, waiting to see her come out.

Over yonder, the Schenley, in its vacant stretch, loomed big and square through the fine rain, the windows of its twelve stories glowing like those of a lighted cardboard house under a Christmas tree. All the actors and singers of the better class stayed there when they were in the city, and a number of the big manufacturers of the place lived there in the winter. Paul had often hung about the hotel, watching the people go in and out, longing to enter and leave schoolmasters and dull care behind him forever.

---
① (French) haughtiness; loftiness.
② In one of the tales of the *Arabian Nights* (also called *Thousand and One Nights*), the fisherman Ali Baba finds a genie imprisoned in a bottle who is able to perform miracles.

At last the singer came out, accompanied by the conductor, who helped her into her carriage and closed the door with a cordial *auf wiedersehen*[①] which set Paul to wondering whether she were not an old sweetheart of his. Paul followed the carriage over to the hotel, walking so rapidly as not to be far from the entrance when the singer alighted, and disappeared behind the swinging glass doors that were opened by a Negro in a tall hat and a long coat. In the moment that the door was ajar it seemed to Paul that he, too, entered. He seemed to feel himself go after her up the steps, into the warm, lighted building, into an exotic, tropical world of shiny, glistening surfaces and basking ease. He reflected upon the mysterious dishes that were brought into the dining room, the green bottles in buckets of ice, as he had seen them in the supper party pictures of the *Sunday World* supplement. A quick gust of wind brought the rain down with sudden vehemence, and Paul was startled to find that he was still outside in the slush of the gravel driveway; that his boots were letting in the water and his scanty overcoat was clinging wet about him; that the lights in front of the concert hall were out and that the rain was driving in sheets between him and the orange glow of the windows above him. There it was, what he wanted—tangibly before him, like the fairy world of a Christmas pantomime, but mocking spirits stood guard at the doors, and, as the rain beat in his face, Paul wondered whether he were destined always to shiver in the black night outside, looking up at it.

He turned and walked reluctantly toward the car[②] tracks. The end had to come sometime; his father in his nightclothes at the top of the stairs, explanations that did not explain, hastily improvised fictions that were forever tripping him up, his upstairs room and its horrible yellow wallpaper, the creaking bureau with the greasy plush collar-box, and over his painted wooden bed the pictures of George Washington and John Calvin[③], and the framed motto, "Feed my Lambs," which had been worked in red worsted by his mother.

Half an hour later Paul alighted from his car and went slowly down one of the side streets off the main thoroughfare. It was a highly respectable street, where all the houses were exactly alike, and where businessmen of moderate means begot and reared large families of children, all of whom went to Sabbath school and learned the shorter catechism, and were interested in arithmetic; all of whom were as exactly alike as their homes, and of a piece with the monotony in which they lived. Paul never went up Cordelia Street without a shudder of loathing. His home was next to the house of the Cumberland[④] minister. He approached it tonight with the nerveless sense of defeat, the hopeless feeling of sinking back forever into ugliness and commonness that he had always had when he came home. The moment he turned into Cordelia Street he felt the waters close above his head. After each of these orgies of living he experienced all the physical depression which follows a debauch; the loathing of respectable beds, of common food, of a

---

① (German) Good-bye. Literally, "to again see."
② Streetcar.
③ French Protestant reformer (1509—1564) who lived in Geneva.
④ A division of the Presbyterian Church in the United States.

Unit Two Setting
Chapter 3 Paul's Case

house penetrated by kitchen odors; a shuddering repulsion for the flavorless, colorless mass of everyday existence; a morbid desire for cool things and soft lights and fresh flowers.

The nearer he approached the house, the more absolutely unequal Paul felt to the sight of it all: his ugly sleeping chamber; the cold bathroom with the grimy zinc tub, the cracked mirror, the dripping spigots; his father, at the top of the stairs, his hairy legs sticking out from his nightshirt, his feet thrust into carpet slippers. He was so much later than usual that there would certainly be inquiries and reproaches. Paul stopped short before the door. He felt that he could not be accosted by his father tonight; that he could not toss again on that miserable bed. He would not go in. He would tell his father that he had no carfare and it was raining so hard he had gone home with one of the boys and stayed all night.

Meanwhile, he was wet and cold. He went around to the back of the house and tried one of the basement windows, found it open, raised it cautiously, and scrambled down the cellar wall to the floor. There he stood, holding his breath, terrified by the noise he had made, but the floor above him was silent, and there was no creak on the stairs. He found a soapbox, and carried it over to the soft ring of light that streamed from the furnace door, and sat down. He was horribly afraid of rats, so he did not try to sleep, but sat looking distrustfully at the dark, still terrified lest he might have awakened his father. In such reactions, after one of the experiences which made days and nights out of the dreary blanks of the calendar, when his senses were deadened, Paul's head was always singularly clear. Suppose his father had heard him getting in at the window and had come down and shot him for a burglar? Then, again, suppose his father had come down, pistol in hand, and he had cried out in time to save himself, and his father had been horrified to think how nearly he had killed him? Then, again, suppose a day should come when his father would remember that night, and wish there had been no warning cry to stay his hand? With this last supposition Paul entertained himself until daybreak.

The following Sunday was fine; the sodden November chill was broken by the last flash of autumnal summer. In the morning Paul had to go to church and Sabbath school, as always. On seasonable Sunday afternoons the burghers① of Cordelia Street always sat out on their front stoops and talked to their neighbors on the next stoop, or called to those across the street in neighborly fashion. The men usually sat on gay cushions placed upon the steps that led down to the sidewalk, while the women, in their Sunday "waists,"② sat in rockers on the cramped porches, pretending to be greatly at their ease. The children played in the streets; there were so many of them that the place resembled the recreation grounds of a kindergarten. The men on the steps—all in their shirt sleeves, their vests unbuttoned—sat with their legs well apart, their stomachs comfortably protruding, and talked of the prices of things, or told anecdotes of the sagacity of their various chiefs and overlords. They occasionally looked over the multitude of squabbling children, listened affectionately to their high-pitched, nasal voices, smiling to see their own pro-

---
① Comfortable or complacent members of the middle class.
② Bodices or blouses.

clivities reproduced in their offspring, and interspersed their legends of the iron kings[①] with remarks about their sons' progress at school, their grades in arithmetic, and the amounts they had saved in their toy banks.

On this last Sunday of November Paul sat all the afternoon on the lowest step of his stoop, staring into the street, while his sisters, in their rockers, were talking to the minister's daughters next door about how many shirtwaists they had made in the last week, and how many waffles someone had eaten at the last church supper. When the weather was warm, and his father was in a particularly jovial frame of mind, the girls made lemonade, which was always brought out in a red-glass pitcher, ornamented with forget-me-nots in blue enamel. This the girls thought very fine, and the neighbors always joked about the suspicious color of the pitcher.

Today Paul's father sat on the top step, talking to a young man who shifted a restless baby from knee to knee. He happened to be the young man who was daily held up to Paul as a model, and after whom it was his father's dearest hope that he would pattern. This young man was of a ruddy complexion, with a compressed, red mouth, and faded, nearsighted eyes, over which he wore thick spectacles, with gold bows that curved about his ears. He was clerk to one of the magnates of a great steel corporation, and was looked upon in Cordelia Street as a young man with a future. There was a story that, some five years ago—he was now barely twenty-six—he had been a trifle dissipated, but in order to curb his appetites and save the loss of time and strength that a sowing of wild oats might have entailed, he had taken his chief's advice, oft reiterated to his employees, and at twenty-one had married the first woman whom he could persuade to share his fortunes. She happened to be an angular schoolmistress, much older than he, who also wore thick glasses, and who had now borne him four children, all nearsighted, like herself.

The young man was relating how his chief, now cruising in the Mediterranean, kept in touch with all the details of the business, arranging his office hours on his yacht just as though he were at home, and "knocking off work enough to keep two stenographers busy." His father told, in turn, the plan his corporation was considering, of putting in an electric railway plant in Cairo. Paul snapped his teeth; he had an awful apprehension that they might spoil it all before he got there. Yet he rather liked to hear these legends of the iron kings that were told and retold on Sundays and holidays; these stories of palaces in Venice, yachts on the Mediterranean, and high play at Monte Carlo[②] appealed to his fancy, and he was interested in the triumphs of these cash boys who had become famous, though he had no mind for the cash-boy stage.

After supper was over and he had helped to dry the dishes, Paul nervously asked his father whether he could go to George's to get some help in his geometry, and still more nervously asked for carfare. This latter request he had to repeat, as his father, on principle, did not like to hear requests for money, whether much or little. He asked Paul whether he could not go to some boy who lived nearer, and told him that he ought not to leave his schoolwork until Sunday; but

---

① Tycoons of the iron and steel industry.
② High-stakes gambling in Monaco's chief city.

he gave him the dime①. He was not a poor man, but he had a worthy ambition to come up in the world. His only reason for allowing Paul to usher was that he thought a boy ought to be earning a little.

Paul bounded upstairs, scrubbed the greasy odor of the dishwater from his hands with the ill-smelling soap he hated, and then shook over his fingers a few drops of violet water from the bottle he kept hidden in his drawer. He left the house with his geometry conspicuously under his arm, and the moment he got out of Cordelia Street and boarded a downtown car, he shook off the lethargy of two deadening days and began to live again.

The leading juvenile② of the permanent stock company③ which played at one of the downtown theaters was an acquaintance of Paul's, and the boy had been invited to drop in at the Sunday-night rehearsals whenever he could. For more than a year Paul had spent every available moment loitering about Charley Edwards's dressing room. He had won a place among Edwards's following not only because the young actor, who could not afford to employ a dresser, often found him useful, but because he recognized in Paul something akin to what churchmen term "vocation."

It was at the theater and at Carnegie Hall that Paul really lived; the rest was but a sleep and a forgetting. This was Paul's fairy tale, and it had for him all the allurement of a secret love. The moment he inhaled the gassy, painty, dusty odor behind the scenes, he breathed like a prisoner set free, and felt within him the possibility of doing or saying splendid, brilliant, poetic things. The moment the cracked orchestra beat out the overture from *Martha*④, or jerked at the serenade from *Rigoletto*⑤, all stupid and ugly things slid from him, and his senses were deliciously, yet delicately fired.

Perhaps it was because, in Paul's world, the natural nearly always wore the guise of ugliness, that a certain element of artificiality seemed to him necessary in beauty. Perhaps it was because his experience of life elsewhere was so full of Sabbath-school picnics, petty economies, wholesome advice as to how to succeed in life, and the inescapable odors of cooking, that he found this existence so alluring, these smartly clad men and women so attractive, that he was so moved by these starry apple orchards that bloomed perennially under the limelight.

It would be difficult to put it strongly enough how convincingly the stage entrance of that theater was for Paul the actual portal of Romance. Certainly none of the company ever suspected it, least of all Charley Edwards. It was very like the old stories that used to float about London of fabulously rich Jews, who had subterranean halls there, with palms, and fountains, and soft lamps and richly appareled women who never saw the disenchanting light of London day. So, in the midst of that smoke-palled city, enamored of figures and grimy toil, Paul had his secret tem-

---

① A coin of the United States worth ten cents.
② The juvenile is the male actor who takes youthful parts; his female equivalent is called an ingénue.
③ A theatrical company that performs several plays in one theater.
④ A romantic opera by Friedrich von Flotow (1812—1883).
⑤ A tragic opera by Giuseppe Verdi (1813—1901).

ple, his wishing carpet, his bit of blue-and-white Mediterranean shore bathed in perpetual sunshine.

Several of Paul's teachers had a theory that his imagination had been perverted by garish fiction, but the truth was that he scarcely ever read at all. The books at home were not such as would either tempt or corrupt a youthful mind, and as for reading the novels that some of his friends urged upon him—well, he got what he wanted much more quickly from music; any sort of music, from an orchestra to a barrel organ. He needed only the spark, the indescribable thrill that made his imagination master of his senses, and he could make plots and pictures enough of his own. It was equally true that he was not stage struck—not, at any rate, in the usual acceptation of that expression. He had no desire to become an actor, any more than he had to become a musician. He felt no necessity to do any of these things; what he wanted was to see, to be in the atmosphere, float on the wave of it, to be carried out, blue league① after blue league, away from everything.

After a night behind the scenes Paul found the schoolroom more than ever repulsive; the bare floors and naked walls; the prosy men who never wore frock coats, or violets in their buttonholes; the women with their dull gowns, shrill voices, and pitiful seriousness about prepositions that govern the dative. He could not bear to have the other pupils think, for a moment, that he took these people seriously; he must convey to them that he considered it all trivial, and was there only by way of a jest, anyway. He had autographed pictures of all the members of the stock company which he showed his classmates, telling them the most incredible stories of his familiarity with these people, of his acquaintance with the soloists who came to Carnegie Hall, his suppers with them and the flowers he sent them. When these stories lost their effect, and his audience grew listless, he became desperate and would bid all the boys good-by, announcing that he was going to travel for a while; going to Naples, to Venice, to Egypt. Then, next Monday, he would slip back, conscious and nervously smiling; his sister was ill, and he should have to defer his voyage until spring.

Matters went steadily worse with Paul at school. In the itch to let his instructors know how heartily he despised them and their homilies, and how thoroughly he was appreciated elsewhere, he mentioned once or twice that he had no time to fool with theorems; adding—with a twitch of the eyebrows and a touch of that nervous bravado which so perplexed them—that he was helping the people down at the stock company; they were old friends of his.

The upshot of the matter was that the Principal went to Paul's father, and Paul was taken out of school and put to work. The manager at Carnegie Hall was told to get another usher in his stead; the doorkeeper at the theater was warned not to admit him to the house; and Charley Edwards remorsefully promised the boy's father not to see him again.

The members of the stock company were vastly amused when some of Paul's stories

---

① A unit of distance equal to 3.0 statute miles (4.8 kilometers).

Unit Two Setting
Chapter 3 Paul's Case

reached them—especially the women. They were hard-working women, most of them supporting indigent husbands or brothers, and they laughed rather bitterly at having stirred the boy to such fervid and florid inventions. They agreed with the faculty and with his father that Paul's was a bad case.

The east-bound train was plowing through a January snowstorm; the dull dawn was beginning to show gray when the engine whistled a mile out of Newark①. Paul started up from the seat where he had lain curled in uneasy slumber, rubbed the breath-misted window glass with his hand, and peered out. The snow was whirling in curling eddies above the white bottom lands, and the drifts lay already deep in the fields and along the fences, while here and there the long dead grass and dried weed stalks protruded black above it. Lights shone from the scattered houses, and a gang of laborers who stood beside the track waved their lanterns.

Paul had slept very little, and he felt grimy and uncomfortable. He had made the all-night journey in a day coach, partly because he was ashamed, dressed as he was, to go into a Pullman②, and partly because he was afraid of being seen there by some Pittsburgh businessman, who might have noticed him in Denny & Carson's office. When the whistle awoke him, he clutched quickly at his breast pocket, glancing about him with an uncertain smile. But the little, clay-bespattered Italians were still sleeping, the slatternly women across the aisle were in open-mouthed oblivion, and even the crumby, crying babies were for the nonce stilled. Paul settled back to struggle with his impatience as best he could.

When he arrived at the Jersey City station he hurried through his breakfast, manifestly ill at ease and keeping a sharp eye about him. After he reached the Twenty-third Street station③, he consulted a cabman and had himself driven to a men's-furnishings establishment that was just opening for the day. He spent upward of two hours there, buying with endless reconsidering and great care. His new street suit he put on in the fitting room; the frock coat and dress clothes he had bundled into the cab with his linen. Then he drove to a hatter's and a shoe house. His next errand was at Tiffany's④, where he selected his silver⑤ and a new scarf pin. He would not wait to have his silver marked⑥, he said. Lastly, he stopped at a trunk shop on Broadway and had his purchases packed into various traveling bags.

It was a little after one o'clock when he drove up to the Waldorf⑦, and after settling with the cabman, went into the office. He registered from Washington; said his mother and father had been abroad, and that he had come down to await the arrival of their steamer. He told his story

---
① The city in New Jersey just outside of New York City.
② The luxurious sleeping car designed by American inventor George M. Pullman.
③ Railway terminal in Manhattan.
④ A fashionable jewelry store in Manhattan.
⑤ A comb and brush set.
⑥ Monogrammed.
⑦ A fashionable hotel in Manhattan.

plausibly and had no trouble, since he volunteered to pay for them in advance, in engaging his rooms; a sleeping room, sitting room, and bath.

Not once, but a hundred times, Paul had planned this entry into New York. He had gone over every detail of it with Charley Edwards, and in his scrapbook at home there were pages of description about New York hotels, cut from the Sunday papers. When he was shown to his sitting room on the eighth floor he saw at a glance that everything was as it should be; there was but one detail in his mental picture that the place did not realize, so he rang for the bellboy and sent him down for flowers. He moved about nervously until the boy returned, putting away his new linen and fingering it delightedly as he did so. When the flowers came he put them hastily into water, and then tumbled into a hot bath. Presently he came out of his white bathroom, resplendent in his new silk underwear, and playing with the tassels of his red robe. The snow was whirling so fiercely outside his windows that he could scarcely see across the street, but within the air was deliciously soft and fragrant. He put the violets and jonquils on the taboret[1] beside the couch, and threw himself down, with a long sigh, covering himself with a Roman blanket. He was thoroughly tired; he had been in such haste, he had stood up to such a strain, covered so much ground in the last twenty-four hours, that he wanted to think how it had all come about. Lulled by the sound of the wind, the warm air, and the cool fragrance of the flowers, he sank into deep, drowsy retrospection.

It had been wonderfully simple; when they had shut him out of the theater and concert hall, when they had taken away his bone, the whole thing was virtually determined. The rest was a mere matter of opportunity. The only thing that at all surprised him was his own courage—for he realized well enough that he had always been tormented by fear, a sort of apprehensive dread that, of late years, as the meshes of the lies he had told closed about him, had been pulling the muscles of his body tighter and tighter. Until now he could not remember the time when he had not been dreading something. Even when he was a little boy it was always there—behind him, or before, or on either side. There had always been the shadowed corner, the dark place into which he dared not look, but from which something seemed always to be watching him—and Paul had done things that were not pretty to watch, he knew.

But now he had a curious sense of relief, as though he had at last thrown down the gauntlet to the thing in the corner.

Yet it was but a day since he had been sulking in the traces[2]; but yesterday afternoon that he had been sent to the bank with Denny & Carson's deposit, as usual—but this time he was instructed to leave the book to be balanced. There was above two thousand dollars in checks, and nearly a thousand in the bank notes which he had taken from the book and quietly transferred to his pocket. At the bank he had made out a new deposit slip. His nerves had been steady enough

---

[1] A small, cylindrical stand.
[2] Traces were straps, ropes, or chains by which an animal pulled a wagon or a carriage. Here, the phrase is metaphoric, referring to Paul's sulky attitude toward the bonds of work.

Unit Two Setting

Chapter 3 Paul's Case

to permit of his returning to the office, where he had finished his work and asked for a full day's holiday tomorrow, Saturday, giving a perfectly reasonable pretext. The bankbook, he knew, would not be returned before Monday or Tuesday, and his father would be out of town for the next week. From the time he slipped the bank notes into his pocket until he boarded the night train for New York, he had not known a moment's hesitation. It was not the first time Paul had steered through treacherous waters.

How astonishingly easy it had all been; here he was, the thing done; and this time there would be no awakening, no figure at the top of the stairs. He watched the snowflakes whirling by his window until he fell asleep.

When he awoke, it was three o'clock in the afternoon. He bounded up with a start; half of one of his precious days gone already! He spent more than an hour in dressing, watching every stage of his toilet carefully in the mirror. Everything was quite perfect; he was exactly the kind of boy he had always wanted to be.

When he went downstairs Paul took a carriage and drove up Fifth Avenue toward the Park①. The snow had somewhat abated; carriages and tradesmen's wagons were hurrying soundlessly to and fro in the winter twilight; boys in woolen mufflers were shoveling off the doorsteps; the avenue stages② made fine spots of color against the white street. Here and there on the corners were stands, with whole flower gardens blooming under glass cases, against the sides of which the snowflakes stuck and melted; violets, roses, carnations, lilies of the valley—somehow vastly more lovely and alluring that they blossomed thus unnaturally in the snow. The Park itself was a wonderful stage winterpiece.

When he returned, the pause of the twilight had ceased and the tune of the streets had changed. The snow was falling faster, lights streamed from the hotels that reared their dozen stories fearlessly up into the storm, defying the raging Atlantic winds. A long, black stream of carriages poured down the avenue, intersected here and there by other streams, tending horizontally. There were a score of cabs about the entrance of his hotel, and his driver had to wait. Boys in livery were running in and out of the awning stretched across the sidewalk, up and down the red velvet carpet laid from the door to the street. Above, about, within it all was the rumble and roar, the hurry and toss of thousands of human beings as hot for pleasure as himself, and on every side of him towered the glaring affirmation of the omnipotence of wealth.

The boy set his teeth and drew his shoulders together in a spasm of realization; the plot of all dramas, the text of all romances, the nerve-stuff of all sensations was whirling about him like the snowflakes. He burnt like a faggot③ in a tempest.

When Paul went down to dinner the music of the orchestra came floating up the elevator shaft to greet him. His head whirled as he stepped into the thronged corridor, and he sank back

---

① Central Park, the principal park in Manhattan.
② Window displays.
③ A bundle of sticks or twigs, tied together for burning.

into one of the chairs against the wall to get his breath. The lights, the chatter, the perfumes, the bewildering medley of color—he had, for a moment, the feeling of not being able to stand it. But only for a moment; these were his own people, he told himself. He went slowly about the corridors, through the writing rooms, smoking rooms, reception rooms, as though he were exploring the chambers of an enchanted palace, built and peopled for him alone.

When he reached the dining room he sat down at a table near a window. The flowers, the white linen, the many-colored wineglasses, the gay toilettes of the women, the low popping of corks, the undulating repetitions of the *Blue Danube*① from the orchestra, all flooded Paul's dream with bewildering radiance. When the roseate tinge of his champagne was added—that cold, precious, bubbling stuff that creamed and foamed in his glass—Paul wondered that there were honest men in the world at all. This was what all the world was fighting for, he reflected; this was what all the struggle was about. He doubted the reality of his past. Had he ever known a place called Cordelia Street, a place where fagged-looking businessmen got on the early car; mere rivets in a machine they seemed to Paul,—sickening men, with combings of children's hair always hanging to their coats, and the smell of cooking in their clothes. Cordelia Street—Ah, that belonged to another time and country; had he not always been thus, had he not sat here night after night, from as far back as he could remember, looking pensively over just such shimmering textures and slowly twirling the stem of a glass like this one between his thumb and middle finger? He rather thought he had.

He was not in the least abashed or lonely. He had no especial desire to meet or to know any of these people; all he demanded was the right to look on and conjecture, to watch the pageant. The mere stage properties were all he contended for. Nor was he lonely later in the evening, in his lodge at the Metropolitan.② He was now entirely rid of his nervous misgivings, of his forced aggressiveness, of the imperative desire to show himself different from his surroundings. He felt now that his surroundings explained him. Nobody questioned the purple;③ he had only to wear it passively. He had only to glance down at his attire to reassure himself that here it would be impossible for anyone to humiliate him.

He found it hard to leave his beautiful sitting room to go to bed that night, and sat long watching the raging storm from his turret window. When he went to sleep it was with the lights turned on in his bedroom; partly because of his old timidity, and partly so that, if he should wake in the night, there would be no wretched moment of doubt, no horrible suspicion of yellow wallpaper, or of Washington and Calvin above his bed.

Sunday morning the city was practically snowbound. Paul breakfasted late, and in the afternoon he fell in with a wild San Francisco boy, a freshman at Yale, who said he had run down for a "little flyer" over Sunday. The young man offered to show Paul the night side of the town, and

---

① Waltz by Johann Strauss (1825—1899), Austrian composer.
② His box at the Metropolitan Opera House.
③ His assumption of a royal robe.

Unit Two Setting
Chapter 3 Paul's Case

the two boys went out together after dinner, not returning to the hotel until seven o'clock the next morning. They had started out in the confiding warmth of a champagne friendship, but their parting in the elevator was singularly cool. The freshman pulled himself together to make his train, and Paul went to bed. He awoke at two o'clock in the afternoon, very thirsty and dizzy, and rang for ice-water, coffee, and the Pittsburgh papers.

On the part of the hotel management, Paul excited no suspicion. There was this to be said for him, that he wore his spoils with dignity and in no way made himself conspicuous. Even under the glow of his wine he was never boisterous, though he found the stuff like a magician's wand for wonder-building. His chief greediness lay in his ears and eyes, and his excesses were not offensive ones. His dearest pleasures were the gray winter twilights in his sitting room; his quiet enjoyment of his flowers, his clothes, his wide divan[①], his cigarette, and his sense of power. He could not remember a time when he had felt so at peace with himself. The mere release from the necessity of petty lying, lying every day and every day, restored his self-respect. He had never lied for pleasure, even at school; but to be noticed and admired, to assert his difference from other Cordelia Street boys; and he felt a good deal more manly, more honest, even, now that he had no need for boastful pretensions, now that he could, as his actor friends used to say, "dress the part." It was characteristic that remorse did not occur to him. His golden days went by without a shadow, and he made each as perfect as he could.

On the eighth day after his arrival in New York he found the whole affair exploited in the Pittsburgh papers, exploited with a wealth of detail which indicated that local news of a sensational nature was at a low ebb. The firm of Denny & Carson announced that the boy's father had refunded the full amount of the theft and that they had no intention of prosecuting. The Cumberland minister had been interviewed, and expressed his hope of yet reclaiming the motherless lad, and his Sabbath-school teacher declared that she would spare no effort to that end. The rumor had reached Pittsburgh that the boy had been seen in a New York hotel, and his father had gone East to find him and bring him home.

Paul had just come in to dress for dinner; he sank into a chair, weak to the knees, and clasped his head in his hands. It was to be worse than jail, even; the tepid waters of Cordelia Street were to close over him finally and forever. The gray monotony stretched before him in hopeless, unrelieved years; Sabbath school, Young People's Meeting, the yellow-papered room, the damp dishtowels; it all rushed back upon him with a sickening vividness. He had the old feeling that the orchestra had suddenly stopped, the sinking sensation that the play was over. The sweat broke out on his face, and he sprang to his feet, looked about him with his white, conscious smile, and winked at himself in the mirror. With something of the old childish belief in miracles with which he had so often gone to class, all his lessons unlearned, Paul dressed and dashed whistling down the corridor to the elevator.

---

① A long backless sofa, especially one set with pillows against a wall.

He had no sooner entered the dining room and caught the measure of the music than his remembrance was lightened by his old elastic power of claiming the moment, mounting with it, and finding it all-sufficient. The glare and glitter about him, the mere scenic accessories had again, and for the last time, their old potency. He would show himself that he was game, he would finish the thing splendidly. He doubted, more than ever, the existence of Cordelia Street, and for the first time he drank his wine recklessly. Was he not, after all, one of those fortunate beings born to the purple, was he not still himself and in his own place? He drummed a nervous accompaniment to the *Pagliacci*① music and looked about him, telling himself over and over that it had paid.

He reflected drowsily, to the swell of the music and the chill sweetness of his wine, that he might have done it more wisely. He might have caught an outbound steamer and been well out of their clutches before now. But the other side of the world had seemed too far away and too uncertain then; he could not have waited for it; his need had been too sharp. If he had to choose over again, he would do the same thing tomorrow. He looked affectionately about the dining room, now gilded with a soft mist. Ah, it had paid indeed!

Paul was awakened next morning by a painful throbbing in his head and feet. He had thrown himself across the bed without undressing, and had slept with his shoes on. His limbs and hands were lead heavy, and his tongue and throat were parched and burnt. There came upon him one of those fateful attacks of clear-headedness that never occurred except when he was physically exhausted and his nerves hung loose. He lay still, closed his eyes, and let the tide of things wash over him.

His father was in New York; "stopping at some joint or other," he told himself. The memory of successive summers on the front stoop fell upon him like a weight of black water. He had not a hundred dollars left; and he knew now, more than ever, that money was everything, the wall that stood between all he loathed and all he wanted. The thing was winding itself up; he had thought of that on his first glorious day in New York, and had even provided a way to snap the thread. It lay on his dressing table now; he had got it out last night when he came blindly up from dinner, but the shiny metal hurt his eyes, and he disliked the looks of it.

He rose and moved about with a painful effort, succumbing now and again to attacks of nausea②. It was the old depression exaggerated; all the world had become Cordelia Street. Yet somehow he was not afraid of anything, was absolutely calm; perhaps because he had looked into the dark corner at last and knew. It was bad enough, what he saw there, but somehow not so bad as his long fear of it had been. He saw everything clearly now. He had a feeling that he had made the best of it, that he had lived the sort of life he was meant to live, and for half an hour he sat staring at the revolver. But he told himself that was not the way, so he went downstairs and took a cab to the ferry.

---

① A tragic opera by Ruggiero Leoncavallo (1857—1919).
② Strong aversion; disgust.

Unit Two Setting
Chapter 3 Paul's Case

When Paul arrived in Newark he got off the train and took another cab, directing the driver to follow the Pennsylvania tracks out of the town. The snow lay heavy on the roadways and had drifted deep in the open fields. Only here and there the dead grass or dried weed stalks projected, singularly black, above it. Once well into the country, Paul dismissed the carriage and walked, floundering along the tracks, his mind a medley of irrelevant things. He seemed to hold in his brain an actual picture of everything he had seen that morning. He remembered every feature of both his drivers, of the toothless old woman from whom he had bought the red flowers in his coat, the agent from whom he had got his ticket, and all of his fellow passengers on the ferry. His mind, unable to cope with vital matters near at hand, worked feverishly and deftly at sorting and grouping these images. They made for him a part of the ugliness of the world, of the ache in his head, and the bitter burning on his tongue. He stooped and put a handful of snow into his mouth as he walked, but that, too, seemed hot. When he reached a little hillside, where the tracks ran through a cut some twenty feet below him, he stopped and sat down.

The carnations in his coat were drooping with the cold, he noticed, their red glory all over. It occurred to him that all the flowers he had seen in the glass cases that first night must have gone the same way, long before this. It was only one splendid breath they had, in spite of their brave mockery at the winter outside the glass; and it was a losing game in the end, it seemed, this revolt against the homilies by which the world is run. Paul took one of the blossoms carefully from his coat and scooped a little hole in the snow, where he covered it up. Then he dozed awhile, from his weak condition, seemingly insensible to the cold.

The sound of an approaching train awoke him, and he started to his feet, remembering only his resolution, and afraid lest he should be too late. He stood watching the approaching locomotive, his teeth chattering, his lips drawn away from them in a frightened smile; once or twice he glanced nervously sidewise, as though he were being watched. When the right moment came, he jumped. As he fell, the folly of his haste occurred to him with merciless clearness, the vastness of what he had left undone. There flashed through his brain, clearer than ever before, the blue of Adriatic water, the yellow of Algerian sands.

He felt something strike his chest, and that his body was being thrown swiftly through the air, on and on, immeasurably far and fast, while his limbs were gently relaxed. Then, because the picture-making mechanism was crushed, the disturbing visions flashed into black, and Paul dropped back into the immense design of things.

Film Comment:
Willa Cather's "Paul's Case": 54 minutes, color
Starring: Eric Roberts
Screenplay by: Ron Cowen
Directed by: Lamont Johnson

   Lost in a world of fantasy, young working-class Paul dreams of escaping his dreary existence in

The American Short Story Through Film

turn-of-the-century Pittsburgh. As fate would have it, Paul gets his chance by stealing some money and subsequently running off to glamorous New York City.

Once there, Paul experiences everything he ever dreamed of... from a luxurious hotel suite to his first taste of champagne. However, when reality finally comes crashing down around him, Paul realizes the desperate course he must now take.

In a powerful and intense performance, Eric Roberts ("Star 80") plays the title role in Willa Cather's "Paul's Case." As the tortured and tragic young man, Roberts brings to life this classic American story of a sensitive soul pitted against an uncaring materialistic society.

Film Scenes:

Scene 1: Dreamer
Scene 2: Art lover
Scene 3: Want to be like you!
Scene 4: Expelled from school
Scene 5: The Waldorf Hotel
Scene 6: End of a dream

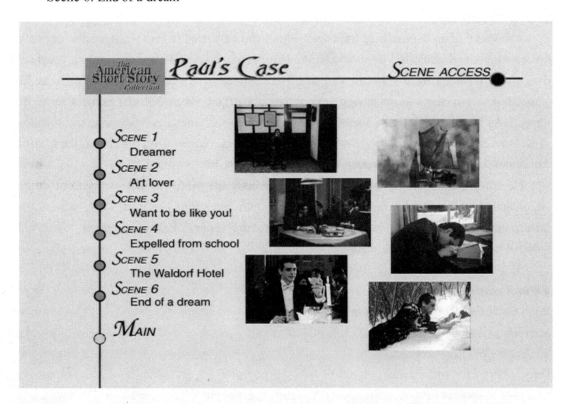

Unit Two Setting
Chapter 3 Paul's Case

Script Excerpts:

Set in 1905, the script opens with Paul, a Pittsburgh high-school student, awaiting "trial" by a group of teachers to determine whether he should be readmitted to classes. Once reprimanded, he runs to the city concert hall where he works as an usher, soaks up the atmosphere of the foyer painting gallery, and is again reprimanded for inattention to duty, this time by the house manager. Once the concert begins, Paul thrills to the beauty of the soprano's voice, and is warmed by the glamour of her presence afterwards. When Paul arrives home late, his widowed father reprimands him a third time, challenging him to do his best, since he has been readmitted to school. After Paul and his father walk home from church the next Sunday afternoon, the following scenes begin.

Interior. Kitchen. Evening.

Paul and his father sit in silence, eating supper. There is a flower in a little vase on the table between them—Paul's touch. Paul finally breaks the silence.

Paul: Did you like the roast?

Father: Very tasty. (*Paul smiles*.) It must've been expensive.

Paul: Not too... I did what you told me, I complained to the butcher. I said, "Twenty-nine a pound is highway robbery!" So he gave it to me for twenty-seven. I made your favorite dessert—rhubarb pie.

Father (*wiping his mouth*): None for me tonight—no room for it.

He pushes his seat away from the table, takes out a pipe from his pocket, and lights it.

Paul rises and clears the table. He carries the dishes to the sink and begins washing them.

Paul: George said if I came over, he'd help me with geometry. Could I have a dime, for car fare?

His father puffs at his pipe to get it lit. He doesn't answer.

Paul (*continuing*): Could I ...please?

Father: What's the point of your being an usher if you don't save your money?

Paul: I try to—

Father: Where's it all go?

Paul looks at the flowers on the table. He doesn't say anything.

Father (*continuing*): I don't know why you can't study with someone who lives in the neighborhood.

Paul: I don't know anybody.

Father: You mean this boy, George, who lives on the other side of town, is the only one who can help you?

Paul doesn't answer. His father begrudgingly digs into his pocket for a dime. He lays it on the kitchen table.

Father: The next time I expect you to pay for it yourself, or else find someone around here to help you.

Paul looks at the dime waiting for him on the table. Finally he goes to it and picks it up.

Paul: Thank you—

Interior. Paul's room. Night.

Paul stands at his dresser, splashing rose water on his hands. He hides the bottle under the clothes in the top drawer. He leaves the room.

Interior. Stairs. Night.

Paul comes down the stairs, book in hand. He takes his coat from the hook and puts it on. He calls to his father.

Paul: Be back soon.

Father (VO): Don't be late!

Paul opens the front door and leaves, closing it behind him.

Interior. Stage of theater. Night.

In bright lights and full costume, an acting company is performing Dumas's *La Dame Aux Camelias*.

Marguerite: Come along, little Saint-Gaudens! I want to dance!

Marguerite polkas with Saint-Gaudens. Armand plays the piano.

Exterior. Alley and stage door behind theater. Night.

Paul walks down the alley to the stage door. Propped up next to it is a signboard that read: "The Pittsburgh Repertory Company presents *La Dame Aux Camelias* by Alexander Dumas."

Paul looks at the sign, then opens the stage door and enters.

Interior. Backstage. Night.

Paul closes the door quietly behind him. In the hallway, a backstage doorman sits by the callboard reading a newspaper. Paul nods to him.

The doorman looks up, nods at Paul, and goes back to reading.

Paul walks down the hallway to a door. He opens it.

Interior. Wings. Night.

Paul closes the door quietly behind him and steps into the darkened wings. He stops and breathes in the intoxicating backstage air. He walks softly to the edge of the wings for a view of the stage.

Unit Two Setting
Chapter 3 Paul's Case

Interior. Stage. Night.

From Paul's POV: A very angled shot of the stage, brightly lit. Heavily made-up actors in full costume move about a French drawing room. The speech and mannerisms are highly exaggerated. Paul watches, transfixed.

Marguerite and Saint-Gaudens are dancing. She stops suddenly and coughs.

Saint-Gaudens: What is the matter?

Marguerite: Nothing—I lost my breath.

Armand (*stops playing the piano*): I am afraid you are ill! (*He goes to her.*)

Marguerite: No, it's nothing. Don't stop.

Prudence: Marguerite is ill!

Marguerite: But it is nothing, really. Please go into the other room. I'll be with you directly.

Prudence (*to Saint-Gaudens*): We had better leave her. She always want to be alone when she feels like that.

Marguerite: Do go, I shall come presently.

Interior. Wings. Night.

Prudence and Saint-Gaudens exit past a starry-eyed Paul. Offstage, the actors appear grotesque in their heavy make-up. Their costumes seem shabby.

Close-up of Paul as he turns to watch them. They walk across the wings, their backs to him. They vanish into the darkness, whispering to each other, while we only hear the voices from the stage.

Marguerite (VO): Take this flower. Bring it back to me.

Armand (VO): When?

Marguerite (VO): When it is faded—

Interior. Wings. Night.

The camera follows the actor and actress from behind, acting once more as Paul's eyes and ears. They climb a circular iron staircase to the second floor dressing rooms. We hear their conversation. In voiceover, they speak "dramatically," as Paul would expect them to do.

Actor (VO): —magic in the air tonight! Did you feel it?

Actress (VO): As if Dumas himself had breathed every word into me!

Actor (VO): I could tell by the way you spoke—your every gesture—

Interior. Second floor hallway. Night.

The camera follows the actor and actress from behind as they walk down the hallway to their dressing rooms. Their imagined conversation continues in voiceover.

Actor (VO): I felt as if the ghosts of the Comedie Francaise were on stage with us tonight! Moliere! Corneille! Racine!

Actress (VO): The Divine Sarah!

Actor (VO): Sarah herself!

Interior. Wings. Night.

Paul, looking off into the darkened wings, in the direction of the actor and actress. A hand is placed on his shoulder. A voice.

Charlie (VO): Hey!

Paul spins around.

Charlie Edwards stands there in front of him, in costume. He was playing the part of Armand. He removes his powdered wig. His makeup is dripping with perspiration.

Charlie: Didn't you hear me calling you?

Paul: No, I—

Charlie takes him by the arm and pull him along.

Charlie: Come on, I have to change for Act Two!

Interior. Dressing room. Night.

Charlie bursts into his dressing room with energy left over from the stage. Paul follows, putting his geometry book down on the makeup table.

Charlie is out of his costume in a flash, handing pieces to Paul to hang up.

Charlie: Did you see the first act?

Paul: The last part—

Charlie: How was I?

Paul (*simply*): You were brilliant.

Charlie (*laughing*): "Brilliant"?

Paul (*feeling he's being made fun of*): I thought so...

Charlie (*convinced*): That good? I suppose I *did* have a special feel for it tonight.

Paul: I could tell.

Charlie hands Paul a piece of his costume to hang up.

Charlie: Here— Where are my pants?

Paul: They're right here—

He hands Charlie his pants for the second act. Charlie puts them on.

Paul (*continuing*): It must be wonderful to say and do splendid things.

Charlie: It is, it is. That's what they call acting, m'boy! I bet you'd like to get out there on the boards yourself, wouldn't you?

Paul: No, I—

Charlie: Come on, you can tell old Charlie!

Paul: No, really—

Charlie: You don't have a great, secret desire to be an actor?

Unit Two Setting
Chapter 3 Paul's Case

Paul: I just want to...

Charlie: ...What?

Paul: Be. Here. In the atmosphere of it. Float on the wave of it, be carried off—

Charlie pulls on his wig.

Charlie: Such poetry!

Paul: Where I live...all the houses are the same. All the people inside the houses are the same...all they think about are their jobs, their suppers, sending their children to school and going to church on Sunday.

Charlie: A bit drab for you?

Paul: I long for cool things...soft lights...fresh flowers...

He picks up a flower bouquet that lies next to his geometry book.

Charlie: They're not real...they'd wilt under the lights...Here, help me with this—

Paul helps him on with his jacket. Charlie sits at his makeup table to touch up his face. Behind him, in the mirror, we see the actress who went up the stairs earlier come into the dressing room. She wears a tattered bathrobe. Her hair is pinned up.

Actress: Charlie, you got some lip rouge?

Charlie: Sure, love, come on in.

She comes into the room. She smiles at Paul. He blushes.

Charlie: That's Paul.

Actress: Hello, Paul.

Charlie: He's a connoisseur of great art!

Paul (*to actress*): I've admired your performance greatly.

The actress curtsies to Paul.

Charlie: Here you go!

He tosses her the lip rouge.

Actress: Thanks—you're a real gent.

She winks at Paul and walks out of the dressing room.

Charlie: You know, you should be in the big time with that act.

Paul: I want to go to New York—some day.

Charlie: Don't we all! Don't we all!

Paul: I have a scrapbook at home...with pictures of New York.

Charlie looks at Paul. His smile vanishes as he realizes how sad Paul really is. He puts his hand on Paul's shoulder.

Charlie: I hope you get there, old man.

He smiles at Paul.

Discussion Questions:

1. If you feel that Paul has been unjustly treated by parents, teachers, or society at large, explain the injustice.
2. If, on the other hand, you feel he suffers from a defect of character, define it.
3. What is the connection between Paul's fascination with the theater and his crime?
4. Why is his father's repayment of the stolen money "worse than jail"?
5. Does Paul repent at the moment of his death? If you think he does not, how do you interpret the ending of the story?

Further Reading and Watching:

The Bohemian Girl

Chapter 4

Bernice Bobs Her Hair

F. Scott Fitzgerald

Author Introduction:

F. Scott Fitzgerald (1896—1940) was born into an upper-middle-class family in St. Paul, Minnesota, and he attended Princeton University until he left in 1917 to enlist in the Army as a second lieutenant. While stationed at the training camp, he met the beautiful girl Zelda in a country club who was to become his wife. He married Zelda Sayre as the novel *This Side of Paradise* (1920) launched Fitzgerald's career as a writer and provided a steady income suitable to Zelda's needs. Acting out the glamorous life-style he wrote of in his most popular magazine fiction, the couple traveled with a well-heeled crowd in New York, Paris, and the French Riviera through the 1920s. Most of their income came from those numerous stories published in magazines such as *The Saturday Evening Post*. Fitzgerald was a spokesman for the so-called Jazz Age, setting a personal as well as literary example for a generation whose first commandment was: Do what you will. He fell from favor as a writer when the indulgent decade of his triumph went down under the impact of a worldwide Depression. Fitzgerald's alcoholism and financial difficulties, in addition to Zelda's mental illness made for difficult years of their marriage. Through years of emotional and physical collapse he struggled to repair his life by writing to Hollywood—producing at the same time a series of stories that exposed his humiliations there. His major novels include *The Beautiful and Damned* (1922), *The Great Gatsby* (1925), and *Tender Is the Night* (1934), and the unfinished novel *The Last Tycoon* (1941) was published posthumously. His stories, many of which treat themes of youth and promise, and age and despair, were collected in *Flappers and Philosophers* (1921), *Tales of the Jazz Age* (1922), *All the Sad Young Men* (1926), and *Taps at Reveille* (1935).

Story Summary:

Bernice is of the pre-flapper generation, but her struggles in learning to "fit in" are as modern as today. Bernice starts out as the prototypical "drag." She is taken in town by her know-it-all cousin, Marjorie, who sets out to remake her. Under Marjorie's tutelage, Bernice becomes so adopt in applying the lessons in how to attract and beguile men that she begins to rival Marjorie at her own game. When Marjorie attempts to humiliate Bernice, and actually succeeds in goading her into bobbing her hair, Bernice strikes back in an act of revenge that gives the story a delightful and ironic twist.

Key Terms:
Flapper, "Bobbed" Hair, Social Elite, Popularity, Jazz Age

Bernice Bobs Her Hair[①]

I

After dark on Saturday night one could stand on the first tee of the golf-course and see the country-club windows as a yellow expanse over a very black and wavy ocean. The waves of this ocean, so to speak, were the heads of many curious caddies[②], a few of the more ingenious chauffeurs, the golf professional's deaf sister—and there were usually several stray, diffident waves who might have rolled inside had they so desired. This was the gallery.

The balcony was inside. It consisted of the circle of wicker chairs that lined the wall of the combination clubroom and ballroom. At these Saturday-night dances it was largely feminine; a great babel[③] of middle-aged ladies with sharp eyes and icy hearts behind lorgnettes and large bosoms. The main function of the balcony was critical. It occasionally showed grudging admiration, but never approval, for it is well known among ladies over thirty-five that when the younger set dance in the summer-time it is with the very worst intentions in the world, and if they are not bombarded with stony eyes stray couples will dance weird barbaric interludes in the corners, and the more popular, more dangerous, girls will sometimes be kissed in the parked limousines of unsuspecting dowagers.

But, after all, this critical circle is not close enough to the stage to see the actors' faces and catch the subtler byplay. It can only frown and lean, ask questions and make satisfactory deductions from its set of postulates, such as the one which states that every young man with a large income leads the life of a hunted partridge. It never really appreciates the drama of the shifting, semi-cruel world of adolescence. No; boxes, orchestra-circle, principals, and chorus are represented by the medley of faces and voices that sway to the plaintive African rhythm of Dyer's dance orchestra.

---

① First published in *Saturday Evening Post* on May 1, 1920, then collected in *Flappers and Philosophers,* 1921.
② Kids hired to serve as an attendant to a golfer, especially by carrying the golf clubs.
③ A confusion of sounds or voices. In the Bible, a city (now thought to be Babylon) in Shinar where construction of a heaven-reaching tower was interrupted when the builders became unable to understand one another's language.

Unit Two Setting
Chapter 4 Bernice Bobs Her Hair

From sixteen-year-old Otis Ormonde, who has two more years at Hill School, to G. Reece Stoddard, over whose bureau at home hangs a Harvard law diploma; from little Madeleine Hogue, whose hair still feels strange and uncomfortable on top of her head, to Bessie MacRae, who has been the life of the party a little too long—more than ten years—the medley is not only the center of the stage but contains the only people capable of getting an un-obstructed view of it.

With a flourish and a bang the music stops. The couples exchange artificial, effortless smiles, facetiously repeat "*la-de-da-da* dum-*dum*," and then the clatter of young feminine voices soars over the burst of clapping.

A few disappointed stags① caught in midfloor as they had been about to cut in subsided listlessly back to the walls, because this was not like the riotous Christmas dances—these summer hops were considered just pleasantly warm and exciting, where even the younger marrieds rose and performed ancient waltzes and terrifying fox trots② to the tolerant amusement of their younger brothers and sisters.

Warren McIntyre, who casually attended Yale, being one of the unfortunate stags, felt in his dinner-coat pocket for a cigarette and strolled out onto the wide, semi-dark veranda③, where couples were scattered at tables, filling the lantern-hung night with vague words and hazy laughter. He nodded here and there at the less absorbed and as he passed each couple some half-forgotten fragment of a story played in his mind, for it was not a large city and every one was Who's Who to every one else's past. There, for example, were Jim Strain and Ethel Demorest, who had been privately engaged for three years. Every one knew that as soon as Jim managed to hold a job for more than two months she would marry him. Yet how bored they both looked, and how wearily Ethel regarded Jim sometimes, as if she wondered why she had trained the vines of her affection on such a wind-shaken poplar.

Warren was nineteen and rather pitying with those of his friends who hadn't gone East to college. But, like most boys, he bragged tremendously about the girls of his city when he was away from it. There was Genevieve Ormonde, who regularly made the rounds of dances, house-parties, and football games at Princeton, Yale, Williams, and Cornell; there was black-eyed Roberta Dillon, who was quite as famous to her own generation as Hiram Johnson or Ty Cobb; and, of course, there was Marjorie Harvey, who besides having a fairylike face and a dazzling, bewildering tongue was already justly celebrated for having turned five cart-wheels④ in succession during the last pump-and-slipper dance at New Haven.

Warren, who had grown up across the street from Marjorie, had long been "crazy about her." Sometimes she seemed to reciprocate his feeling with a faint gratitude, but she had tried

---
① Those who attend a social gathering unaccompanied by a woman.
② A ballroom dance in 2/4 or 4/4 time, encompassing a variety of slow and fast steps.
③ A porch or balcony, usually roofed and often partly enclosed, extending along the outside of a building.
④ A handspring in which the body turns over sideways with the arms and legs spread like the spokes of a wheel.

him by her infallible test and informed him gravely that she did not love him. Her test was that when she was away from him she forgot him and had affairs with other boys. Warren found this discouraging, especially as Marjorie had been making little trips all summer, and for the first two or three days after each arrival home he saw great heaps of mail on the Harveys' hall table addressed to her in various masculine handwritings. To make matters worse, all during the month of August she had been visited by her cousin Bernice from Eau Claire[①], and it seemed impossible to see her alone. It was always necessary to hunt round and find someone to take care of Bernice. As August waned this was becoming more and more difficult.

Much as Warren worshipped Marjorie, he had to admit that Cousin Bernice was sorta hopeless. She was pretty, with dark hair and high color, but she was no fun on a party. Every Saturday night he danced a long arduous duty dance with her to please Marjorie, but he had never been anything but bored in her company.

"Warren"—a soft voice at his elbow broke in upon his thoughts, and he turned to see Marjorie, flushed and radiant as usual. She laid a hand on his shoulder and a glow settled almost imperceptibly over him.

"Warren," she whispered, "do something for me—dance with Bernice. She's been stuck with little Otis Ormonde for almost an hour."

Warren's glow faded.

"Why—sure," he answered half-heartedly.

"You don't mind, do you? I'll see that you don't get stuck."

"'Sall right."

Marjorie smiled—that smile that was thanks enough.

"You're an angel, and I'm obliged loads."

With a sigh the angel glanced round the veranda, but Bernice and Otis were not in sight. He wandered back inside, and there in front of the women's dressing-room he found Otis in the center of a group of young men who were convulsed with laughter. Otis was brandishing a piece of timber he had picked up, and discoursing volubly.

"She's gone in to fix her hair," he announced wildly. "I'm waiting to dance another hour with her."

Their laughter was renewed.

"Why don't some of you cut in[②]?" cried Otis resentfully. "She likes more variety."

"Why, Otis," suggested a friend, "you've just barely got used to her."

"Why the two-by-four, Otis?" inquired Warren, smiling.

"The two-by-four? Oh, this? This is a club. When she comes out I'll hit her on the head and knock her in again."

---

① A city of west-central Wisconsin at the mouth of the Eau Clair River.
② To interrupt a dancing couple in order to dance with one of them.

Unit Two Setting

Chapter 4 Bernice Bobs Her Hair

Warren collapsed on a settee① and howled with glee.

"Never mind, Otis," he articulated finally. "I'm relieving you this time."

Otis simulated a sudden fainting attack and handed the stick to Warren.

"If you need it, old man," he said hoarsely.

No matter how beautiful or brilliant a girl may be, the reputation of not being frequently cut in on makes her position at a dance unfortunate. Perhaps boys prefer her company to that of the butterflies with whom they dance a dozen times an evening, but youth in this jazz-nourished generation is temperamentally restless, and the idea of fox-trotting more than one full fox trot with the same girl is distasteful, not to say odious. When it comes to several dances and the intermissions between she can be quite sure that a young man, once relieved, will never tread on her wayward toes again.

Warren danced the next full dance with Bernice, and finally, thankful for the intermission, he led her to a table on the veranda. There was a moment's silence while she did unimpressive things with her fan.

"It's hotter here than in Eau Claire," she said.

Warren stifled a sigh and nodded. It might be for all he knew or cared. He wondered idly whether she was a poor conversationalist because she got no attention or got no attention because she was a poor conversationalist.

"You going to be here much longer?" he asked, and then turned rather red. She might suspect his reasons for asking.

"Another week," she answered, and stared at him as if to lunge at his next remark when it left his lips.

Warren fidgeted. Then with a sudden charitable impulse he decided to try part of his line② on her. He turned and looked at her eyes.

"You've got an awfully kissable mouth," he began quietly.

This was a remark that he sometimes made to girls at college proms③ when they were talking in just such half dark as this. Bernice distinctly jumped. She turned an ungraceful red and became clumsy with her fan. No one had ever made such a remark to her before.

"Fresh!"—the word had slipped out before she realized it, and she bit her lip. Too late she decided to be amused, and offered him a flustered smile.

Warren was annoyed. Though not accustomed to have that remark taken seriously, still it usually provoked a laugh or a paragraph of sentimental banter. And he hated to be called fresh, except in a joking way. His charitable impulse died and he switched the topic.

"Jim Strain and Ethel Demorest sitting out as usual," he commented.

This was more in Bernice's line, but a faint regret mingled with her relief as the subject

---

① A long wooden bench with a back.
② Glib or insincere talk, usually intended to deceive or impress.
③ A formal dance held for a high-school or college class typically at or near the end of the academic year.

changed. Men did not talk to her about kissable mouths, but she knew that they talked in some such way to other girls.

"Oh, yes," she said, and laughed. "I hear they've been mooning round for years without a red penny. Isn't it silly?"

Warren's disgust increased. Jim Strain was a close friend of his brother's, and anyway he considered it bad form to sneer at people for not having money. But Bernice had had no intention of sneering. She was merely nervous.

II

When Marjorie and Bernice reached home at half after midnight they said good night at the top of the stairs. Though cousins, they were not intimates. As a matter of fact Marjorie had no female intimates—she considered girls stupid. Bernice on the contrary all through this parent-arranged visit had rather longed to exchange those confidences flavored with giggles and tears that she considered an indispensable factor in all feminine intercourse. But in this respect she found Marjorie rather cold; felt somehow the same difficulty in talking to her that she had in talking to men. Marjorie never giggled, was never frightened, seldom embarrassed, and in fact had very few of the qualities which Bernice considered appropriately and blessedly feminine.

As Bernice busied herself with tooth-brush and paste this night she wondered for the hundredth time why she never had any attention when she was away from home. That her family were the wealthiest in Eau Claire; that her mother entertained tremendously, gave little dinners for her daughter before all dances and bought her a car of her own to drive round in, never occurred to her as factors in her home-town social success. Like most girls she had been brought up on the warm milk prepared by Annie Fellows Johnston and on novels in which the female was beloved because of certain mysterious womanly qualities, always mentioned but never displayed.

Bernice felt a vague pain that she was not at present engaged in being popular. She did not know that had it not been for Marjorie's campaigning she would have danced the entire evening with one man; but she knew that even in Eau Claire other girls with less position and less pulchritude[1] were given a much bigger rush. She attributed this to something subtly unscrupulous[2] in those girls. It had never worried her, and if it had her mother would have assured her that the other girls cheapened themselves and that men really respected girls like Bernice.

She turned out the light in her bathroom, and on an impulse decided to go in and chat for a moment with her aunt Josephine, whose light was still on. Her soft slippers bore her noiselessly down the carpeted hall, but hearing voices inside she stopped near the partly opened door. Then she caught her own name, and without any definite intention of eavesdropping lingered—and the thread of the conversation going on inside pierced her consciousness sharply as if it had been

---

[1] Great physical beauty and appeal.
[2] Devoid of scruples; oblivious to or contemptuous of what is right or honorable.

drawn through with a needle.

"She's absolutely hopeless!" It was Marjorie's voice. "Oh, I know what you're going to say! So many people have told you how pretty and sweet she is, and how she can cook! What of it? She has a bum time. Men don't like her."

"What's a little cheap popularity?"

Mrs. Harvey sounded annoyed.

"It's everything when you're eighteen," said Marjorie emphatically. "I've done my best. I've been polite and I've made men dance with her, but they just won't stand being bored. When I think of that gorgeous coloring wasted on such a ninny①, and think what Martha Carey could do with it—oh!"

"There's no courtesy these days."

Mrs. Harvey's voice implied that modern situations were too much for her. When she was a girl all young ladies who belonged to nice families had glorious times.

"Well," said Marjorie, "no girl can permanently bolster up a lame-duck visitor, because these days it's every girl for herself. I've even tried to drop her hints about clothes and things, and she's been furious—given me the funniest looks. She's sensitive enough to know she's not getting away with much, but I'll bet she consoles herself by thinking that she's very virtuous and that I'm too gay and fickle and will come to a bad end. All unpopular girls think that way. Sour grapes! Sarah Hopkins refers to Genevieve and Roberta and me as gardenia② girls! I'll bet she'd give ten years of her life and her European education to be a gardenia girl and have three or four men in love with her and be cut in on every few feet at dances."

"It seems to me," interrupted Mrs. Harvey rather wearily, "that you ought to be able to do something for Bernice. I know she's not very vivacious."

Marjorie groaned.

"Vivacious! Good grief! I've never heard her say anything to a boy except that it's hot or the floor's crowded or that she's going to school in New York next year. Sometimes she asks them what kind of car they have and tells them the kind she has. Thrilling!"

There was a short silence, and then Mrs. Harvey took up her refrain:

"All I know is that other girls not half so sweet and attractive get partners. Martha Carey, for instance, is stout and loud, and her mother is distinctly common. Roberta Dillon is so thin this year that she looks as though Arizona were the place for her. She's dancing herself to death."

"But, mother," objected Marjorie impatiently, "Martha is cheerful and awfully witty and an awfully slick girl, and Roberta's a marvelous dancer. She's been popular for ages!"

Mrs. Harvey yawned.

"I think it's that crazy Indian blood in Bernice," continued Marjorie. "Maybe she's a rever-

---

① A fool; a simpleton.
② A type of large, white or yellow flower with a very pleasant smell.

sion to type. Indian women all just sat round and never said anything."

"Go to bed, you silly child," laughed Mrs. Harvey. "I wouldn't have told you that if I'd thought you were going to remember it. And I think most of your ideas are perfectly idiotic," she finished sleepily.

There was another silence, while Marjorie considered whether or not convincing her mother was worth the trouble. People over forty can seldom be permanently convinced of anything. At eighteen our convictions are hills from which we look; at forty-five they are caves in which we hide.

Having decided this, Marjorie said good night. When she came out into the hall it was quite empty.

III

While Marjorie was breakfasting late next day Bernice came into the room with a rather formal good morning, sat down opposite, stared intently over and slightly moistened her lips.

"What's on your mind?" inquired Marjorie, rather puzzled.

Bernice paused before she threw her hand-grenade.

"I heard what you said about me to your mother last night."

Marjorie was startled, but she showed only a faintly heightened color and her voice was quite even when she spoke.

"Where were you?"

"In the hall. I didn't mean to listen—at first."

After an involuntary look of contempt Marjorie dropped her eyes and became very interested in balancing a stray corn-flake on her finger.

"I guess I'd better go back to Eau Claire—if I'm such a nuisance." Bernice's lower lip was trembling violently and she continued on a wavering note: "I've tried to be nice, and—and I've been first neglected and then insulted. No one ever visited me and got such treatment."

Marjorie was silent.

"But I'm in the way, I see. I'm a drag on you. Your friends don't like me." She paused, and then remembered another one of her grievances. "Of course I was furious last week when you tried to hint to me that that dress was unbecoming. Don't you think I know how to dress myself?"

"No," murmured Marjorie less than half-aloud.

"What?"

"I didn't hint anything," said Marjorie succinctly. "I said, as I remember, that it was better to wear a becoming dress three times straight than to alternate it with two frights."

"Do you think that was a very nice thing to say?"

"I wasn't trying to be nice." Then after a pause: "When do you want to go?"

Bernice drew in her breath sharply.

Unit Two Setting
Chapter 4 Bernice Bobs Her Hair

"Oh!" It was a little half-cry.

Marjorie looked up in surprise.

"Didn't you say you were going?"

"Yes, but——"

"Oh, you were only bluffing①!"

They stared at each other across the breakfast-table for a moment. Misty waves were passing before Bernice's eyes, while Marjorie's face wore that rather hard expression that she used when slightly intoxicated undergraduates were making love to her.

"So you were bluffing," she repeated as if it were what she might have expected.

Bernice admitted it by bursting into tears. Marjorie's eyes showed boredom.

"You're my cousin," sobbed Bernice. "I'm v-v-visiting you. I was to stay a month, and if I go home my mother will know and she'll wah-wonder——"

Marjorie waited until the shower of broken words collapsed into little sniffles.

"I'll give you my month's allowance," she said coldly, "and you can spend this last week anywhere you want. There's a very nice hotel——"

Bernice's sobs rose to a flute note, and rising of a sudden she fled from the room.

An hour later, while Marjorie was in the library absorbed in composing one of those non-committal, marvelously elusive letters that only a young girl can write, Bernice reappeared, very red-eyed and consciously calm. She cast no glance at Marjorie but took a book at random from the shelf and sat down as if to read. Marjorie seemed absorbed in her letter and continued writing. When the clock showed noon Bernice closed her book with a snap.

"I suppose I'd better get my railroad ticket."

This was not the beginning of the speech she had rehearsed upstairs, but as Marjorie was not getting her cues—wasn't urging her to be reasonable; it's all a mistake—it was the best opening she could muster.

"Just wait till I finish this letter," said Marjorie without looking round. "I want to get it off in the next mail."

After another minute, during which her pen scratched busily, she turned round and relaxed with an air of "at your service." Again Bernice had to speak.

"Do you want me to go home?"

"Well," said Marjorie, considering, "I suppose if you're not having a good time you'd better go. No use being miserable."

"Don't you think common kindness—"

"Oh, please don't quote *Little Women*②!" cried Marjorie impatiently. "That's out of style."

"You think so?"

---

① Misleading or deceiving.
② A novel by Louisa May Alcott.

"Heavens, yes! What modern girl could live like those inane females?"

"They were the models for our mothers."

Marjorie laughed.

"Yes, they were—not! Besides, our mothers were all very well in their way, but they know very little about their daughters' problems."

Bernice drew herself up.

"Please don't talk about my mother."

Marjorie laughed.

"I don't think I mentioned her."

Bernice felt that she was being led away from her subject.

"Do you think you've treated me very well?"

"I've done my best. You're rather hard material to work with."

The lids of Bernice's eyes reddened.

"I think you're hard and selfish, and you haven't a feminine quality in you."

"Oh, my Lord!" cried Marjorie in desperation. "You little nut! Girls like you are responsible for all the tiresome colorless marriages; all those ghastly① inefficiencies that pass as feminine qualities. What a blow it must be when a man with imagination marries the beautiful bundle of clothes that he's been building ideals round, and finds that she's just a weak, whining, cowardly mass of affectations!"

Bernice's mouth had slipped half open.

"The womanly woman!" continued Marjorie. "Her whole early life is occupied in whining criticisms of girls like me who really do have a good time."

Bernice's jaw descended farther as Marjorie's voice rose.

"There's some excuse for an ugly girl whining. If I'd been irretrievably ugly I'd never have forgiven my parents for bringing me into the world. But you're starting life without any handicap —" Marjorie's little fist clinched. "If you expect me to weep with you you'll be disappointed. Go or stay, just as you like." And picking up her letters she left the room.

Bernice claimed a headache and failed to appear at luncheon. They had a matinée date for the afternoon, but the headache persisting, Marjorie made explanation to a not very downcast boy. But when she returned late in the afternoon she found Bernice with a strangely set face waiting for her in her bedroom.

"I've decided," began Bernice without preliminaries, "that maybe you're right about things—possibly not. But if you'll tell me why your friends aren't—aren't interested in me I'll see if I can do what you want me to."

Marjorie was at the mirror shaking down her hair.

"Do you mean it?"

---

① Extremely unpleasant or bad.

Unit Two Setting
Chapter 4 Bernice Bobs Her Hair

"Yes."

"Without reservations? Will you do exactly what I say?"

"Well, I—"

"Well nothing! Will you do exactly as I say?"

"If they're sensible things."

"They're not! You're no case for sensible things."

"Are you going to make—to recommend—"

"Yes, everything. If I tell you to take boxing-lessons you'll have to do it. Write home and tell your mother you're going to stay another two weeks."

"If you'll tell me—"

"All right—I'll just give you a few examples now. First, you have no ease of manner. Why? Because you're never sure about your personal appearance. When a girl feels that she's perfectly groomed and dressed she can forget that part of her. That's charm. The more parts of yourself you can afford to forget the more charm you have."

"Don't I look all right?"

"No; for instance, you never take care of your eyebrows. They're black and lustrous, but by leaving them straggly① they're a blemish. They'd be beautiful if you'd take care of them in one-tenth the time you take doing nothing. You're going to brush them so that they'll grow straight."

Bernice raised the brows in question.

"Do you mean to say that men notice eyebrows?"

"Yes—subconsciously. And when you go home you ought to have your teeth straightened a little. It's almost imperceptible, still—"

"But I thought," interrupted Bernice in bewilderment, "that you despised little dainty② feminine things like that."

"I hate dainty minds," answered Marjorie. "But a girl has to be dainty in person. If she looks like a million dollars she can talk about Russia, ping-pong, or the League of Nations③ and get away with it."

"What else?"

"Oh, I'm just beginning! There's your dancing."

"Don't I dance all right?"

"No, you don't—you lean on a man; yes, you do—ever so slightly. I noticed it when we were dancing together yesterday. And you dance standing up straight instead of bending over a little. Probably some old lady on the side-line once told you that you looked so dignified that

---

① Growing or spread out in a disorderly or aimless way.
② Overly fastidious; squeamish.
③ A world organization established in 1920 to promote international cooperation and peace. It was first proposed in 1918 by President Woodrow Wilson, although the United States never joined the League. Essentially powerless, it was officially dissolved in 1946.

way. But except with a very small girl it's much harder on the man, and he's the one that counts."

"Go on." Bernice's brain was reeling.

"Well, you've got to learn to be nice to men who are sad birds. You look as if you'd been insulted whenever you're thrown with any except the most popular boys. Why, Bernice, I'm cut in on every few feet—and who does most of it? Why, those very sad birds. No girl can afford to neglect them. They're the big part of any crowd. Young boys too shy to talk are the very best conversational practice. Clumsy boys are the best dancing practice. If you can follow them and yet look graceful you can follow a baby tank across a barb-wire sky-scraper."

Bernice sighed profoundly, but Marjorie was not through.

"If you go to a dance and really amuse, say, three sad birds that dance with you; if you talk so well to them that they forget they're stuck with you, you've done something. They'll come back next time, and gradually so many sad birds will dance with you that the attractive boys will see there's no danger of being stuck—then they'll dance with you."

"Yes," agreed Bernice faintly. "I think I begin to see."

"And finally," concluded Marjorie, "poise and charm will just come. You'll wake up some morning knowing you've attained it, and men will know it too."

Bernice rose.

"It's been awfully kind of you—but nobody's ever talked to me like this before, and I feel sort of startled."

Marjorie made no answer but gazed pensively at her own image in the mirror.

"You're a peach to help me," continued Bernice.

Still Marjorie did not answer, and Bernice thought she had seemed too grateful.

"I know you don't like sentiment," she said timidly.

Marjorie turned to her quickly.

"Oh, I wasn't thinking about that. I was considering whether we hadn't better bob your hair."

Bernice collapsed backward upon the bed.

IV

On the following Wednesday evening there was a dinner-dance at the country club. When the guests strolled in Bernice found her place-card with a slight feeling of irritation. Though at her right sat G. Reece Stoddard, a most desirable and distinguished young bachelor, the all-important left held only Charley Paulson. Charley lacked height, beauty, and social shrewdness, and in her new enlightenment Bernice decided that his only qualification to be her partner was that he had never been stuck with her. But this feeling of irritation left with the last of the soup-plates, and Marjorie's specific instruction came to her. Swallowing her pride she turned to Charley Paulson and plunged.

Unit Two Setting
Chapter 4 Bernice Bobs Her Hair

"Do you think I ought to bob my hair, Mr. Charley Paulson?"

Charley looked up in surprise.

"Why?"

"Because I'm considering it. It's such a sure and easy way of attracting attention."

Charley smiled pleasantly. He could not know this had been rehearsed. He replied that he didn't know much about bobbed hair. But Bernice was there to tell him.

"I want to be a society vampire①, you see," she announced coolly, and went on to inform him that bobbed hair was the necessary prelude. She added that she wanted to ask his advice, because she had heard he was so critical about girls.

Charley, who knew as much about the psychology of women as he did of the mental states of Buddhist contemplatives, felt vaguely flattered.

"So I've decided," she continued, her voice rising slightly, "that early next week I'm going down to the Sevier Hotel barber-shop, sit in the first chair, and get my hair bobbed." She faltered, noticing that the people near her had paused in their conversation and were listening; but after a confused second Marjorie's coaching told, and she finished her paragraph to the vicinity at large. "Of course I'm charging admission, but if you'll all come down and encourage me I'll issue passes for the inside seats."

There was a ripple of appreciative laughter, and under cover of it G. Reece Stoddard leaned over quickly and said close to her ear: "I'll take a box right now."

She met his eyes and smiled as if he had said something surpassingly brilliant.

"Do you believe in bobbed hair?" asked G. Reece in the same undertone.

"I think it's unmoral," affirmed Bernice gravely. "But, of course, you've either got to amuse people or feed 'em or shock 'em." Marjorie had culled this from Oscar Wilde②. It was greeted with a ripple of laughter from the men and a series of quick, intent looks from the girls. And then as though she had said nothing of wit or moment Bernice turned again to Charley and spoke confidentially in his ear.

"I want to ask you your opinion of several people. I imagine you're a wonderful judge of character."

Charley thrilled faintly—paid her a subtle compliment by overturning her water.

Two hours later, while Warren McIntyre was standing passively in the stag line abstractedly watching the dancers and wondering whither and with whom Marjorie had disappeared, an unrelated perception began to creep slowly upon him—a perception that Bernice, cousin to Marjorie, had been cut in on several times in the past five minutes. He closed his eyes, opened them and looked again. Several minutes back she had been dancing with a visiting boy, a matter

---

① A reanimated corpse that is believed to rise from the grave at night to suck the blood of sleeping people.

② Irish-born writer. Renowned as a wit in London literary circles, he achieved recognition with *The Picture of Dorian Gray* (1891), a novel. He also wrote plays of lively dialogue, such as *The Importance of Being Earnest* (1895), and poetry, including *The Ballad of Reading Gaol* (1898).

easily accounted for; a visiting boy would know no better. But now she was dancing with some one else, and there was Charley Paulson headed for her with enthusiastic determination in his eye. Funny—Charley seldom danced with more than three girls an evening.

Warren was distinctly surprised when—the exchange having been effected—the man relieved proved to be none other than G. Reece Stoddard himself. And G. Reece seemed not at all jubilant at being relieved. Next time Bernice danced near, Warren regarded her intently. Yes, she was pretty, distinctly pretty; and to-night her face seemed really vivacious. She had that look that no woman, however histrionically proficient, can successfully counterfeit—she looked as if she were having a good time. He liked the way she had her hair arranged, wondered if it was brilliantine① that made it glisten so. And that dress was becoming—a dark red that set off her shadowy eyes and high coloring. He remembered that he had thought her pretty when she first came to town, before he had realized that she was dull. Too bad she was dull—dull girls unbearable—certainly pretty though.

His thoughts zigzagged back to Marjorie. This disappearance would be like other disappearances. When she reappeared he would demand where she had been—would be told emphatically that it was none of his business. What a pity she was so sure of him! She basked in the knowledge that no other girl in town interested him; she defied him to fall in love with Genevieve or Roberta.

Warren sighed. The way to Marjorie's affections was a labyrinth indeed. He looked up. Bernice was again dancing with the visiting boy. Half unconsciously he took a step out from the stag line in her direction, and hesitated. Then he said to himself that it was charity. He walked toward her—collided suddenly with G. Reece Stoddard.

"Pardon me," said Warren.

But G. Reece had not stopped to apologize. He had again cut in on Bernice.

That night at one o'clock Marjorie, with one hand on the electric-light switch in the hall, turned to take a last look at Bernice's sparkling eyes.

"So it worked?"

"Oh, Marjorie, yes!" cried Bernice.

"I saw you were having a gay time."

"I did! The only trouble was that about midnight I ran short of talk. I had to repeat myself—with different men of course. I hope they won't compare notes."

"Men don't," said Marjorie, yawning, "and it wouldn't matter if they did—they'd think you were even trickier."

She snapped out the light, and as they started up the stairs Bernice grasped the banister thankfully. For the first time in her life she had been danced tired.

---

① An oily, perfumed hairdressing.

Unit Two Setting
Chapter 4 Bernice Bobs Her Hair

"You see," said Marjorie at the top of the stairs, "one man sees another man cut in and he thinks there must be something there. Well, we'll fix up some new stuff tomorrow. Good night."

"Good night."

As Bernice took down her hair she passed the evening before her in review. She had followed instructions exactly. Even when Charley Paulson cut in for the eighth time she had simulated① delight and had apparently been both interested and flattered. She had not talked about the weather or Eau Claire or automobiles or her school, but had confined her conversation to me, you, and us.

But a few minutes before she fell asleep a rebellious thought was churning drowsily in her brain—after all, it was she who had done it. Marjorie, to be sure, had given her her conversation, but then Marjorie got much of her conversation out of things she read. Bernice had bought the red dress, though she had never valued it highly before Marjorie dug it out of her trunk—and her own voice had said the words, her own lips had smiled, her own feet had danced. Marjorie nice girl—vain, though—nice evening—nice boys—like Warren—Warren—Warren—what's-his-name—Warren—

She fell asleep.

V

To Bernice the next week was a revelation. With the feeling that people really enjoyed looking at her and listening to her came the foundation of self-confidence. Of course there were numerous mistakes at first. She did not know, for instance, that Draycott Deyo was studying for the ministry; she was unaware that he had cut in on her because he thought she was a quiet, reserved girl. Had she known these things she would not have treated him to the line which began "Hello, Shell Shock②!" and continued with the bathtub story—"It takes a frightful lot of energy to fix my hair in the summer—there's so much of it—so I always fix it first and powder my face and put on my hat; then I get into the bathtub, and dress afterward. Don't you think that's the best plan?"

Though Draycott Deyo was in the throes of difficulties concerning baptism by immersion and might possibly have seen a connection, it must be admitted that he did not. He considered feminine bathing an immoral subject, and gave her some of his ideas on the depravity of modern society.

But to offset that unfortunate occurrence Bernice had several signal successes to her credit. Little Otis Ormonde pleaded off from a trip East and elected instead to follow her with a puppy-like devotion, to the amusement of his crowd and to the irritation of G. Reece Stoddard, several of whose afternoon calls Otis completely ruined by the disgusting tenderness of the glances he bent on Bernice. He even told her the story of the two-by-four and the dressing-room

---

① Pretend.
② Any of the various acute, often hysterical neuroses originating in trauma suffered under fire in modern warfare.

to show her how frightfully mistaken he and every one else had been in their first judgment of her. Bernice laughed off that incident with a slight sinking sensation.

Of all Bernice's conversation perhaps the best known and most universally approved was the line about the bobbing of her hair.

"Oh, Bernice, when you goin' to get the hair bobbed?"

"Day after to-morrow maybe," she would reply, laughing. "Will you come and see me? Because I'm counting on you, you know."

"Will we? You know! But you better hurry up."

Bernice, whose tonsorial① intentions were strictly dishonorable, would laugh again.

"Pretty soon now. You'd be surprised."

But perhaps the most significant symbol of her success was the gray car of the hypercritical Warren McIntyre, parked daily in front of the Harvey house. At first the parlor-maid was distinctly startled when he asked for Bernice instead of Marjorie; after a week of it she told the cook that Miss Bernice had gotta holda Miss Marjorie's best fella.

And Miss Bernice had. Perhaps it began with Warren's desire to rouse jealousy in Marjorie; perhaps it was the familiar though unrecognized strain of Marjorie in Bernice's conversation; perhaps it was both of these and something of sincere attraction besides. But somehow the collective mind of the younger set knew within a week that Marjorie's most reliable beau had made an amazing face-about and was giving an indisputable rush to Marjorie's guest. The question of the moment was how Marjorie would take it. Warren called Bernice on the 'phone twice a day, sent her notes, and they were frequently seen together in his roadster②, obviously engrossed in one of those tense, significant conversations as to whether or not he was sincere.

Marjorie on being twitted only laughed. She said she was mighty glad that Warren had at last found some one who appreciated him. So the younger set laughed, too, and guessed that Marjorie didn't care and let it go at that.

One afternoon when there were only three days left of her visit Bernice was waiting in the hall for Warren, with whom she was going to a bridge party. She was in rather a blissful mood, and when Marjorie—also bound for the party—appeared beside her and began casually to adjust her hat in the mirror, Bernice was utterly unprepared for anything in the nature of a clash. Marjorie did her work very coldly and succinctly in three sentences.

"You may as well get Warren out of your head," she said coldly.

"What?" Bernice was utterly astounded.

"You may as well stop making a fool of yourself over Warren McIntyre. He doesn't care a snap of his fingers about you."

For a tense moment they regarded each other—Marjorie scornful, aloof; Bernice astounded,

---

① Of or relating to barbering or a barber.

② An open automobile having a single seat in the front for two or three people and a rumble seat or luggage compartment in the back.

Unit Two Setting
Chapter 4 Bernice Bobs Her Hair

half-angry, half-afraid. Then two cars drove up in front of the house and there was a riotous honking. Both of them gasped faintly, turned, and side by side hurried out.

All through the bridge party Bernice strove in vain to master a rising uneasiness. She had offended Marjorie, the sphinx① of sphinxes. With the most wholesome and innocent intentions in the world she had stolen Marjorie's property. She felt suddenly and horribly guilty. After the bridge game, when they sat in an informal circle and the conversation became general, the storm gradually broke. Little Otis Ormonde inadvertently precipitated it.

"When you going back to kindergarten, Otis?" some one had asked.

"Me? Day Bernice gets her hair bobbed."

"Then your education's over," said Marjorie quickly. "That's only a bluff② of hers. I should think you'd have realized."

"That a fact?" demanded Otis, giving Bernice a reproachful glance.

Bernice's ears burned as she tried to think up an effectual come-back. In the face of this direct attack her imagination was paralyzed.

"There's a lot of bluffs in the world," continued Marjorie quite pleasantly. "I should think you'd be young enough to know that, Otis."

"Well," said Otis, "maybe so. But gee! With a line like Bernice's—"

"Really?" yawned Marjorie. "What's her latest bon mot?"

No one seemed to know. In fact, Bernice, having trifled with her muse's beau, had said nothing memorable of late.

"Was that really all a line?" asked Roberta curiously.

Bernice hesitated. She felt that wit in some form was demanded of her, but under her cousin's suddenly frigid eyes she was completely incapacitated.

"I don't know," she stalled.

"Splush!" said Marjorie. "Admit it!"

Bernice saw that Warren's eyes had left a ukulele③ he had been tinkering with and were fixed on her questioningly.

"Oh, I don't know!" she repeated steadily. Her cheeks were glowing.

"Splush!" remarked Marjorie again.

"Come through, Bernice," urged Otis. "Tell her where to get off."

Bernice looked round again—she seemed unable to get away from Warren's eyes.

"I like bobbed hair," she said hurriedly, as if he had asked her a question, "and I intend to bob mine."

"When?" demanded Marjorie.

---

① A winged creature having the head of a woman and the body of a lion, noted for killing those who could not answer its riddle.

② Trickery.

③ A small four-stringed guitar popularized in Hawaii.

"Any time."

"No time like the present," suggested Roberta.

Otis jumped to his feet.

"Good stuff!" he cried. "We'll have a summer bobbing party. Sevier Hotel barber-shop, I think you said."

In an instant all were on their feet. Bernice's heart throbbed violently.

"What?" she gasped.

Out of the group came Marjorie's voice, very clear and contemptuous.

"Don't worry—she'll back out!"

"Come on, Bernice!" cried Otis, starting toward the door.

Four eyes—Warren's and Marjorie's—stared at her, challenged her, defied her. For another second she wavered wildly.

"All right," she said swiftly, "I don't care if I do."

An eternity of minutes later, riding down-town through the late afternoon beside Warren, the others following in Roberta's car close behind, Bernice had all the sensations of Marie Antoinette① bound for the guillotine② in a tumbrel③. Vaguely she wondered why she did not cry out that it was all a mistake. It was all she could do to keep from clutching her hair with both hands to protect it from the suddenly hostile world. Yet she did neither. Even the thought of her mother was no deterrent now. This was the test supreme of her sportsmanship; her right to walk unchallenged in the starry heaven of popular girls.

Warren was moodily silent, and when they came to the hotel he drew up at the curb and nodded to Bernice to precede him out. Roberta's car emptied a laughing crowd into the shop, which presented two bold plate-glass windows to the street.

Bernice stood on the curb and looked at the sign, Sevier Barber-Shop. It was a guillotine indeed, and the hangman was the first barber, who, attired in a white coat and smoking a cigarette, leaned nonchalantly against the first chair. He must have heard of her; he must have been waiting all week, smoking eternal cigarettes beside that portentous, too-often-mentioned first chair. Would they blindfold her? No, but they would tie a white cloth round her neck lest any of her blood—nonsense—hair—should get on her clothes.

"All right, Bernice," said Warren quickly.

With her chin in the air she crossed the sidewalk, pushed open the swinging screen-door, and giving not a glance to the uproarious, riotous row that occupied the waiting bench, went up to the first barber.

"I want you to bob my hair."

The first barber's mouth slid somewhat open. His cigarette dropped to the floor.

---

① Marie Antoinette (1755—1793), Queen of France. Her husband was King Louis XVI.
② A device consisting of a heavy blade held aloft between upright guides and dropped to behead the victim below.
③ A crude cart used to carry condemned prisoners to their place of execution, as during the French Revolution.

Unit Two Setting
Chapter 4 Bernice Bobs Her Hair

"Huh?"

"My hair—bob it!"

Refusing further preliminaries, Bernice took her seat on high. A man in the chair next to her turned on his side and gave her a glance, half lather, half amazement. One barber started and spoiled little Willy Schuneman's monthly haircut. Mr. O'Reilly in the last chair grunted and swore musically in ancient Gaelic as a razor bit into his cheek. Two bootblacks[①] became wide-eyed and rushed for her feet. No, Bernice didn't care for a shine.

Outside a passer-by stopped and stared; a couple joined him; half a dozen small boys' noses sprang into life, flattened against the glass; and snatches of conversation borne on the summer breeze drifted in through the screen-door.

"Lookada long hair on a kid!"

"Where'd yuh get 'at stuff? 'At's a bearded lady he just finished shavin'."

But Bernice saw nothing, heard nothing. Her only living sense told her that this man in the white coat had removed one tortoise-shell comb and then another; that his fingers were fumbling clumsily with unfamiliar hairpins; that this hair, this wonderful hair of hers, was going—she would never again feel its long voluptuous pull as it hung in a dark-brown glory down her back. For a second she was near breaking down, and then the picture before her swam mechanically into her vision—Marjorie's mouth curling in a faint ironic smile as if to say:

"Give up and get down! You tried to buck me and I called your bluff. You see you haven't got a prayer."

And some last energy rose up in Bernice, for she clinched her hands under the white cloth, and there was a curious narrowing of her eyes that Marjorie remarked on to some one long afterward.

Twenty minutes later the barber swung her round to face the mirror, and she flinched at the full extent of the damage that had been wrought. Her hair was not curly, and now it lay in lank lifeless blocks on both sides of her suddenly pale face. It was ugly as sin—she had known it would be ugly as sin. Her face's chief charm had been a Madonna[②]-like simplicity. Now that was gone and she was—well, frightfully mediocre—not stagy; only ridiculous, like a Greenwich Villager who had left her spectacles at home.

As she climbed down from the chair she tried to smile—failed miserably. She saw two of the girls exchange glances; noticed Marjorie's mouth curved in attenuated mockery—and that Warren's eyes were suddenly very cold.

"You see"—her words fell into an awkward pause—"I've done it."

"Yes, you've—done it," admitted Warren.

"Do you like it?"

There was a half-hearted "Sure" from two or three voices, another awkward pause, and

---

① Kids who clean and polish shoes for a living.
② The Virgin Mary.

then Marjorie turned swiftly and with serpent-like intensity to Warren.

"Would you mind running me down to the cleaners?" she asked. "I've simply got to get a dress there before supper. Roberta's driving right home and she can take the others."

Warren stared abstractedly at some infinite speck[①] out the window. Then for an instant his eyes rested coldly on Bernice before they turned to Marjorie.

"Be glad to," he said slowly.

VI

Bernice did not fully realize the outrageous trap that had been set for her until she met her aunt's amazed glance just before dinner.

"Why, Bernice!"

"I've bobbed it, Aunt Josephine."

"Why, child!"

"Do you like it?"

"Why, Ber-nice!"

"I suppose I've shocked you."

"No, but what'll Mrs. Deyo think tomorrow night? Bernice, you should have waited until after the Deyos' dance—you should have waited if you wanted to do that."

"It was sudden, Aunt Josephine. Anyway, why does it matter to Mrs. Deyo particularly?"

"Why, child," cried Mrs. Harvey, "in her paper on 'The Foibles[②] of the Younger Generation' that she read at the last meeting of the Thursday Club she devoted fifteen minutes to bobbed hair. It's her pet abomination. And the dance is for you and Marjorie!"

"I'm sorry."

"Oh, Bernice, what'll your mother say? She'll think I let you do it."

"I'm sorry."

Dinner was an agony. She had made a hasty attempt with a curling-iron, and burned her finger and much hair. She could see that her aunt was both worried and grieved, and her uncle kept saying, "Well, I'll be darned!" over and over in a hurt and faintly hostile tone. And Marjorie sat very quietly, intrenched behind a faint smile, a faintly mocking smile.

Somehow she got through the evening. Three boys called; Marjorie disappeared with one of them, and Bernice made a listless unsuccessful attempt to entertain the two others—sighed thankfully as she climbed the stairs to her room at half past ten. What a day!

When she had undressed for the night the door opened and Marjorie came in.

"Bernice," she said, "I'm awfully sorry about the Deyo dance. I'll give you my word of honor I'd forgotten all about it."

"'Sall right," said Bernice shortly. Standing before the mirror she passed her comb slowly

---

① A small spot, mark, or discoloration.
② Minor weakness or failing of character.

Unit Two Setting
Chapter 4 Bernice Bobs Her Hair

through her short hair.

"I'll take you down-town to-morrow," continued Marjorie, "and the hairdresser'll fix it so you'll look slick①. I didn't imagine you'd go through with it. I'm really mighty sorry."

"Oh, 'sall right!"

"Still it's your last night, so I suppose it won't matter much."

Then Bernice winced as Marjorie tossed her own hair over her shoulders and began to twist it slowly into two long blond braids until in her cream-colored negligée she looked like a delicate painting of some Saxon princess. Fascinated, Bernice watched the braids grow. Heavy and luxurious they were, moving under the supple fingers like restive snakes—and to Bernice remained this relic and the curling-iron and a to-morrow full of eyes. She could see G. Reece Stoddard, who liked her, assuming his Harvard manner and telling his dinner partner that Bernice shouldn't have been allowed to go to the movies so much; she could see Draycott Deyo exchanging glances with his mother and then being conscientiously charitable to her. But then perhaps by to-morrow Mrs. Deyo would have heard the news; would send round an icy little note requesting that she fail to appear—and behind her back they would all laugh and know that Marjorie had made a fool of her; that her chance at beauty had been sacrificed to the jealous whim of a selfish girl. She sat down suddenly before the mirror, biting the inside of her cheek.

"I like it," she said with an effort. "I think it'll be becoming."

Marjorie smiled.

"It looks all right. For heaven's sake, don't let it worry you!"

"I won't."

"Good night, Bernice."

But as the door closed something snapped within Bernice. She sprang dynamically to her feet, clinching her hands, then swiftly and noiselessly crossed over to her bed and from underneath it dragged out her suitcase. Into it she tossed toilet articles and a change of clothing. Then she turned to her trunk and quickly dumped in two drawerfuls of lingerie② and summer dresses. She moved quietly, but with deadly efficiency, and in three-quarters of an hour her trunk was locked and strapped and she was fully dressed in a becoming new traveling suit that Marjorie had helped her pick out.

Sitting down at her desk she wrote a short note to Mrs. Harvey, in which she briefly outlined her reasons for going. She sealed it, addressed it, and laid it on her pillow. She glanced at her watch. The train left at one, and she knew that if she walked down to the Marborough Hotel two blocks away she could easily get a taxicab.

Suddenly she drew in her breath sharply and an expression flashed into her eyes that a practiced character reader might have connected vaguely with the set look she had worn in the barber's chair—somehow a development of it. It was quite a new look for Bernice and it carried

---

① Smooth, glossy, and slippery.
② Women's underclothes.

consequences.

She went stealthily to the bureau, picked up an article that lay there, and turning out all the lights stood quietly until her eyes became accustomed to the darkness. Softly she pushed open the door to Marjorie's room. She heard the quiet, even breathing of an untroubled conscience asleep.

She was by the bedside now, very deliberate and calm. She acted swiftly. Bending over she found one of the braids of Marjorie's hair, followed it up with her hand to the point nearest the head, and then holding it a little slack so that the sleeper would feel no pull, she reached down with the shears and severed it. With the pigtail in her hand she held her breath. Marjorie had muttered something in her sleep. Bernice deftly amputated the other braid, paused for an instant, and then flitted swiftly and silently back to her own room.

Down-stairs she opened the big front door, closed it carefully behind her, and feeling oddly happy and exuberant stepped off the porch into the moonlight, swinging her heavy grip like a shopping-bag. After a minute's brisk walk she discovered that her left hand still held the two blond braids. She laughed unexpectedly—had to shut her mouth hard to keep from emitting an absolute peal. She was passing Warren's house now, and on the impulse she set down her baggage, and swinging the braids like pieces of rope flung them at the wooden porch, where they landed with a slight thud. She laughed again, no longer restraining herself.

"Huh!" she giggled wildly. "Scalp[①] the selfish thing!"

Then picking up her suitcase she set off at a half-run down the moonlit street.

Film Comment:

F. Scott Fitzgerald's *Bernice Bobs Her Hair*: 48 minutes, color
Starring: Shelley Duvall & Bud Cort
Screenplay by: Joan Micklin Silver
Directed by: Joan Micklin Silver

It's the hot summer of 1919. Visiting her cousin Marjorie (Veronica Cartwright), sweet-but-dull Bernice (Shelley Duvall) is transformed into a smooth-talking man-trap by her vampish kin. However, the "make-over" works too well, Bernice becomes the belle of the ball, captivating every boy's interest... even Marjorie's boyfriend Warren (Bud Cort).

The now worldly Bernice has the last laugh...a clever and ironic twist. One of the best screen translations of F. Scott Fitzgerald's literary work, "Bernice Bobs Her Hair" also includes the delightful supporting role performances of Dennis Christopher ("Breaking Away") and Polly Holliday ("Alice").

---

① The skin that covers the top of the head, taken as a trophy of victory for American Indians. Remove the scalp of, when used as a verb.

Unit Two Setting
Chapter 4 Bernice Bobs Her Hair

Film Scenes:

Scene 1: the cousin
Scene 2: transformation
Scene 3: jealousy
Scene 4: Bernice bobs her hair
Scene 5: revenge

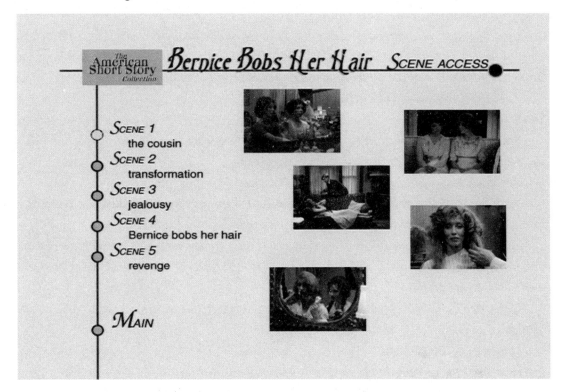

Script Excerpts:

A Midwestern town of medium size in the late summer of 1919.

Interior. Country club. Women's dressing room. Saturday night.

The room is empty. Faint band music can be heard...a Saturday night country club combo. As the door opens, and Marjorie Harvey and Roberta Dillon enter, the music blares briefly, becoming faint again as they close the door after them.

Marjorie is eighteen, dark-haired and pretty. Roberta is seventeen, small and thin with a delicate wisp. Like all the women in the script, they wear their long, thick hair piled on top of their heads in an arrangement of tendrils and curls. Numerous tortoise shell combs support these hair-dos.

If Marjorie and Roberta were not yet flappers, it is only because full-scale flapperdom hasn't reached their particular corner of the Midwest.

Still, they are close to it, impudent, good-looking, self-assured, not at all giggly, girlish or demure.

A long horizontal mirror against one wall; beneath it a long table on which women have left their purses. Marjorie finds hers, opens it and carefully removes her handkerchief. We move in for an ECU as she opens the handkerchief. In it is...a red jelly bean. She offers it to Roberta, who takes it eagerly.

Roberta: Marjorie, you saved my life.

(*The two girls sit at the mirror. Roberta licks the jelly bean, then uses it as a lipstick. It leaves a faint red stain on her lips. Marjorie has a fresh gardenia; idly she positions it here and there on her dress, in her hair, all the while staring intently at herself in the mirror.*)

Roberta: Who gave you that gardenia?

Marjorie: Warren.

Roberta: Warren McIntyre? I thought he'd get over you when he went away to Yale.

Marjorie: No. All that happened was I got over him.

Roberta: I know about three girls in the East that are wild about him.

Marjorie (*profoundly, as she gazes at herself in the mirror*): Roberta, when you've grown up across the street from someone, he loses his mystery.

(*A brief flurry as the door opens and several young women enter...among them Genevieve Ormonde, eighteen, and along with Marjorie and Roberta one of the popular set. Genevieve hurries over to her friends.*)

Genevieve (*sotto voce*): Honestly, Marjorie, my brother has been stuck with your cousin Bernice for an hour.

Marjorie (*sighs*): All right.

(*She drops the gardenia in the wastebasket, rises.*)

Genevieve: Roberta, is that your jelly bean?

Marjorie: It's mine but you can borrow it.

(*Marjorie starts toward dressing room door; Genevieve sits down, starts to apply jelly bean.*)

Int. Bernice's room. Day.

She looks down at the trio from her window.

From her POV, we see Carpenter, then Reece, jump over the car door without opening it, landing one on either side of Marjorie.

Nothing will do but for Marjorie to try it. The boys demur, she insists, standing up on the car seat, until Carpenter gets out, Marjorie following.

Carpenter closes the car door. Marjorie now gets in by jumping over it. She pats her hair delicately. Before Carpenter can follow suit, Reece pulls the car out. Carpenter must now enter in a flying leap, landing half on Marjorie, who yelps.

Bernice watches the car until it is out of view, then with a sigh she pulls the curtain closed,

Unit Two Setting
Chapter 4 Bernice Bobs Her Hair

as if to shut out the pain of the outside world.

Bernice sits down at her desk. We hear the front door chimes. Bernice takes stationery and pen and begins a letter. She gets as far as the date, "August 20, 1919" and "Dear Mother," when there is a knock on her door.

Mrs. Harvey's Voice: Bernice?

Bernice: Come in.

(*Mrs. Harvey enters.*)

Mrs. Harvey: Are you feeling better, dear?

Bernice: I'm all right, Aunt Josephine.

Mrs. Harvey: Will you come down? Young Draycott Deyo is here.

Ext. Porch. Day

The girls are now rocking back and forth on the porch glider.

Marjorie: If you must mention college, do it like this. You be warren. (*Bernice nods.*) Is it true what I hear about Yale men, Warren McIntyre? (*Nudges Bernice.*)

Bernice: What did you hear?

Marjorie (*with great charm*): That they're fickler than other men. He'd probably say, who told you, and I'd say, never mind, I just hope it's true, because I think fickle men are more interesting, more of a challenge.

(*Bernice drinks this in as though it is the revealed word.*)

Marjorie: That's sure fire, actually. I used it all the time.

Bernice (*with a studied casualness*): What would you say if he said something like, you've got an awfully kissable mouth?

Marjorie: (*again, intensely charming and flirtatious*): What's your criterion for a kissable mouth? One that looks like it's been kissed a lot or one you'd like to kiss?

(*Bernice is shocked but ashamed to let Marjorie know it. She pretends to be busy with a strand of wayward hair. Suddenly...*)

Bernice: Marjorie, have you ever...

Marjorie: Lots of times.

(*Bernice thinks this over.*)

Bernice: But if you're a nice girl from a good family...

Marjorie: ...you like to have as much fun as anybody else.

Bernice: Did you ever kiss Warren?

Marjorie (*a bored tone*): Oh Warren...I have an infallible test and he flunked it. I think if you really love someone, you love them even when they aren't around. When Warren went away to school, I fell in love with four men before he got home for Christmas.

(*Bernice listens closely.*)

Marjorie: I'm afraid he'll never get over me, though. Poor thing.

Int. Marjorie's room. Night.

The two girls are brushing and braiding their hair for the night. They sit on Marjorie's bed.

Marjorie: You've got the smile down pat, but you've got to perfect a pathetic look, too.

Bernice: Why?

Marjorie: You need it sometimes in certain situations.

Bernice (*puzzled*): With men?

Marjorie: Of course with men. Next year when you go East to school, you'll run into Babs Finley.

Bernice: The one who got fired from Miss Walker's?

Marjorie: Oh, she's been fired from three schools that I know of and maybe more. Anyway, she's probably got the greatest pathetic look of any girl in our generation.

Bernice (*awestruck*): How do you do it?

Marjorie: Open your eyes wide. That's it. Now droop your mouth a little. Now... (*Marjorie tips her head slightly and Bernice copies her*) ...look right in the man's eyes and say, "I hardly have any beaux at all."

Bernice: I hardly have any beaux at all.

Marjorie: Not bad.

Bernice: But I thought the idea was to seem popular.

Marjorie: It only works if you're popular. An unpopular girl couldn't use it at all. If she said, "I don't have any beaux," what could a man say? But if a popular girl says it...see?

Bernice (*nods*): Do you think I'll ever know all these things like you do?

Marjorie: I don't know. You got a late start.

Bernice (*that rebellious feeling again*): I think I'm doing all right. How did you like my bathtub line?

Marjorie: Snazzy.

Bernice (*feeling better*): You can use it if you want to.

Marjorie: Bernice, I don't have to use other people's lines.

(*Bernice feels the implicit put-down, of course. She frowns just a little.*)

Discussion Questions:

1. What's the role of country club among the upper-class people in the story?
2. How do the young ladies catch and maintain the masculine attention? How is it different for the young men?
3. Bernice learns very fast and soon outdoes her teacher, Marjorie. How does she make that possible?
4. What do you think of rivalry, trap and even revenge between girls?

5. What does the long hair mean for young girls? Can you see the twisting irony in the story ending?

Further Reading and Watching:

Babylon Revisited

Unit Three

Point of View

Chapter 5

I'm a Fool

Sherwood Anderson

Author Introduction:

Sherwood Anderson (1876—1941) was born in Camden, Ohio, and spent most of his childhood in small Midwestern towns. After some intermittent schooling, Anderson enlisted in the Army for service in Cuba during the Spanish-American War. Self-educated, he rose to become a successful copywriter and business owner in Cleveland and Elyria, Ohio. A few years later, in the spirit of rebellion against industrial and commercial civilization which was to color his writing thereafter, Anderson had a nervous breakdown that led him to abandon his business  and family to become a writer. Going to Chicago, he was eventually married three more times. In the ferment of a literary renaissance, Anderson made friends with writers and began to publish his own poetry and fiction. He became famous with the appearance of his most enduring work *Winesburg, Ohio* (1919), the stories of which show life and desire frustrated by the provincialism of the Midwest. Characteristic of Anderson's work is a tone of melancholy reminiscence in which he projects remembered realities on the screen of a philosophic imagination. Anderson might be most remembered for his influential effect on the next generation of young writers, as he inspired and helped gain publication for William Faulkner and Ernest Hemingway. His autobiography, *A Story-Teller's Story* (1924), is partly fictional, as most of his fiction is partly autobiographical. His novels include *Windy McPherson's Son* (1916), *Poor White* (1920), *Many Marriages* (1923), and *Dark Laughter* (1925). His later collections of stories are *The Triumph of the Egg* (1921), *Horses and Men* (1923), and *Death in the Woods and Other Stories* (1933).

Story Summary:

Andy ("I") is a young boy, making it on his own as a "swipe" on the Ohio racetrack circuit in the 1900s. One day, as a spectator in the grandstand, he meets a beautiful young lady—his feminine ideal comes to life—to whom he tells some monumental lies about his wealth and his position in an attempt to win her. When she reveals a fondness for him and a desire to keep in touch, Andy is trapped—hopelessly enmeshed in the web of his own falsehoods. Like a typical human, after he makes his mistake, he finds something and someone to blame it on. Andy, the young "fool" in the story, is therefore a good example of an actual 19-year-old boy trying to impress a girl.

Key Terms:
Contemporary, Loneliness, Material Possession, Deceit, Realism

I'm a Fool[①]

It was a hard jolt for me, one of the most bitterest I ever had to face. And it all came about through my own foolishness, too. Even yet sometimes, when I think of it, I want to cry or swear or kick myself. Perhaps, even now, after all this time, there will be a kind of satisfaction in making myself look cheap by telling of it.

It began at three o'clock one October afternoon as I sat in the grandstand[②] at the fall trotting and pacing meet[③] at Sandusky, Ohio.

To tell the truth, I felt a little foolish that I should be sitting in the grandstand at all. During the summer before I had left my home town with Harry Whitehead and, with a nigger named Burt, had taken a job as swipe[④] with one of the two horses Harry was campaigning through the fall race meets that year. Mother cried and my sister Mildred, who wanted to get a job as a school teacher in our town that fall, stormed and scolded about the house all during the week before I left. They both thought it something disgraceful that one of our family should take a place as a swipe with race horses. I've an idea Mildred thought my taking the place would stand in the way of her getting the job she'd been working so long for.

But after all I had to work, and there was no other work to be got. A big lumbering fellow of nineteen couldn't just hang around the house and I had got too big to mow people's lawns and sell newspapers. Little chaps who could get next to people's sympathies by their sizes were always getting jobs away from me. There was one fellow who kept saying to everyone who wanted a lawn mowed or a cistern cleaned, that he was saving money to work his way through college, and I used to lay awake nights thinking up ways to injure him without being found out. I kept thinking of wagons running over him and bricks falling on his head as he walked along the street. But never mind him.

---

① First published in the little literary magazine *Dial* in 1922, and later collected in *Horses and Men* (1923).
② A roofed stand for spectators at a stadium or racetrack.
③ The racing in the story is harness racing, in which the horse draws a light two-wheeled vehicle seating the driver.
④ A horse trainer.

Unit Three Point of View
Chapter 5 I'm a Fool

I got the place with Harry and I liked Burt fine. We got along splendid together. He was a big nigger with a lazy sprawling body and soft, kind eyes, and when it came to a fight he could hit like Jack Johnson①. He had Bucephalus②, a big black pacing stallion③ that could do 2.09 or 2.10, if he had to, and I had a little gelding④ named Doctor Fritz that never lost a race all fall when Harry wanted him to win.

We set out from home late in July in a box car with the two horses and after that, until late November, we kept moving along to the race meets and the fairs. It was a peachy time for me, I'll say that. Sometimes now I think that boys who are raised regular in houses, and never have a fine nigger like Burt for best friend, and go to high schools and college, and never steal anything, or get drunk a little, or learn to swear from fellows who know how, or come walking up in front of a grandstand in their shirt sleeves and with dirty horsey pants on when the races are going on and the grandstand is full of people all dressed up—What's the use of talking about it? Such fellows don't know nothing at all. They've never had no opportunity.

But I did. Burt taught me how to rub down a horse and put the bandage on after a race and steam a horse out and a lot of valuable things for any man to know. He could wrap a bandage on a horse's leg so smooth that if it had been the same color you would think it was his skin, and I guess he'd have been a big driver, too, and got to the top like Murphy and Walter Cox and the others if he hadn't been black.

Gee whizz, it was fun. You got to a county seat town, maybe say on a Saturday or Sunday, and the fair began the next Tuesday and lasted until Friday afternoon. Doctor Fritz would be, say in the 2.25 trot on Tuesday afternoon and on Thursday afternoon Bucephalus would knock 'em cold in the "free-for-all" pace. It left you a lot of time to hang around and listen to horse talk, and see Burt knock some yap cold that got too gay, and you'd find out about horses and men and pick up a lot of stuff you could use all the rest of your life, if you had some sense and salted down what you heard and felt and saw.

And then at the end of the week when the race meet was over, and Harry had run home to tend up to his livery stable business, you and Burt hitched the two horses to carts and drove slow and steady across country, to the place for the next meeting, so as to not overheat the horses, etc., etc., you know.

Gee whizz, Gosh amighty, the nice hickorynut and beechnut and oaks and other kind of trees along the roads, all brown and red, the good smells, and Burt singing a song that was called Deep River⑤, and the country girls at the windows of houses and everything. You can stick your colleges up your nose for all me. I guess I know where I got my education.

Why, one of those little burgs of towns you come to on the way, say now on a Saturday

---

① World heavyweight boxing champion, 1908—1915, black.
② Alexander the Great's war horse.
③ An adult male horse that has not been castrated, especially one kept for breeding.
④ A castrated animal, especially a male horse.
⑤ An old song of African-Americans.

afternoon, and Burt says, "let's lay up here." And you did.

And you took the horses to a livery stable and fed them, and you got your good clothes out of a box and put them on.

And the town was full of farmers gaping, because they could see you were race-horse people, and the kids maybe never see a nigger before and was afraid and run away when the two of us walked down their main street.

And that was before prohibition① and all that foolishness, and so you went into a saloon, the two of you, and all the yaps come and stood around, and there was always someone pretended he was horsey and knew things and spoke up and began asking questions, and all you did was to lie and lie all you could about that horses you had, and I said I owned them, and then some fellow said "will you have a drink of whisky" and Burt knocked his eye out the way he could say, offhand-like, "Oh well, all right, I'm agreeable to a little nip. I'll split a quart② with you." Gee whizz.

But that isn't what I want to tell my story about. We got home late in November and I promised mother I'd quit the race horses for good. There's a lot of things you've got to promise a mother because she don't know any better.

And so, there not being any work in our town any more than when I left there to go to the races, I went off to Sandusky and got a pretty good place taking care of horses for a man who owned a teaming and delivery and storage and coal and real estate business there. It was a pretty good place with good eats, and a day off each week, and sleeping on a cot in a big barn, and mostly just shoveling in hay and oats to a lot of big good-enough skates of horses, that couldn't have trotted a race with a load. I wasn't dissatisfied and I could send money home.

And then, as I started to tell you, the fall races come to Sandusky and I got the day off and I went. I left the job at noon and had on my good clothes and my new brown derby③ hat, I'd just bought the Saturday before, and a stand-up collar.

First of all I went downtown and walked about with the dudes④. I've always thought to myself, "put up a good front" and so I did it. I had forty dollars in my pocket and so I went into the West House, a big hotel, and walked up to the cigar stand. "Give me three twenty-five cent cigars," I said. There was a lot of horsemen and strangers and dressed-up people from other towns standing around in the lobby and in the bar, and I mingled amongst them. In the bar there was a fellow with a cane and a Windsor tie⑤ on, that it made me sick to look at him. I like a man

---

① The period (1920—1933) during which the 18th Amendment forbidding the manufacture and sale of alcoholic beverages was in force in the United States.

② A unit of volume or capacity in the U.S. Customary System, used in liquid measure, equal to ¼ gallon or 32 ounces (0.946 liter).

③ A stiff felt hat with a round crown and a narrow, curved brim.

④ Those who are very fancy or sharp in dress and demeanor.

⑤ A wide silk necktie tied in a loose bow.

Unit Three Point of View
Chapter 5 I'm a Fool

to be a man and dress up, but not to go put on that kind of airs. So I pushed him aside, kind of rough, and had me a drink of whisky. And then he looked at me, as though he thought maybe he'd get gay, but he changed his mind and didn't say anything. And then I had another drink of whisky, just to show him something, and went out and had a hack① out to the races, all to myself, and when I got there I bought myself the best seat I could get up in the grandstand, but didn't go in for any of these boxes. That's putting on too many airs.

And so there I was, sitting up in the grandstand as gay as you please and looking down on the swipes coming out with their horses, and with their dirty horsey pants on and the horse blankets swung over their shoulders, same as I had been doing all the year before. I liked one thing about the same as the other, sitting up there and feeling grand and being down there and looking up at the yaps and feeling grander and more important, too. One thing's about as good as another, if you take it just right. I've often said that.

Well, right in front of me, in the grandstand that day, there was a fellow with a couple of girls and they was about my age. The young fellow was a nice guy all right. He was the kind maybe that goes to college and then comes to be a lawyer or maybe a newspaper editor or something like that, but he wasn't stuck on himself. There are some of that kind are all right and he was one of the ones.

He had his sister with him and another girl and the sister looked around over his shoulder, accidental at first, not intending to start anything—she wasn't that kind—and her eyes and mine happened to meet.

You know how it is. Gee, she was a peach! She had on a soft dress, kind of a blue stuff and it looked carelessly made, but was well sewed and made and everything. I knew that much. I blushed when she looked right at me and so did she. She was the nicest girl I've ever seen in my life. She wasn't stuck on herself and she could talk proper grammar without being like a school teacher or something like that. What I mean is, she was O.K. I think maybe her father was well-to-do, but not rich to make her chesty② because she was his daughter, as some are. Maybe he owned a drugstore or a drygoods store in their home town, or something like that. She never told me and I never asked.

My own people are all O.K. too, when you come to that. My grandfather was Welsh and over in the old country, in Wales he was— But never mind that.

The first heat of the first race come off and the young fellow setting there with the two girls left them and went down to make a bet. I knew what he was up to, but he didn't talk big and noisy and let everyone around know he was a sport, as some do. He wasn't that kind. Well, he come back and I heard him tell the two girls what horse he'd bet on, and when the heat was trotted they all half got to their feet and acted in the excited, sweaty way people do when they've got

---
① A carriage or hackney for hire.
② Arrogant or proud; conceited.

money down on a race, and the horse they bet on is up there pretty close at the end, and they think maybe he'll come on with a rush, but he never does because he hasn't got the old juice in him, come right down to it.

And then, pretty soon, the horses came out for the 2.18 pace and there was a horse in it I knew. He was a horse Bob French had in his string but Bob didn't own him. He was a horse owned by a Mr. Mathers down at Marietta, Ohio.

This Mr. Mathers had a lot of money and owned some coal miners or something, and he had a swell place out in the country, and he was stuck on race horses, but was a Presbyterian[①] or something, and I think more than likely his wife was one, too, maybe a stiffer one than himself. So he never raced his horses himself, and the story round the Ohio race tracks was that when one of his horses got ready to go to the races he turned him over to Bob French and pretended to his wife he was sold.

So Bob had the horses and he did pretty much as he pleased and you can't blame Bob, at least, I never did. Sometimes he was out to win and sometimes he wasn't. I never cared much about that when I was swiping a horse. What I did want to know was that my horse had the speed and could go out in front, if you wanted him to.

And, as I'm telling you, there was Bob in his race with one of Mr. Mathers' horses, was named "About Ben Ahem"[②] or something like that, and was fast as a steak. He was a gelding and had a mark of 2.21, but could step in .08 or .09.

Because when Burt and I were out, as I've told you, the year before, there was a nigger, Burt knew, worked for Mr. Mathers and we went out there one day when we didn't have no race on at the Marietta Fair and our boss Harry was gone home.

And so everyone was gone to the fair but just this one nigger and he took us all through Mr. Mathers' swell house and he and Burt tapped a bottle of wine Mr. Mathers had hid in his bedroom, back in a closet, without his wife knowing, and he showed us this Ahem horse. Burt was always stuck on being a driver but didn't have much chance to get to the top, being a nigger, and he and the other nigger gulped that whole bottle of wine and Burt got a little lit up.

So the nigger let Burt take this About Ben Ahem and step him a mile in a track Mr. Mathers had all to himself, right there on the farm. And Mr. Mathers had one child, a daughter, kinda sick and not very good-looking, and she came home and we had to hustle and get About Ben Ahem stuck back in the barn.

I'm only telling you to get everything straight. At Sandusky, that afternoon I was at the fair, this young fellow with two girls was fussed, being with the girls and losing his bet. You know how a fellow is that way. One of them was his girl and the other his sister I had figured that out.

---

① A member or an adherent of a Presbyterian Church.
② Abou Ben Adhem is the title character of a well-known poem by Leigh Hunt.

Unit Three Point of View
Chapter 5 I'm a Fool

"Gee whizz," I says to myself, "I'm going to give him the dope①".

He was mighty nice when I touched him on the shoulder. He and the girls were nice to me right from the start and clear to the end. I'm not blaming them.

And so he leaned back and I give him the dope on About Ben Ahem. "Don't bet a cent on this first heat because he'll go like an oxen hitched to a plow, but when the first heat is over go right down and lay on your pile." That's what I told him.

Well, I never saw a fellow treat anyone sweller. There was a fat man sitting beside the little girl, that had looked at me twice by this time, and I at her, and both blushing, and what did he do but have the nerve to turn and ask the fat man to get up and change places with me so I could set with his crowd.

Gee whizz, craps amighty. There I was. What a chump② I was to go and get gay up there in the West House bar, and just because that dude was standing there with a cane and that kind of a necktie on, to go and get all balled up and drink that whisky, just to show off.

Of course she would know, me setting right beside her and letting her smell of my breath. I could have kicked myself right down out of that grandstand and all around that race track and made a faster record than most of the skates of horses they had there that year.

Because that girl wasn't any mutt of a girl. What wouldn't I have give right then for a stick of chewing gum to chew, or a lozenger, or some liquorice, or most anything. I was glad I had those twenty-five cent cigars in my pocket and right away I give that fellow one and lit one myself. Then that fat man got up and we changed places and there I was, plunked right down beside her.

They introduced themselves and the fellow's best girl, he had with him, was named Miss Elinor Woodbury, and her father was a manufacturer of barrels from a place called Tiffin, Ohio. And the fellow himself was named Wilbur Wessen and his sister was Miss Lucy Wessen.

I suppose it was their having such swell names got me off my trolley. A fellow, just because he has been a swipe with a race horse, and works taking care of horses for a man in the teaming, delivery, and storage business, isn't any better or worse than anyone else. I've often thought that, and said it too.

But you know how a fellow is. There's something in that kind of nice clothes, and the kind of nice eyes she had, and the way she had looked at me, awhile before, over her brother's shoulder, and me looking back at her, and both of us blushing.

I couldn't show her up for a boob③, could I?

I made a fool of myself, that's what I did. I said my name was Walter Mathers from Marietta, Ohio, and then I told all three of them the smashingest④ lie you ever heard. What I said

---

① Factual information, especially of a private nature.
② A stupid or foolish person; a dolt.
③ A stupid or foolish person.
④ Extraordinarily impressive or fine; wonderful.

was that my father owned the horse About Ben Ahem and that he had let him out to this Bob French for racing purposes, because our family was proud and had never gone into racing that way, in our own name, I mean. Then I had got started and they were all leaning over and listening, and Miss Lucy Wessen's eyes were shining, and I went the whole log.

I told about our place down at Marietta, and about the big stables and the grand brick house we had on a hill, up above the Ohio River, but I knew enough not to do it in no bragging way. What I did was to start things and then let them drag the rest out of me. I acted just as reluctant to tell as I could. Our family hasn't got any barrel factory, and, since I've known us, we've always been pretty poor, but not asking anything of anyone at that, and my grandfather, over in Wales—but never mind that.

We set there talking like we had known each other for years and years, and I went and told them that my father had been expecting maybe this Bob French wasn't on the square, and had sent me up to Sandusky on the sly[①] to find out what I could.

And I buffed it through I had found out all about the 2.18 pace, in which About Ben Ahem was to start.

I said he would lose the first heat by pacing like a lame cow and then he would come back and skin 'em alive after that. And to back up what I said I took thirty dollars out of my pocket and handed it to Mr. Wilbur Wessen and asked him, would he mind, after the first heat, to go down and place it on About Ben Ahem for whatever odds he could get. What I said was that I didn't want Bob French to see me and none of the swipes.

Sure enough the first heat come off and About Ben Ahem went off his stride, up the back stretch, and looked like a wooden horse or a sick one, and come in to be last. Then this Wilbur Wessen went down to the betting place and when that Miss Woodbury was looking the other way once, Lucy Wessen kinda, with her shoulder you know, kinda touched me. Not just tucking down, I don't mean. You know how a woman can do. They get close, but not getting gay either. You know what they do. Gee whizz.

And then they give me a jolt. What they had done, when I didn't know, was to get together, and they had decided Wilber Wessen would bet fifty dollars, and the two girls had gone and put in ten dollars each, of their own money, too. I was sick then, but I was sicker later.

About the gelding, About Ben Ahem, and their winning their money, I wasn't worried a lot about that. It come out O.K. Ahem stepped the next three heats like a bushel of spoiled eggs going to market before they could be found out, and Wilber Wessen had got nine to two for the money. There was something else eating at me.

Because Wilbur come back, after he had bet the money, and after that he spent most of his time talking to that Miss Woodbury, and Lucy Wessen and I was left alone together like on a

---

① Secretly.

Unit Three Point of View
Chapter 5 I'm a Fool

desert island. Gee, if I'd only been on the square or if there had been any way of getting myself on the square. There ain't any Walter Mathers, like I said to her and them, and there hasn't ever been one, but if there was, I bet I'd go to Marietta, Ohio, and shoot him tomorrow.

There I was, big boob that I am. Pretty soon the race was over, and Wilbur had gone down and collected our money, and we had a hack downtown, and he stood us a swell supper at the West House, and a bottle of champagne beside.

And I was with that girl and she wasn't saying much, and I wasn't saying much either. One thing I know. She wasn't stuck on me because of the lie about my father being rich and all that. There's a way you know....Craps amighty. There's a kind of girl, you see just once in your life, and if you don't get busy and make hay, then you're gone for good and all, and might as well go jump off a bridge. They give you a look from inside of them somewhere, and it ain't no vamping, and what it means is—you want that girl to be your wife, and you want nice things around her like flowers and swell clothes, and you want her to have the kids you're going to have, and you want good music played and no ragtime[①]. Gee whizz.

There's a place over near Sandusky, across a kind of bay, and it's called Cedar Point. And after we had supper we went over to it in a launch, all by ourselves. Wilbur and Miss Lucy and that Miss Woodbury had to catch a ten o'clock train back to Tiffin, Ohio, because, when you're out with girls like that you can't get careless and miss any trains and stay out all night, like you can with some kinds of Janes.

And Wilbur blowed himself to the launch and it cost him fifteen cold plunks, but I wouldn't never have knew if I hadn't listened. He wasn't no tin horn kind of a sport.

Over at the Cedar Point place, we didn't stay around where there was a gang of common kind of cattle at all.

There was big dance halls and dining places for yaps, and there was a beach you could walk along and get where it was dark, and we went there.

She didn't talk hardly at all and neither did I, and I was thinking how glad I was my mother was all right, and always made us kids learn to eat with a fork at table, and not swill soup, and not be noisy and rough like a gang you see around a race track that way.

Then Wilbur and his girl went away up the beech and Lucy and I sat down in a dark place, where there was some roots of old trees, the water had washed up, and after that the time, till we had to go back in the launch and they had to catch their trains, wasn't nothing at all. It went like winking your eye.

Here's how it was. The place we were setting in was dark, like I said, and there was the roots from that old stump[②] sticking up like arms, and there was a watery smell, and the night was like—as if you could put your hand out and feel it—so warm and soft and dark and sweet like an orange.

---

① A style of jazz characterized by elaborately syncopated rhythm in the melody and a steadily accented accompaniment.
② The part of a tree trunk left protruding from the ground after the tree has fallen or has been felled.

I most cried and I most swore and I most jumped up and danced, I was so mad and happy and sad.

When Wilbur come back from being alone with his girl, and she saw him coming, Lucy she says, "we got to go to the train now," and she was most crying too, but she never knew nothing I knew, and she couldn't be so all busted up. And then, before Wilbur and Miss Woodbury got up to where we was, she put her face up and kissed me quick and put her head up against me and she was all quivering and—Gee whizz.

Sometimes I hope I have cancer and die. I guess you know what I mean. We went in the launch across the bay to the train like that, and it was dark, too. She whispered and said it was like she and I could get out of the boat and walk on the water, and it sounded foolish, but I knew what she meant.

And then quick we were right at the depot①, and there was a big gang of yaps, the kind that goes to the fairs, and crowded and milling around like cattle, and how could I tell her? "It won't be long because you'll write and I'll write to you." That's all she said.

I got a chance like a hay barn afire. A swell chance I got.

And maybe she would write to me, down at Marietta that way, and the letter would come back, and stamped on the front of it by the U.S.A. "there ain't any such guy," or something like that, whatever they stamp on a letter that way.

And me trying to pass myself off for a bigbug and a swell—to her, as decent a little body as God ever made. Craps amighty—a swell chance I got!

And then the train come in, and she got on it, and Wilbur Wessen he come and shook hands with me, and that Miss Woodbury was nice too and bowed to me, and I at her, and the train went and I busted out and cried like a kid.

Gee, I could have run after that train and made Dan Patch② look like a freight train after a wreck but, socks amighty, what was the use? Did you ever see such a fool?

I'll bet you what—if I had an arm broke right now or a train had run over my foot—I wouldn't go to no doctor at all. I'd go set down and let her hurt and hurt—that's what I'd do.

I'll bet you what—if I hadn't a drunk that booze③ I'd a never been such a boob as to go tell such a lie—that couldn't never be made straight to a lady like her.

I wish I had that fellow right here that had on a Windsor tie and carried a cane. I'd smash him for fair. Gosh darn his eyes. He's a big fool—that's what he is.

And if I'm not another you just go find me one and I'll quit working and be a bum and give him my job. I don't care nothing for working, and earning money, and saving it for no such boob as myself.

---

① A railroad or bus station.
② One of the fastest harness horses in history.
③ Heavy drinking.

Unit Three　Point of View
Chapter 5　I'm a Fool

Film Comment:

Sherwood Anderson's *I'm a Fool*: 38 minutes, color
Starring: Ron Howard & Amy Irving
Screenplay by: Ron Cowen
Directed by: Dan McCann

　　Traveling from town to town during the summer of 1919, young Andy (Ron Howard) has left his Ohio home in search of adventure and romance as a horse trainer on the country fair racing circuit.

　　More than a little "wet behind the ears," Andy learns a bittersweet lesson about life when he meets Lucy (Amy Irving), the girl of his dreams, at the race track one day. Ashamed of his occupation, Andy leads Lucy to believe he's wealthy. Soon one lie leads to another until there is no way to tell Lucy the truth.

　　The irony of the story is that Lucy and Andy have fallen deeply in love. As Andy dejectedly admits on his way out of town, all is lost because "I'm a Fool."

Film Scenes:

　　Scene 1: The journey
　　Scene 2: Walter L. Mathers Farm
　　Scene 3: At the race track
　　Scene 4: The embellishment
　　Scene 5: The goodbye

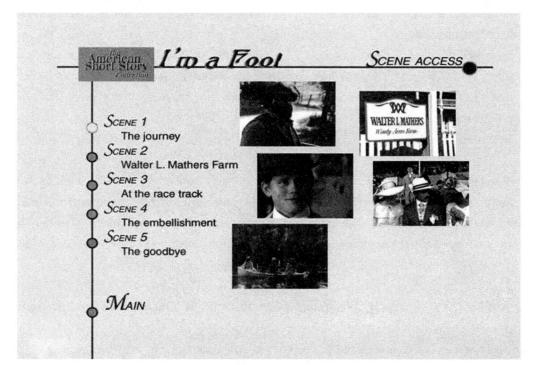

The American Short Story Through Film

Script Excerpts:

In his late teens at the beginning of this century, Andy has spent the summer wandering through Ohio in the company of Burt, a fellow racetrack swipe older than he. Together they drive a horse or two from track to track, caring for them en route. As the summer ends, they stop to visit George, a friend of Burt's and a stablehand on the estate of a wealthy man, Mr. Walter Mathers. There Andy drinks a bit and reveals his desire for a woman, and Burt wears himself out racing Big Ben, Mr. Mather's prize horse, on the sly. A day or two later Andy decides to view a race from the grandstand. Already feeling rather insecure in his fine clothes, he becomes more so when taunted by a dude in a bar. As a result, he drinks a couple of neat whiskies and buys some fine cigars just before the following scene begins.

Exterior. Racetrack. Grandstand. Day.

Andy weaves past small crowd.

Cut to

Andy making way across an aisle of grandstand.

Andy: 'Scuse me...beg pardon.

He sits down and wipes sweat from his forehead. Beginning to feel effects of liquor. Squints into sun.

Cut to Exterior. Racetrack.

Andy sees George leading Big Ben. He rubs his eyes and squints again. Looks in pocket for a candy and pops it in his mouth. Eyes people sitting on either side of him, older and well dressed. Straightens his tie.

In boxes, just four or five rows below, Andy sees Wilbur Wessen, Lucy Wessen and Elinor Woodbury take their seats. They are his age. Attractive and well dressed.

Lucy turns to adjust her hat and her eyes meet Andy's. They stare at each other. Then look away. Embarrassed.

The sound of gunshot.

Exterior. Racetrack. Day.

An empty stretch of track. The sound of horses thundering off in distance growing louder. Finally we see a horse race across the screen, momentarily filling blank stretch of track. Then they're gone again and the track is empty.

Cut to

Andy point of view—sees Wilbur and Elinor shake heads in disappointment. Lucy slowly tears losing tickets into small pieces.

Andy gets up and excuses himself. Point of view of spectators who are perturbed.

Unit Three   Point of View
Chapter 5   I'm a Fool

Andy finds a seat just behind Wesson. Leans forward and taps Wilbur on the shoulder.

Andy: 'Scuse me. Hope I'm not bein' too forward. I couldn't help noticin' your bad luck. I've had it on several occasions at the races myself. If you're thinkin' about placin' another bet, you might take a look at a horse comin' up named Big Ben. Right below.

Wilber (*big smile*): Why, thanks. Big Ben. My, he is a handsome horse. Isn't he, Lucy?

(*They are looking at the warm-ups.*)

Lucy (*demurely*): He certainly is.

Wilbur: Have you bet on him before?

Andy: Wouldn't be fair if I said right now. But I can tell you he's got a time of 2.18 and he'll come in well under that.

Wilbur: You sure?

Andy: I'm positive. But don't bet a cent on this first heat 'cause he'll run it like...like a mule in a snowstorm. After that, he'll skin 'em alive.

Wilbur: Why thank you...Mr....Mr.?

Andy: Don't mention it. (*Hesitates and doesn't identify himself.*)

Wilbur (*offering his hand*): My name's Wilbur Wessen and this is my sister Lucy Wessen and my fiancée, Miss Elinor Woodbury.

(*Andy shakes Wilbur's hand and tips his hat to both ladies. Andy's expression glazes over as his eyes and Lucy's meet.*)

Andy: How do you do. I'm—uh...Mr. Walter Mathers Jr. of Marietta, Ohio...Our family has this place nearby, a grand old brick house up on a hill, and big stables...(*His hesitancy gives way to bravado.*)

Elinor: What brings you up to Sandusky, Mr. Mathers?

Andy: What brings me? Well...you see, my father owns that horse, Big Ben...which he lets out to a Mr. Bob French for racing purposes. You see, being Presbyterian, our family's never gone into racing that way. In our own name, I mean....

(*He smiles at Lucy. She smiles back.*)

Well, my father thinks this Bob French may not be on the square, so he's sent me up here to Sandusky on the sly...

Elinor: You mean you're a spy? How exciting! Isn't that exciting, Lucy?

(*Lucy smiles at Andy. Andy smiles back.*)

Andy: Wilbur, can I offer you a cigar?

(*He reaches in his pocket and pulls out two cigars.*)

Wilbur: Thank you, Walter. Don't mind if I do.

(*Andy lights the two cigars.*)

Andy: And, Wilbur, I was wonderin' if you wouldn't mind placin' this for me on Big Ben for the second heat. Might not look right for me to...ownin' him and all.

(*He takes three ten-dollar bills from his pocket and hands them one by one to Wilbur.*)

...for whatever odds you can get.

(*Wilbur starts to leave.*)

Lucy: Wait, Wilbur! After what Mr. Mathers had told us, Elinor and I would be missing a golden opportunity if we didn't each put in something.

Elinor: That's right, Wilbur. We all want to be millionaires.

Lucy: Is ten dollars enough?

Cut to Andy's face. His large smile vanishes.

Cut to

Exterior. Racetrack. The field. Day

A pack of horses crosses the finish line. The sequence is repeated two more times, possibly from different points of view.

Cut to

Andy's sigh of relief and hysterics and hugging. Wilbur and Elinor hug. Andy and Lucy want to hug. He pulls back slightly.

Cut to

Exterior. Dusk

Montage of four young people walking slowly along bankside of lake. In the distance, soft colored lights are strung out at the fair across the lake. They are supposed to be choosing a picnic spot but are more engrossed in enjoying one another's company during the leisurely stroll, as we hear Andy in voice over:

Andy: So Big Ben came through and all, then what am I gettin' so worked up for, right? Well, I'll tell you. Miss Lucy wasn't stuck on me 'count of the lie about my father being rich. She really liked me! Now that's the kind of girl you see just once in your life, and if you don't make hay, then she's gone and you may as well jump off a bridge. They give you a look from inside them somewhere, and it ain't no vampin'. What it means is...you want that girl to be your wife and you want nice things around her and you want her to have your kids and you want good music played and no ragtime!

Discussion Questions:

1. What did Andy get from the wandering year as a horse swipe? What's the opinion from his family?
2. Why did Andy lie to Lucy? What are the consequences of such a big lie?
3. Do you really think Andy "a Fool"? Put in his position, what would you do?

Unit Three Point of View
Chapter 5 I'm a Fool

4. Can you see the irony that Lucy and Andy have really fallen in love?
5. What does Andy learn from the lesson of being "a Fool"? How can the story apply to the modern young men?

Further Reading and Watching:

Death in the Woods

Chapter 6

The Golden Honeymoon

Ring Lardner

Author Introduction:

Ring Lardner (1885—1933) was born in Niles, Michigan. His father was rich, the town's leading citizen, and his lively, talented mother wrote plays, stories, and poems. Lardner graduated from high school at 16, but he had little interest in going to college. Lardner started his writing career as a sports columnist. In 1905 he got a job as a reporter for the South Bend, Indiana, *Times*, and within three years he became a sports writer for the *Chicago Examiner* and finally a sports columnist for the *Chicago Tribune*. Working for a big-city newspaper brought Lardner into contact with the professional athletes and with the vernacular American speech he later presented in the stories that earned him nationwide popularity. In 1914 he published a series of six stories in the *Saturday Evening Post* describing the life and attitudes of a bush-league baseball player "Jack Keefe." Two years later the stories were issued in a single volume under the title *You Know Me, Al* (1916). In spite of his successes, Lardner disparaged his reputation as a literary artist and called himself a journalist. Yet his work covered a far wider range than just journalism. In addition to newspaper articles and short stories he wrote song lyrics, movie scenarios, verse, and essays. He wrote skits for Broadway shows and a self-mocking autobiography, *The Story of a Wonder Man* (1927). Eventually he wrote more than twenty volumes, but most notable were two collections of his short stories, *How to Write Short Stories* (1924) and *The Love Nest* (1926). Lardner influenced the writing of Ernest Hemingway, and he was a good friend of F. Scott Fitzgerald and other authors of the Jazz Age. In short fiction like the much-anthologized "Haircut," "I Can't Breathe," and "The Golden Honeymoon," Lardner proves himself a master of dramatic irony: the narrators' voices reveal their own utter lack of insight to create both wonderful comedy and a deeply bitter vision of human folly.

Unit Three Point of View
Chapter 6 The Golden Honeymoon

Story Summary:

Lucy and Charley Tate travel from New Jersey to Florida to enjoy their golden wedding anniversary in the warm sunshine of Tampa. However, early in their trip they run into the Hartsells. Fifty years before, Charley had won Lucy away from Frank Hartsell, to whom Lucy had been engaged. Pettiness and jealousy prevail, and Charley and Frank spend several days trying to prove that the other is the lesser man. Naturally, they only embarrass themselves, and when Charley finally confronts Frank directly, telling him that if he was really the better man he would never have lost Lucy to him, the explosion is at hand.

Key Terms:

Satire, Cynical, Humorist, Social Observation, Vanity, Realism

The Golden Honeymoon[①]

Mother says that when I start talking I never know when to stop. But I tell her the only time I get a chance is when she ain't around, so I have to make the most of it. I guess the fact is neither one of us would be welcome in a Quaker[②] meeting, but as I tell Mother, what did God give us tongues for if He didn't want we should use them? Only she says He didn't give them to us to say the same thing over and over again, like I do, and repeat myself. But I say:

"Well, Mother," I say, "when people is like you and I and been married fifty years, do you expect everything I say will be something you ain't heard me say before? But it may be new to others, as they ain't nobody else lived with me as long as you have."

So she says:

"You can bet they ain't, as they couldn't nobody else stand you that long."

"Well," I tell her, "you look pretty healthy."

"Maybe I do," she will say, "but I looked even healthier before I married you."

You can't get ahead of Mother.

Yes, sir, we was married just fifty years ago the seventeenth day of last December and my daughter and son-in-law was over from Trenton[③] to help us celebrate the Golden Wedding. My son-in-law is John H. Kramer, the real estate man. He made $12,000 one year and is pretty well thought of around Trenton; a good, steady, hard worker. The Rotarians[④] was after him a long time to join, but he kept telling them his home was his club. But Edie finally made him join. That's my daughter.

[①] First published in *Cosmopolitan*, 73 (July, 1922), 59—64.
[②] A person who belongs to a Christian group called the Society of Friends.
[③] The capital of New Jersey.
[④] Members of the local Rotary clubs, which form Rotary International, an international association of professionals and businessmen founded in the US in 1905 to promote community service.

Well, anyway, they come over to help us celebrate the Golden Wedding and it was pretty crimpy weather and the furnace don't seem to heat up no more like it used to and Mother made the remark that she hoped this winter wouldn't be as cold as the last, referring to the winter previous. So Edie said if she was us, and nothing to keep us home, she certainly wouldn't spend no more winters up here and why didn't we just shut off the water and close up the house and go down to Tampa, Florida? You know we was there four winters ago and staid five weeks, but it cost us over three hundred and fifty dollars for hotel bill alone. So Mother said we wasn't going no place to be robbed. So my son-in-law spoke up and said that Tampa wasn't the only place in the South, and besides we didn't have to stop at no high price hotel but could rent us a couple rooms and board out somewheres, and he had heard that St. Petersburg, Florida, was *the* spot and if we said the word he would write down there and make inquiries.

Well, to make a long story short, we decided to do it and Edie said it would be our Golden Honeymoon and for a present my son-in-law paid the difference between a section and a compartment so as we could have a compartment and have more privatecy. In a compartment you have an upper and lower berth just like the regular sleeper, but it is a shut in room by itself and got a wash bowl. The car we went in was all compartments and no regular berths at all. It was all compartments.

We went to Trenton the night before and staid at my daughter and son-in-law and we left Trenton the next afternoon at 3:23 P.M.

This was the twelfth day of January. Mother set facing the front of the train, as it makes her giddy to ride backwards. I set facing her, which does not affect me. We reached North Philadelphia at 4:03 P.M. and we reached West Philadelphia at 4:14, but did not go into Broad Street. We reached Baltimore at 6:30 and Washington, D.C., at 7:25. Our train laid over in Washington two hours till another train come along to pick us up and I got out and strolled up the platform and into the Union Station①. When I come back, our car had been switched on to another track, but I remembered the name of it, the La Belle, as I had once visited my aunt out in Oconomowoc, Wisconsin, where there was a lake of that name, so I had no difficulty in getting located. But Mother had nearly fretted herself sick for fear I would be left.

"Well," I said, "I would of followed you on the next train."

"You could of," said Mother, and she pointed out that she had the money.

"Well," I said, "we are in Washington and I could of borrowed from the United States Treasury. I would of pretended I was an Englishman."

Mother caught the point and laughed heartily.

Our train pulled out of Washington at 9:40 P.M. and Mother and I turned in early, I taking the upper. During the night we passed through the green fields of old Virginia, though it was too dark to tell if they was green or what color. When we got up in the morning, we was at Fayette-

---

① The traffic hub of Washington, D.C.

Unit Three Point of View
Chapter 6 The Golden Honeymoon

ville, North Carolina. We had breakfast in the dining car and after breakfast I got in conversation with the man in the next compartment to ours. He was from Lebanon, New Hampshire, and a man about eighty years of age. His wife was with him, and two unmarried daughters and I made the remark that I should think the four of them would be crowded in one compartment, but he said they had made the trip every winter for fifteen years and knowed how to keep out of each other's way. He said they was bound for Tarpon Springs.

We reached Charleston, South Carolina, at 12:50 P.M. and arrived at Savannah, Georgia, at 4:20. We reached Jacksonville, Florida, at 8:45 P.M. and had an hour and a quarter to lay over there, but Mother made a fuss about me getting off the train, so we had the darky make up our berths and retired before we left Jacksonville. I didn't sleep good as the train done a lot of hemming and hawing, and Mother never sleeps good on a train as she says she is always worrying that I will fall out. She says she would rather have the upper herself, as then she would not have to worry about me, but I tell her I can't take the risk of having it get out that I allowed my wife to sleep in an upper berth. It would make talk.

We was up in the morning in time to see our friends from New Hampshire get off at Tarpon Springs, which we reached at 6:53 A.M.

Several of our fellow passengers got off at Clearwater and some at Belleair, where the train backs right up to the door of the mammoth① hotel. Belleair is the winter headquarters for the golf dudes and everybody that got off there had their bag of sticks, as many as ten and twelve in a bag. Women and all. When I was a young man we called it shinny and only needed one club to play with and about one game of it would of been a-plenty for some of these dudes, the way we played it.

The train pulled into St. Petersburg at 8:20 and when we got off the train you would think they was a riot, what with all the darkies barking for the different hotels.

I said to Mother, I said:

"It is a good thing we have got a place picked out to go to and don't have to choose a hotel, as it would be hard to choose amongst them if every one of them is the best."

She laughed.

We found a jitney② and I give him the address of the room my son-in-law had got for us and soon we was there and introduced ourselves to the lady that owns the house, a young widow about forty-eight years of age. She showed us our room, which was light and airy with a comfortable bed and bureau and washstand. It was twelve dollars a week, but the location was good, only three blocks from Williams Park.

St. Pete is what folks calls the town, though they also call it the Sunshine City, as they claim they's no other place in the country where they's fewer days when Old Sol don't smile down on Mother Earth, and one of the newspapers gives away all their copies free every day

---
① An animal like an elephant, with very long tusks and long hair, that lived a long time ago but no longer exists.
② A small bus that carries passengers for a low price, originally five cents.

when the sun don't shine. They claim to of only give them away some sixty-odd times in the last eleven years. Another nickname they have got for the town is "the Poor Man's Palm Beach," but I guess they's men that comes there that could borrow as much from the bank as some of the Willie boys over to the other Palm Beach.

During our stay we paid a visit to the Lewis Tent City, which is the headquarters for the Tin Can Tourists. But maybe you ain't heard about them. Well, they are an organization that takes their vacation trips by auto and carries everything with them. That is, they bring along their tents to sleep in and cook in and they don't patronize no hotels or cafeterias, but they have got to be bona fide auto campers or they can't belong to the organization.

They tell me they's over 200,000 members to it and they call themselves the Tin Canners on account of most of their food being put up in tin cans. One couple we seen in the Tent City was a couple from Brady, Texas, named Mr. and Mrs. Pence, which the old man is over eighty years of age and they had come in their auto all the way from home, a distance of 1,641 miles. They took five weeks for the trip, Mr. Pence driving the entire distance.

The Tin Canners hails from every State in the Union and in the summer time they visit places like New England and the Great Lakes region, but in the winter the most of them comes to Florida and scatters all over the State. While we was down there, they was a national convention of them at Gainesville, Florida, and they elected a Fredonia, New York, man as their president. His title is Royal Tin Can Opener of the World. They have got a song wrote up which everybody has got to learn it before they are a member:

"The tin can forever! Hurrah, boys! Hurrah!

Up with the tin can! Down with the foe!

We will rally round the campfire, we'll rally once again,

Shouting, 'We auto camp forever!'"

That is something like it. And the members has also got to have a tin can fastened on to the front of their machine.

I asked Mother how she would like to travel around that way and she said:

"Fine, but not with an old rattle brain like you driving."

"Well," I said, "I am eight years younger than this Mr. Pence who drove here from Texas."

"Yes," she said, "but he is old enough to not be skittish."

You can't get ahead of Mother.

Well, one of the first things we done in St. Petersburg was to go to the Chamber of Commerce and register our names and where we was from as they's great rivalry amongst the different States in regards to the number of their citizens visiting in town and of course our little State don't stand much of a show, but still every little bit helps, as the fella says. All and all, the man told us, they was eleven thousand names registered, Ohio leading with some fifteen hundred-odd and New York State next with twelve hundred. Then come Michigan, Pennsylvania and so on down, with one man each from Cuba and Nevada.

Unit Three Point of View
Chapter 6 The Golden Honeymoon

The first night we was there, they was a meeting of the New York-New Jersey Society at the Congregational Church and a man from Ogdensburg, New York State, made the talk. His subject was Rainbow Chasing. He is a Rotarian and a very convicting speaker, though I forget his name.

Our first business, of course, was to find a place to eat and after trying several places we run on to a cafeteria on Central Avenue that suited us up and down. We eat pretty near all our meals there and it averaged about two dollars per day for the two of us, but the food was well cooked and everything nice and clean. A man don't mind paying the price if things is clean and well cooked.

On the third day of February, which is Mother's birthday, we spread ourselves and eat supper at the Poinsettia Hotel and they charged us seventy-five cents for a sirloin steak that wasn't hardly big enough for one.

I said to Mother: "Well," I said, "I guess it's a good thing every day ain't your birthday or we would be in the poorhouse."

"No," says Mother, "because if every day was my birthday, I would be old enough by this time to of been in my grave long ago."

You can't get ahead of Mother.

In the hotel they had a card-room where they was several men and ladies playing five hundred and this new fangled whist bridge. We also seen a place where they was dancing, so I asked Mother would she like to trip the light fantastic toe and she said no, she was too old to squirm like you have got to do now days. We watched some of the young folks at it awhile till Mother got disgusted and said we would have to see a good movie to take the taste out of our mouth. Mother is a great movie heroyne and we go twice a week here at home.

But I want to tell you about the Park. The second day we was there we visited the Park, which is a good deal like the one in Tampa, only bigger, and they's more fun goes on here every day than you could shake a stick at. In the middle they's a big bandstand and chairs for the folks to set and listen to the concerts, which they give you music for all tastes, from "Dixie"① up to classical pieces like "Hearts and Flowers."

Then all around they's places marked off for different sports and games—chess and checkers and dominoes for folks that enjoys those kind of games, and roque② and horse-shoes for the nimbler ones. I used to pitch a pretty fair shoe myself, but ain't done much of it in the last twenty years.

Well, anyway, we bought a membership ticket in the club which costs one dollar for the season, and they tell me that up to a couple years ago it was fifty cents, but they had to raise it to keep out the riffraff.

---

① A war song popular in the Southern States since the American Civil War.
② A game developed from croquet, played on a hard surface with a resilient surrounding border from which the ball can rebound.

Well, Mother and I put in a great day watching the pitchers and she wanted I should get in the game, but I told her I was all out of practice and would make a fool of myself, though I seen several men pitching who I guess I could take their measure without no practice. However, they was some good pitchers, too, and one boy from Akron, Ohio, who could certainly throw a pretty shoe. They told me it looked like he would win them championship of the United States in the February tournament. We come away a few days before they held that and I never did hear if he win. I forget his name, but he was a clean cut young fella and he has got a brother in Cleveland that's a Rotarian.

Well, we just stood around and watched the different games for two or three days and finally I set down in a checker game with a man named Weaver from Danville, Illinois. He was a pretty fair checker player, but he wasn't no match for me, and I hope that don't sound like bragging. But I always could hold my own on a checker-board and the folks around here will tell you the same thing. I played with this Weaver pretty near all morning for two or three mornings and he beat me one game and the only other time it looked like he had a chance, the noon whistle blowed and we had to quit and go to dinner.

While I was playing checkers, Mother would set and listen to the band, as she loves music, classical or no matter what kind, but anyway she was setting there one day and between selections the woman next to her opened up a conversation. She was a woman about Mother's own age, seventy or seventy-one, and finally she asked Mother's name and Mother told her her name and where she was from and Mother asked her the same question, and who do you think the woman was?

Well, sir, it was the wife of Frank M. Hartsell, the man who was engaged to Mother till I stepped in and cut him out, fifty-two years ago!

Yes, sir!

You can imagine Mother's surprise! And Mrs. Hartsell was surprised, too, when Mother told her she had once been friends with her husband, though Mother didn't say how close friends they had been, or that Mother and I was the cause of Hartsell going out West. But that's what we was. Hartsell left his town a month after the engagement was broke off and ain't never been back since. He had went out to Michigan and become a veterinary[1], and that is where he had settled down, in Hillsdale, Michigan, and finally married his wife.

Well, Mother screwed up her courage to ask if Frank was still living and Mrs. Hartsell took her over to where they was pitching horse-shoes and there was old Frank, waiting his turn. And he knowed Mother as soon as he seen her, though it was over fifty years. He said he knowed her by her eyes.

"Why, it's Lucy Frost!" he says, and he throwed down his shoes and quit the game.

Then they come over and hunted me up and I will confess I wouldn't of knowed him. Him

---

[1] A person whose job is to treat sick or injured animals, or to describe the medical treatment of animals.

Unit Three Point of View
Chapter 6   The Golden Honeymoon

and I is the same age to the month, but he seems to show it more, some way. He is balder for one thing. And his beard is all white, where mine has still got a streak of brown in it. The very first thing I said to him, I said:

"Well, Frank, that beard of yours makes me feel like I was back north. It looks like a regular blizzard."

"Well," he said, "I guess yourn would be just as white if you had it dry cleaned."

But Mother wouldn't stand that.

"Is that so!" she said to Frank. "Well, Charley ain't had no tobacco in his mouth for over ten years!"

And I ain't!

Well, I excused myself from the checker game and it was pretty close to noon, so we decided to all have dinner together and they was nothing for it only we must try their cafeteria on Third Avenue. It was a little more expensive than ours and not near as good, I thought. I and Mother had about the same dinner we had been having every day and our bill was $1.10. Frank's check was $1.20 for he and his wife. The same meal wouldn't of cost them more than a dollar at our place.

After dinner we made them come up to our house and we all set in the parlor, which the young woman had give us the use of to entertain company. We begun talking over old times and Mother said she was a-scared Mrs. Hartsell would find it tiresome listening to we three talk over old times, but as it turned out they wasn't much chance for nobody else to talk with Mrs. Hartsell in the company. I have heard lots of women that could go it, but Hartsell's wife takes the cake of all the women I ever seen. She told us the family history of everybody in the State of Michigan and bragged for a half hour about her son, who she said is in the drug business in Grand Rapids, and a Rotarian.

When I and Hartsell could get a word in edgeways we joked one another back and forth and I chafed him about being a horse doctor.

"Well, Frank," I said, "you look pretty prosperous, so I suppose they's been plenty of glanders[①] around Hillsdale."

"Well," he said, "I've managed to make more than a fair living. But I've worked pretty hard."

"Yes," I said, "and I suppose you get called out all hours of the night to attend births and so on."

Mother made me shut up.

Well, I thought they wouldn't never go home and I and Mother was in misery trying to keep awake, as the both of us generally always takes a nap after dinner. Finally they went, after we had made an engagement to meet them in the Park the next morning, and Mrs. Hartsell also

---

① A highly infectious bacterial disease of horses, sometimes transmitted to man.

invited us to come to their place the next night and play five hundred. But she had forgot that they was a meeting of the Michigan Society that evening, so it was not till two evenings later that we had our first card game.

Hartsell and his wife lived in a house on Third Avenue North and had a private setting room besides their bedroom. Mrs. Hartsell couldn't quit talking about their private setting room like it was something wonderful. We played cards with them, with Mother and Hartsell partners against his wife and I. Mrs. Hartsell is a miserable card player and we certainly got the worst of it.

After the game she brought out a dish of oranges and we had to pretend it was just what we wanted, though oranges down there is like a young man's whiskers; you enjoy them at first, but they get to be a pesky nuisance.

We played cards again the next night at our place with the same partners and I and Mrs. Hartsell was beat again. Mother and Hartsell was full of compliments for each other on what a good team they made, but the both of them knowed well enough where the secret of their success laid. I guess all and all we must of played ten different evenings and they was only one night when Mrs. Hartsell and I come out ahead. And that one night wasn't no fault of hern.

When we had been down there about two weeks, we spent one evening as their guest in the Congregational Church[①], at a social give by the Michigan Society. A talk was made by a man named Bitting of Detroit, Michigan, on How I was Cured of Story Telling. He is a big man in the Rotarians and give a witty talk.

A woman named Mrs. Oxford rendered some selections which Mrs. Hartsell said was grand opera music, but whatever they was my daughter Edie could of give her cards and spades and not made such a hullaballoo about it neither.

Then they was a ventriloquist from Grand Rapids and a young woman about forty-five years of age that mimicked different kinds of birds. I whispered to Mother that they all sounded like a chicken, but she nudged me to shut up.

After the show we stopped in a drug store and I set up the refreshments and it was pretty close to ten o'clock before we finally turned in. Mother and I would of preferred tending the movies, but Mother said we mustn't offend Mrs. Hartsell, though I asked her had we came to Florida to enjoy ourselves or to just not offend an old chatter-box from Michigan.

I felt sorry for Hartsell one morning. The women folks both had an engagement down to the chiropodist's[②] and I run across Hartsell in the Park and he foolishly offered to play me checkers.

It was him that suggested it, not me, and I guess he repented himself before we had played one game. But he was too stubborn to give up and set there while I beat him game after game and the worst part of it was that a crowd of folks had got in the habit of watching me play and there they all was, hooking on, and finally they seen what a fool Frank was making of himself, and they began to chafe him and pass remarks. Like one of them said:

---

① An evangelical Protestant Christian Church that is governed according to the principles of Congregationalism.
② A clinic to treat and care for people's feet.

Unit Three   Point of View
Chapter 6   The Golden Honeymoon

"Who ever told you you was a checker player!"

And:

"You might maybe be good for tiddle-de-winks, but not checkers!"

I almost felt like letting him beat me a couple games. But the crowd would of knowed it was a put up job.

Well, the women folks joined us in the Park and I wasn't going to mention our little game, but Hartsell told about it himself and admitted he wasn't no match for me.

"Well," said Mrs. Hartsell, "checkers ain't much of a game anyway, is it?" She said: "It's more of a children's game, ain't it? At least, I know my boy's children used to play it a good deal."

"Yes, ma'am," I said. "It's a children's game the way your husband plays it, too."

Mother wanted to smooth things over, so she said:

"Maybe they's other games where Frank can beat you."

"Yes," said Mrs. Hartsell, "and I bet he could beat you pitching horse-shoes."

"Well," I said, "I would give him a chance to try, only I ain't pitched a shoe in over sixteen years."

"Well," said Hartsell, "I ain't played checkers in twenty years."

"You ain't never played it," I said.

"Anyway," says Frank, "Lucy and I is your master at five hundred."

Well, I could of told him why that was, but had decency enough to hold my tongue.

It had got so now that he wanted to play cards every night and when I or Mother wanted to go to a movie, any one of us would have to pretend we had a headache and then trust to goodness that they wouldn't see us sneak into the theater. I don't mind playing cards when my partner keeps their mind on the game, but you take a woman like Hartsell's wife and how can they play cards when they have got to stop every couple seconds and brag about their son in Grand Rapids?

Well, the New York-New Jersey Society announced that they was goin' to give a social evening too and I said to Mother, I said:

"Well, that is one evening when we will have an excuse not to play five hundred."

"Yes," she said, "but we will have to ask Frank and his wife to go to the social with us as they asked us to go to the Michigan social."

"Well," I said, "I had rather stay home than drag that chatterbox everywheres we go."

So Mother said:

"You are getting too cranky. Maybe she does talk a little too much but she is good hearted. And Frank is always good company."

So I said:

"I suppose if he is such good company you wished you had of married him."

Mother laughed and said I sounded like I was jealous. Jealous of a cow doctor!

Anyway we had to drag them along to the social and I will say that we give them a much better entertainment than they had given us.

Judge Lane of Paterson made a fine talk on business conditions and a Mrs. Newell of Westfield imitated birds, only you could really tell what they was the way she done it. Two young women from Red Bank sung a choral selection and we clapped them back and they gave us "Home to Our Mountains" and Mother and Mrs. Hartsell both had tears in their eyes. And Hartsell, too.

Well, some way or another the chairman got wind① that I was there and asked me to make a talk and I wasn't even going to get up, but Mother made me, so I got up and said:

"Ladies and gentlemen," I said. "I didn't expect to be called on for a speech on an occasion like this or no other occasion as I do not set myself up as a speech maker, so will have to do the best I can, which I often say is the best anybody can do."

Then I told them the story about Pat and the motorcycle, using the brogue,② and it seemed to tickle them and I told them one or two other stories, but altogether I wasn't on my feet more than twenty or twenty-five minutes and you ought to of heard the clapping and hollering when I set down. Even Mrs. Hartsell admitted that I am quite a speechifier and said if I ever went to Grand Rapids, Michigan, her son would make me talk to the Rotarians.

When it was over, Hartsell wanted we should go to their house and play cards, but his wife reminded him that it was after 9:30 P.M., rather a late hour to start a card game, but he had went crazy on the subject of cards, probably because he didn't have to play partners with his wife. Anyway, we got rid of them and went home to bed.

It was the next morning, when we met over to the Park, that Mrs. Hartsell made the remark that she wasn't getting no exercise so I suggested that why didn't she take part in the roque game.

She said she had not played a game of roque in twenty years, but if Mother would play she would play. Well, at first Mother wouldn't hear of it, but finally consented, more to please Mrs. Hartsell than anything else.

Well, they had a game with a Mrs. Ryan from Eagle, Nebraska, and a young Mrs. Morse from Rutland, Vermont, who Mother had met down to the chiropodist's. Well, Mother couldn't hit a flea and they all laughed at her and I couldn't help from laughing at her myself and finally she quit and said her back was too lame to stoop over. So they got another lady and kept on playing and soon Mrs. Hartsell was the one everybody was laughing at, as she had a long shot to hit the black ball, and as she made the effort her teeth fell out on to the court. I never seen a woman so flustered in my life. And I never heard so much laughing, only Mrs. Hartsell didn't join in and she was madder than a hornet and wouldn't play no more, so the game broke up.

Mrs. Hartsell went home without speaking to nobody, but Hartsell stayed around and finally

---

① Get to know.
② Speaking English with a strong accent, especially Irish or Scottish.

Unit Three Point of View
Chapter 6 The Golden Honeymoon

he said to me, he said:

"Well, I played you checkers the other day and you beat me bad and now what do you say if you and me play a game of horseshoes?"

I told him I hadn't pitched a shoe in sixteen years, but Mother said:

"Go ahead and play. You used to be good at it and maybe it will come back to you."

Well, to make a long story short, I give in. I oughtn't to of never tried it, as I hadn't pitched a shoe in sixteen years, and I only done it to humor Hartsell.

Before we started, Mother patted me on the back and told me to do my best, so we started in and I seen right off that I was in for it, as I hadn't pitched a shoe in sixteen years and didn't have my distance. And besides, the plating① had wore off the shoes so that they was points right where they stuck into my thumb and I hadn't throwed more than two or three times when my thumb was raw and it pretty near killed me to hang on to the shoe, let alone pitch it.

Well, Hartsell throws the awkwardest shoe I ever seen pitched and to see him pitch you wouldn't think he would ever come nowheres near, but he is also the luckiest pitcher I ever seen and he made some pitches where the shoe lit five and six feet short and then schoonered up and was a ringer. They's no use trying to beat that kind of luck.

They was a pretty fair size crowd watching us and four or five other ladies besides Mother, and it seems like, when Hartsell pitches, he has got to chew and it kept the ladies on the anxious seat as he don't seem to care which way he is facing when he leaves go.

You would think a man as old as him would of learnt more manners.

Well, to make a long story short, I was just beginning to get my distance when I had to give up on account of my thumb, which I showed it to Hartsell and he seen I couldn't go on, as it was raw and bleeding. Even if I could of stood it to go on myself, Mother wouldn't of allowed it after she seen my thumb. So anyway I quit and Hartsell said the score was nineteen to six, but I don't know what it was. Or don't care, neither.

Well, Mother and I went home and I said I hoped we was through with the Hartsells as I was sick and tired of them, but it seemed like she had promised we would go over to their house that evening for another game of their everlasting cards.

Well, my thumb was giving me considerable pain and I felt kind of out of sorts and I guess maybe I forgot myself, but anyway, when we was about through playing Hartsell made the remark that he wouldn't never lose a game of cards if he could always have Mother for a partner.

So I said:

"Well, you had a chance fifty years ago to always have her for a partner, but you wasn't man enough to keep her."

I was sorry the minute I had said it and Hartsell didn't know what to say and for once his wife couldn't say nothing. Mother tried to smooth things over by making the remark that I must

---

① A covering of metal plates.

of had something stronger than tea or I wouldn't talk so silly. But Mrs. Hartsell had froze up like an iceberg and hardly said good night to us and I bet her and Frank put in a pleasant hour after we was gone.

As we was leaving, Mother said to him: "Never mind Charley's nonsense, Frank. He is just mad because you beat him all hollow pitching horseshoes and playing cards."

She said that to make up for my slip, but at the same time she certainly riled me. I tried to keep ahold of myself, but as soon as we was out of the house she had to open up the subject and begun to scold me for the break I had made.

Well, I wasn't in no mood to be scolded. So I said:

"I guess he is such a wonderful pitcher and card player that you wished you had married him."

"Well," she said, "at least he ain't a baby to give up pitching because his thumb has got a few scratches."

"And how about you," I said, "making a fool of yourself on the roque court and then pretending your back is lame and you can't play no more!"

"Yes," she said, "but when you hurt your thumb I didn't laugh at you, and why did you laugh at me when I sprained my back?"

"Who could help from laughing!" I said.

"Well," she said, "Frank Hartsell didn't laugh."

"Well," I said, "why didn't you marry him?"

"Well," said Mother, "I almost wished I had!"

"And I wished so, too!" I said.

"I'll remember that!" said Mother, and that's the last word she said to me for two days.

We seen the Hartsells the next day in the Park and I was willing to apologize, but they just nodded to us. And a couple days later we heard they had left for Orlando, where they have got relatives.

I wished they had went there in the first place.

Mother and I made it up setting on a bench.

"Listen, Charley," she said. "This is our Golden Honeymoon and we don't want the whole thing spoilt with a silly old quarrel."

"Well," I said, "did you mean that about wishing you had married Hartsell?"

"Of course not," she said, "that is, if you didn't mean that you wished I had, too." So I said:

"I was just tired and all wrought up. I thank God you chose me instead of him as they's no other woman in the world who I could of lived with all these years."

"How about Mrs. Hartsell?" says Mother.

"Good gracious!" I said. "Imagine being married to a woman that plays five hundred like she does and drops her teeth on the roque court!"

"Well," said Mother, "it wouldn't be no worse than being married to a man that expecto-

Unit Three Point of View
Chapter 6 The Golden Honeymoon

rates[1] towards ladies and is such a fool in a checker game."

So I put my arm around her shoulder and she stroked my hand and I guess we got kind of spoony.

They was two days left of our stay in St. Petersburg and the next to the last day Mother introduced me to a Mrs. Kendall from Kingston, Rhode Island, who she had met at the chiropodist's.

Mrs. Kendall made us acquainted with her husband, who is in the grocery business. They have got two sons and five grandchildren and one great-grandchild. One of their sons lives in Providence and is way up in the Elks as well as a Rotarian.

We found them very congenial people and we played cards with them the last two nights we was there. They was both experts and I only wished we had met them sooner instead of running into the Hartsells. But the Kendalls will be there again next winter and we will see more of them, that is, if we decide to make the trip again.

We left the Sunshine City on the eleventh day of February, at 11 A.M. This give us a day trip through Florida and we seen all the country we had passed through at night on the way down.

We reached Jacksonville at 7 P.M. and pulled out of there at 8:10 P.M. We reached Fayetteville, North Carolina, at nine o'clock the following morning, and reached Washington, D. C., at 6:30 P.M., laying over there half an hour.

We reached Trenton at 11:01 P.M. and had wired ahead to my daughter and son-in-law and they met us at the train and we went to their house and they put us up for the night. John would of made us stay up all night, telling about our trip, but Edie said we must be tired and made us go to bed. That's my daughter.

The next day we took our train for home and arrived safe and sound, having been gone just one month and a day.

Here comes Mother, so I guess I better shut up.

Film Comment:

Ring Lardner's *The Golden Honeymoon*: 52 minutes, color
Starring: James Whitmore & Teresa Wright
Screenplay by: Frederic Hunter
Directed by: Noel Black

Charley Tate (James Whitmore, two time Academy Award nominee & Tony Award Winner) is an old windbag, often a braggart, but somehow always lovable. Married over fifty years to his ever-patient wife Lucy (Teresa Wright, Academy Award Winner), the two of them are on their Golden Honeymoon in Florida.

---

[1] To cough up and spit out.

The American Short Story Through Film

Everything goes on perfectly...until Lucy meets her former fiancé who's also vacationing with his wife. Suddenly there's a comic competition between Charley and the old boyfriend for Lucy's attention. After fifty years, cantankerous Charley has to win his girl all over again!

Film Scenes:

Scene 1: Celebration
Scene 2: The old boyfriend
Scene 3: The checker game
Scene 4: The speech
Scene 5: The horse shoe game

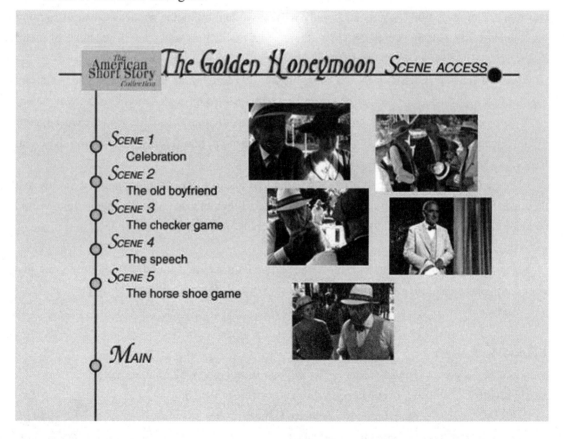

Script Excerpts:

The following scene opens the script.
Fade in:
Exterior. Railway platform, Trenton, New Jersey. Afternoon.
It is a mid-January in the early 1920s. A black porter stands at the steps leading onto the Pullman car vestibule, slapping himself against the cold, boredly overhearing the chatter of the platform, especially one cheery, persistently loquacious voice. As steam hisses from beneath the

Unit Three　Point of View
Chapter 6　*The Golden Honeymoon*

car, the camera pans to the placard indicating its number, "314," and the destination "TAMPA." Then it pans on passengers waiting to board the train. They are bundled against the cold in heavy coats, mufflers, and hats and their breath turns to white as they speak. The camera rests on seventy-two-year-old

　Charley Tate

Dressed almost too colorfully, he is blending the ear of a fellow passenger, a sophisticated-looking man of some eighty years who stand with his wife and two daughters, listening patiently, amusedly. We recognize Charley's as the voice predominating over other platform sounds from the beginning shot.

　Charley: Yessir, we was married just fifty years ago the seventeenth day of last December, and my daughter and son-in-law was over—it was just a month ago, come to think of it—to help us celebrate the Golden Wedding.

　Charley reaches over to take the arm of John Kramer, his son-in-law, who is talking with a redcap about baggage. At first Kramer shrugs off Charley's grasp, a gesture by now almost second nature.

　Charley: This here's my son-in-law. John. John H. Kramer, the real estate man.

　Under Charley's persistence Kramer turns.

　Charley: These folks are bound for Tarpon Springs.

　Kramer shakes hands awkwardly with the travelers. Charley watches proudly. Kramer steps back, off screen, to continue with the redcap as Charley confides:

　Charley: He made twelve thousand dollars one year. Pretty well thought of around here. A good, steady, hard worker. The Rotarians was after him a long time to join. He told them his home was his club. (*Laughs at this.*) Edie finally made him join. Edie's my daughter. (*To the man.*) Are you a Rotarian?

　Traveler: No, I'm an Elk.

　Charley: Yessir, John finally become a Rotarian, Edie—that's my daughter—she made him! (*Chuckles, smiles.*)

Interior. Pullman compartment. Afternoon.

　Lucy Tate sits tensely with her daughter Edie as Charley, visible through the window, continues to talk on the platform. Lucy is bundled up. Her outfit is gray, and the small, gray buds on her hat look permanently shut. She is very keyed up about the trip, almost fretful that it has not yet started.

　Lucy: Talk, talk, talk! Listen to him go on! (*She laughs!*)

　Edie: He does enjoy people.

　Lucy: Yep. He's excited about meeting new ones....

　Edie: You got everything, Mama?

　Lucy: ...He can tell them all the stories he's been telling me for fifty years. And he prob'ly will.

Lucy jumps up nervously from her seat.

Lucy: Let's not stay in here! I need to get out and walk!

Exterior. Railway platform.

Charley continues to talk to the newfound listeners, the Pullman car vestibule visible behind him.

Charley: Well, anyway, it was pretty crimpy weather that day and the furnace don't seem to heat up no more like it used to....

Lucy appears in the Pullman car vestibule and descends to the platform, Edie accompanying her. Lucy gives Charley an impatient look and begins to walk off her excitement.

Charley: ...And Mother made the remark that she hoped this winter wouldn't be as cold as the last, referring to the winter previous.

Two women, good natured, but worldly looking, come along the platform. One, Mrs. Ryan, is a passenger. The other, her sister, carries a miniature poodle under her arm. As the two women pass, Lucy and Edie glance at them. Charley's voice continues.

Charley: So Edie said if she was us, and nothing to keep us home, she certainly wouldn't spend no more winters up here....

The two women start to board the train. The porter stops them, Charley's voice rattling along in the background.

Porter: I'm sorry, ma'am. We don't allow dogs on the train.

Mrs. Ryan: They'll only stay a minute.

Porter: I'm sorry, ma'am.

While talking uninterruptedly, Charley has noticed the women's approach.

Charley: ...And why didn't we just shut off the water and close up the house and go down to Tampa, Florida?

Charley steps up to the women.

Charley: I'll hold him for you, madam.

Sister: Why, thank you!

Charley: Glad to do it.

Charley takes the dog as the women board the train. The women bound for Tarpon Springs take this chance to board the train as well.

Charley (*to the dog*): Hello there, Rover. Arf! Arf! (*To his listener.*) So anyway, Edie—that's my daughter—said why not close up the house and go down to Tampa, Florida. Well, I wasn't so sure. We was there four winters ago and stayed five weeks, but it cost us over three hundred and fifty dollars for the hotel bill alone!

While Charley talks on, his voice clear, but muted in the background, Lucy and Edie have been pacing on the platform.

Unit Three Point of View
Chapter 6 *The Golden Honeymoon*

Edie: My, but you're keyed up!

Lucy: Well, why shouldn't I be? At last something's happening!

Lucy glances down the platform to where Charley is talking.

Charley: Well, Mother said we wasn't going no place to be robbed. So my son-in-law—the one you just met—he spoke up and said that Tampa wasn't the only place in the South....

Lucy: I've heard so much talk for so many years—not that I mind talk. But now we're going somewheres! Maybe something'll happen to us.

Edie smiles with affection at her obviously excited mother. In the background Charley's voice is still heard.

Charley: ...And besides we didn't have to stop at no high-price hotel but could rent us a couple rooms and board out somewheres....

Edie: What do you wish would happen?

Lucy (*smiles, half-embarrassed*): Sometimes I wish some strange, mysterious sheik would come riding out of the desert and carry me off on his white horse.

Edie: Why, Mother!

Lucy: Ain't it shameful that notions the movies'll give a grown woman!

The two women laugh together. Behind them Charley talks on.

Charley: ...Well, he had heard that St. Petersburg, Florida, was *the* spot, and if we said the word, he would write down there and make inquiries.

Kramer approaches Lucy, baggage checks in his hand.

Kramer: Here are the baggage checks, Mother. Be sure you don't lose them.

Lucy: Yes, give them to me. Charley's talking so hard he'll forget he ever had them,

Lucy takes the baggage checks and puts them into her purse. Charley continues to talk in the background.

Charley: Some folks call "St. Pete" the "Poor Man's Palm Beach." So I hear tell. But I guess they's men that comes there that could borrow as much from the bank as some of the Willie boys over to the other Palm Beach.

The porter glances at his watch and calls into the train.

Porter: All visitors off the train! All visitors off the train.

Edie smiles at her mother as Kramer stands by.

Edie: Have a good time, Mama.

Lucy: We will. We always have a good time.

Edie: Don't let any sheik steak into your tent.

Lucy: Any sheik who steals into my tent has got the wrong address!

Lucy and Edie giggle as they return toward the Pullman vestibule. At this moment the woman who owns the dog descends the vestibule stairs and starts waving to her sister, having completely forgotten the dog. Charley's voice drones on.

Charley: Well, to make a long story short, we decided to do what Edie said and take a Golden Honeymoon trip to Florida.

Lucy mounts the vestibule steps, stops, turns toward Charley.

Lucy: I hope you won't be left on the platform, Charley, when the train pulls out!

Charley nods to Lucy, acknowledging her warning. She kisses Edie and Kramer and boards the train, as Charley continues to talk.

Charley: For a present my son-in-law paid the difference between two regular sleepers and a compartment.

Charley and the traveler are the only passengers remaining on the platform. Offscreen a conductor yells: "All aboard!" Edie and Kramer stand off by themselves.

Porter: Gentlemen, we're fixing to leave!

Charley: That way we could have a room by itself with a washbowl and much more privacy.

Traveler: I 'spect we ought to get on board.

The two men move toward the vestibule stairs. The porter stops Charley.

Porter: I'm sorry, sir. No dogs allowed.

The traveler boards the train and disappears. Surprised that he is still holding the dog, Charley looks around confusedly for its owner. And talks on.

Charley: So Mother and me is going to Florida the right way.

Charley is baffled at this predicament. Lucy watches exasperatedly from the compartment window. In the background a conductor moves toward the camera. Charley laughs.

Charley (*to the dog*): Left talking to a dog. Well, it's happened before.

The conductor passes, walking beside the train.

Conductor: All aboard, sir! Are you boarding?

Taking a dislike to the conductor, the dog begins to bark at him.

Edie: Dad, you better get on the train!

The dog jumps out of Charley's arms and runs after the conductor, barking. Charley scurries after it. A voice calls commandingly:

Lucy: Charley Tate, you get on this train!

Lucy stands in the vestibule looking anxiously down the platform.

Lucy: I ain't going on my Golden Honeymoon trip alone!

Kramer restrains Charley as in the background of the shot the dog runs to the arms of its mistress.

Kramer: We'll get the dog, Dad! You get the train!

Charley turns around and, followed by Edie and Kramer, rushes toward the vestibule stairs which the porter is now closing. Lucy watches anxiously. Steam hisses and mists. The dog barks. Offscreen, the conductor calls: "All aboard! All aboard!" Charley jumps aboard, the porter scrambling on beside him. The train pulls out. Lucy and Charley wave good-bye. Edie and Kramer—and behind them the woman with the barking dog—wave from the platform.

Unit Three　Point of View
Chapter 6　The Golden Honeymoon

Discussion Questions:

1. Compare and contrast Charley and Frank. What are their character traits?
2. Why is Charley so envious of Frank? Is the jealousy Charley feels towards Frank rational?
3. Why are the couples drawn together? What causes them to spend so much time together if it is apparently so unpleasant?
4. Consider the ending, are the issues truly resolved, or just avoided? Has Charley changed?
5. What effect does the narrator have on your perception of the story? Is the narrator reliable?
6. Would you consider Lardner's satire the good-natured type that seeks to correct shortcomings with wit and humor, or is it more of a derisive and indignant look at human nature, inviting scornful laughter?

Further Reading and Watching:

Haircut

Unit Four
Character

Chapter 7

Soldier's Home

Ernest Hemingway

Author Introduction:

Ernest Hemingway (1899—1961) was born in Oak Park, Illinois, the son of a doctor, who gave him an enduring enthusiasm for the outdoor life. As a boy, Hemingway spent most of his summers in the woods of upper Michigan that became the setting for some of his best-known stories. Toward the end of the First World War, he volunteered for service as an ambulance driver with the Italian Army and was seriously wounded in the fighting on the Austrian front. Recovering from his wounds, he went to Paris as a correspondent for the *Toronto*  *Star* and there met, among other writers, Ezra Pound and Gertrude Stein. They encouraged him in the invention of his own style, and Hemingway won swift acclaim for his early stories, *In Our Time* (1925), and for his first novel, *The Sun Also Rises* (1926), which portrays the "Lost Generation" of postwar American expatriate community in France and Spain. Later, he became a celebrity, often photographed as a marlin fisherman or a lion hunter. A fan of bullfighting, he wrote one nonfiction book on the subject, *Death in the Afternoon* (1932). The Hemingway hero and his code of conduct—living with "grace under pressure"—were as widely emulated and admired as the style of his short stories and novels. During the Spanish Civil War he went to Spain as a war correspondent and wrote one of his best novels, *For Whom the Bell Tolls* (1940), about that conflict. Afterwards, he followed the American Army in Europe as a correspondent before returning to peacetime life at his home in Cuba, where he wrote *The Old Man and the Sea* (1952). He was awarded the Nobel Prize for literature in 1954, but in 1961, mentally distressed and physically ailing, Hemingway killed himself with his favorite shotgun. His other novels include *A Farewell to Arms* (1929), *To Have and Have Not* (1937), and *Across the River and Into the Trees* (1950). In *A Movable Feast* (1964) he recreates the Paris of his earlier years. His later collections of stories are *Men without Women* (1927) and *Winner Take Nothing* (1933).

Story Summary:

Harold Krebs is a soldier returned. Quietly and without ceremony he comes home after the First World War. No longer does he fit into the life he left. Despite gentle pressure from family and friends, he cannot get hold of his own future. Between the non-changed hero and his past there is a desperate incompatibility. A climatic scene between mother and son foreshadows Krebs' decision to find himself again in a new place, away from the old and familiar, which, for all time, he has outgrown.

Key Terms:

Unexpressive, Conformance, Society, Psychological, Lost Generation

Soldier's Home[1]

Krebs went to the war from a Methodist[2] college in Kansas. There is a picture which shows him among his fraternity brothers, all of them wearing exactly the same height and style collar. He enlisted in the Marines in 1917 and did not return to the United States until the second division returned from the Rhine[3] in the summer of 1919.

There is a picture which shows him on the Rhone[4] with two German girls and another corporal. Krebs and the corporal look too big for their uniforms. The German girls are not beautiful. The Rhine does not show in the picture.

By the time Krebs returned to his home town in Oklahoma the greeting of heroes was over. He came back much too late. The men from the town who had been drafted had all been welcomed elaborately on their return. There had been a great deal of hysteria. Now the reaction had set in. People seemed to think it was rather ridiculous for Krebs to be getting back so late, years after the war was over.

At first Krebs, who had been at Belleau Wood, Soissons, the Champagne, St. Mihiel and in the Argonne[5] did not want to talk about the war at all. Later he felt the need to talk but no one wanted to hear about it. His town had heard too many atrocity stories to be thrilled by actualities. Krebs found that to be listened to at all he had to lie and after he had done this twice he, too, had a reaction against the war and against talking about it. A distaste for everything that had happened to him in the war set in because of the lies he had told. All of the times that had been able to make him feel cool and clear inside himself when he thought of them; the times so long back

---

[1] First published in *In Our Time* (1925).
[2] A denomination of Protestant Christianity that follows the teachings of John Wesley and who have their own branch of the Christian church and their own form of worship.
[3] A river of Western Europe flowing through Germany and the Netherlands to the North Sea.
[4] A river rising in Switzerland, flowing through France and into the Mediterranean Sea.
[5] These places are in the areas of northern and northwestern France. All are the major battlegrounds during the First World War.

Unit Four Character
Chapter 7 Soldier's Home

when he had done the one thing, the only thing for a man to do, easily and naturally, when he might have done something else, now lost their cool, valuable quality and then were lost themselves.

His lies were quite unimportant lies and consisted in attributing to himself things other men had seen, done or heard of, and stating as facts certain apocryphal incidents familiar to all soldiers. Even his lies were not sensational at the pool① room. His acquaintances, who had heard detailed accounts of German women found chained to machine guns in the Argonne and who could not comprehend, or were barred by their patriotism from interest in, any German machine gunners who were not chained, were not thrilled by his stories.

Krebs acquired the nausea in regard to experience that is the result of untruth or exaggeration, and when he occasionally met another man who had really been a soldier and they talked a few minutes in the dressing room at a dance he fell into the easy pose of the old soldier among other soldiers: that he had been badly, sickeningly frightened all the time. In this way he lost everything.

During this time, it was late summer, he was sleeping late in bed, getting up to walk down town to the library to get a book, eating lunch at home, reading on the front porch until he became bored and then walking down through the town to spend the hottest hours of the day in the cool dark of the pool room. He loved to play pool.

In the evening he practiced on his clarinet, strolled down town, read and went to bed. He was still a hero to his two young sisters. His mother would have given him breakfast in bed if he had wanted it. She often came in when he was in bed and asked him to tell her about the war, but her attention always wandered. His father was non-committal.

Before Krebs went away to the war he had never been allowed to drive the family motor car. His father was in the real estate business and always wanted the car to be at his command when he required it to take clients out into the country to show them a piece of farm property. The car always stood outside the First National Bank building where his father had an office on the second floor. Now, after the war, it was still the same car.

Nothing was changed in the town except that the young girls had grown up. But they lived in such a complicated world of already defined alliances and shifting feuds that Krebs did not feel the energy or the courage to break into it. He liked to look at them, though. There were so many good-looking young girls. Most of them had their hair cut short. When he went away only little girls wore their hair like that or girls that were fast. They all wore sweaters and shirt waists with round Dutch collars. It was a pattern. He liked to look at them from the front porch as they walked on the other side of the street. He liked to watch them walking under the shade of the trees. He liked the round Dutch collars above their sweaters. He liked their silk stockings and flat shoes. He liked their bobbed hair and the way they walked.

---

① Any of several games played on a six-pocket billiard table usually with 15 object balls and a cue ball.

When he was in town their appeal to him was not very strong. He did not like them when he saw them in the Greek's ice cream parlor. He did not want them themselves really. They were too complicated. There was something else. Vaguely he wanted a girl but he did not want to have to work to get her. He would have liked to have a girl but he did not want to have to spend a long time getting her. He did not want to get into the intrigue① and the politics. He did not want to have to do any courting. He did not want to tell any more lies. It wasn't worth it.

He did not want any consequences. He did not want any consequences ever again. He wanted to live along without consequences. Besides he did not really need a girl. The army had taught him that. It was all right to pose as though you had to have a girl. Nearly everybody did that. But it wasn't true. You did not need a girl. That was the funny thing. First a fellow boasted how girls mean nothing to him, that he never thought of them, that they could not touch him. Then a fellow boasted that he could not get along without girls, that he had to have them all the time, that he could not go to sleep without them.

That was all a lie. It was all a lie both ways. You did not need a girl unless you thought about them. He learned that in the army. Then sooner or later you always got one. When you were really ripe for a girl you always got one. You did not have to think about it. Sooner or later it could come. He had learned that in the army.

Now he would have liked a girl if she had come to him and not wanted to talk. But here at home it was all too complicated. He knew he could never get through it all again. It was not worth the trouble. That was the thing about French girls and German girls. There was not all this talking. You couldn't talk much and you did not need to talk. It was simple and you were friends. He thought about France and then he began to think about Germany. On the whole he had liked Germany better. He did not want to leave Germany. He did not want to come home. Still, he had come home. He sat on the front porch.

He liked the girls that were walking along the other side of the street. He liked the look of them much better than the French girls or the German girls. But the world they were in was not the world he was in. He would like to have one of them. But it was not worth it. They were such a nice pattern. He liked the pattern. It was exciting. But he would not go through all the talking. He did not want one badly enough. He liked to look at them all, though. It was not worth it. Not now when things were getting good again.

He sat there on the porch reading a book on the war. It was a history and he was reading about all the engagements he had been in. It was the most interesting reading he had ever done. He wished there were more maps. He looked forward with a good feeling to reading all the really good histories when they would come out with good detail maps. Now he was really learning about the war. He had been a good soldier. That made a difference.

One morning after he had been home about a month his mother came into his bedroom and

---

① Trickery.

Unit Four Character
Chapter 7 Soldier's Home

sat on the bed. She smoothed her apron.

"I had a talk with your father last night, Harold," she said, "and he is willing for you to take the car out in the evenings."

"Yeah?" said Krebs, who was not fully awake. "Take the car out? Yeah?"

"Yes. Your father has felt for some time that you should be able to take the car out in the evenings whenever you wished but we only talked it over last night."

"I'll bet you made him," Krebs said.

"No. It was your father's suggestion that we talk the matter over."

"Yeah. I'll bet you made him," Krebs sat up in bed.

"Will you come down to breakfast, Harold?" his mother said.

"As soon as I get my clothes on," Krebs said.

His mother went out of the room and he could hear her frying something downstairs while he washed, shaved and dressed to go down into the dining-room for breakfast. While he was eating breakfast, his sister brought in the mail.

"Well, Hare," she said. "You old sleepy-head. What do you ever get up for?"

Krebs looked at her. He liked her. She was his best sister.

"Have you got the paper?" he asked.

She handed him *The Kansas City Star* and he shucked off its brown wrapper and opened it to the sporting page. He folded *The Star* open and propped it against the water pitcher① with his cereal dish to steady it, so he could read while he ate.

"Harold," his mother stood in the kitchen doorway, "Harold, please don't muss up the paper. Your father can't read his *Star* if it's been mussed."

"I won't muss it," Krebs said.

His sister sat down at the table and watched him while he read.

"We're playing indoor over at school this afternoon," she said. "I'm going to pitch."

"Good," said Krebs. "How's the old wing?"

"I can pitch better than lots of the boys. I tell them all you taught me. The other girls aren't much good."

"Yeah?" said Krebs.

"I tell them all you're my beau②. Aren't you my beau, Hare?"

"You bet."

"Couldn't your brother really be your beau just because he's your brother?"

"I don't know."

"Sure you know. Couldn't you be my beau, Hare, if I was old enough and if you wanted to?"

---

① A container for liquids, usually having a handle and a lip or spout for pouring; this word also has another meaning: the player who throws the ball from the mound to the batter.

② The boyfriend of a woman or girl.

"Sure. You're my girl now."

"Am I really your girl?"

"Sure."

"Do you love me?"

"Uh, huh."

"Do you love me always?"

"Sure."

"Will you come over and watch me play indoor?"

"Maybe."

"Aw, Hare, you don't love me. If you loved me, you'd want to come over and watch me play indoor."

Krebs's mother came into the dining-room from the kitchen. She carried a plate with two fried eggs and some crisp bacon on it and a plate of buckwheat cakes.

"You run along, Helen," she said. "I want to talk to Harold."

She put the eggs and bacon down in front of him and brought in a jug of maple syrup① for the buckwheat cakes. Then she sat down across the table from Krebs.

"I wish you'd put down the paper a minute, Harold," she said.

Krebs took down the paper and folded it.

"Have you decided what you are going to do yet, Harold?" his mother said, taking off her glasses.

"No," said Krebs.

"Don't you think it's about time?" His mother did not say this in a mean way. She seemed worried.

"I hadn't thought about it," Krebs said.

"God has some work for every one to do," his mother said. "There can be no idle hands in His Kingdom."

"I'm not in His Kingdom," Krebs said.

"We are all of us in His Kingdom."

Krebs felt embarrassed and resentful as always.

"I've worried about you too much, Harold," his mother went on. "I know the temptations you must have been exposed to. I know how weak men are. I know what your own dear grandfather, my own father, told us about the Civil War and I have prayed for you. I pray for you all day long, Harold."

Krebs looked at the bacon fat hardening on his plate.

"Your father is worried, too," his mother went on. "He thinks you have lost your ambition, that you haven't got a definite aim in life. Charley Simmons, who is just your age, has a good

---

① The juice of a fruit or plant boiled with sugar until thick and sticky.

job and is going to be married. The boys are all settling down; they're all determined to get somewhere; you can see that boys like Charley Simmons are on their way to being really a credit to the community."

Krebs said nothing.

"Don't look that way, Harold," his mother said. "You know we love you and I want to tell you for your own good how matters stand. Your father does not want to hamper① your freedom. He thinks you should be allowed to drive the car. If you want to take some of the nice girls out riding with you, we are only too pleased. We want you to enjoy yourself. But you are going to have to settle down to work, Harold. Your father doesn't care what you start in at. All work is honorable as he says. But you've got to make a start at something. He asked me to speak to you this morning and then you can stop in and see him at his office."

"Is that all?" Krebs said.

"Yes. Don't you love your mother, dear boy?"

"No," Krebs said.

His mother looked at him across the table. Her eyes were shiny. She started crying.

"I don't love anybody," Krebs said.

It wasn't any good. He couldn't tell her, he couldn't make her see it. It was silly to have said it. He had only hurt her. He went over and took hold of her arm. She was crying with her head in her hands.

"I didn't mean it," he said. "I was just angry at something. I didn't mean I didn't love you."

His mother went on crying. Krebs put his arm on her shoulder.

"Can't you believe me, mother?"

His mother shook her head.

"Please, please, mother. Please believe me."

"All right," his mother said chokily. She looked up at him. "I believe you, Harold."

Krebs kissed her hair. She put her face up to him.

"I'm your mother," she said. "I held you next to my heart when you were a tiny baby."

Krebs felt sick and vaguely nauseated.

"I know, Mummy," he said. "I'll try and be a good boy for you."

"Would you kneel and pray with me, Harold?" his mother asked.

They knelt down beside the dining-room table and Krebs's mother prayed.

"Now, you pray, Harold," she said.

"I can't," Krebs said.

"Try, Harold."

"I can't."

---

① To prevent the free movement, action, or progress of.

"Do you want me to pray for you?"

"Yes."

So his mother prayed for him and then they stood up and Krebs kissed his mother and went out of the house. He had tried so to keep his life from being complicated. Still, none of it had touched him. He had felt sorry for his mother and she had made him lie. He would go to Kansas City and get a job and she would feel all right about it. There would be one more scene maybe before he got away. He would not go down to his father's office. He would miss that one. He wanted his life to go smoothly. It had just gotten going that way. Well, that was all over now, anyway. He would go over to the schoolyard and watch Helen play indoor baseball.

Film Comment:

Ernest Hemingway's *Soldier's Home*: 42 minutes, color

Starring: Richard Backus & Nancy Marchand

Screenplay by: Robert Geller

Directed by: Robert Young

Harold Krebs (Richard Backus) went off to fight the First World War, "the war to end all wars." Then he came home...and found himself wishing it had never ended. To Ernest Hemingway, the hardest part of the war was coming home. This is the essence of "Soldier's Home"—a story with many similarities to the recent experience of those Vietnam veterans.

Harold finds he doesn't fit in anymore. He's outgrown his old life and now needs peace and quiet to work things out for himself. Yet he's pressured by his mother (Nancy Marchand), loving but misunderstanding, to rejoin a community in which he feels alien.

An intense and personal character study from the giant of American Literature, Harold discovers going home is never easy—and maybe it isn't even possible.

Film Scenes:

Scene 1: Coming home

Scene 2: Old friends

Scene 3: Socializing

Scene 4: The conversation

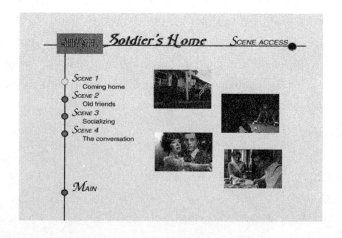

Unit Four Character
Chapter 7 Soldier's Home

Script Excerpts:

Prologue in Sepia.

Eight or ten young men are being huddled together for a fraternity picture. All dressed in high white collars. Most wear silver-rimmed glasses. Austere building in background. No laugher or chatter.

Narrator (*off camera*): Krebs went to the war from a Methodist college in Kansas. There is a picture which shows him among his fraternity brothers....

Photographer motions them to close ranks, and sheep-like they shuffle closer. One young man, Harold Krebs, stands slightly to the side and moves just a fraction after the command "hold it."

Narrator (*off camera*): He enlisted in the Army in 1917....

Cut to

Photographer and "explosion" of his camera gun.

Cut to

Stock footage of WWI, expository in nature, and of returning veterans. Not meant to editorialize about the war.

Narrator (*off camera*): ...and did not return to the United States until the second division returned from the Rhine in 1919.

Exterior. Dusk.

Empty train depot in rural town. Krebs with duffle bag. Platform is deserted, with the exception of the station master and one passenger, neither of whom pays Krebs any attention.

Krebs crosses tracks deftly. Stops at depot to catch breath. Tattered signs flap in wind: "Buy U.S. Bonds," etc. At the front end of the platform a banner with "Welcome Home Yanks" droops limply from a worn cornice.

Narrator (*off camera*): By the time Krebs returned to his home town the greeting of heroes was over. He came back much too late.

Interior. Night.

Dissolve to dining room of Krebs house. Dinner is over. Harold is still in uniform. Mr. and Mrs. Krebs and Marge hunt for words. There is no real jubilation or ease. Harold is lighting up. Faces of family watch.

Mr. Krebs: Son...You smoke lots in battle? You seem to do it...naturally.

Harold: Not really...I just picked it up.

Marge (*enthusiastic*): Did you actually smoke, in the war, Hare? Didn't they see you lighting up? The Germans?

Harold: Uh...uh. We smoked mostly when we were bored.

Mrs. Krebs: Bored! Little chance you had to be bored...

Harold: We were. I was. A lot of time.

(*Silence. Ticking of clock. It is after 11:00 p.m.*)

Mrs. Krebs: Harold, you must be tired...All that traveling. And we've asked so many questions.

Harold: I'm fine.

Mr. Krebs: Well...it's gettin' late. I gotta go out in the county tomorrow. We'll get to talk...about what you wanna be doin'. Plenty of time.

Harold: Yes...I'll need a week or so...

Mrs. Krebs: Of course. Let's just be thankful that you're home safe. Let us be thankful to our Dear Lord (*her eyes are raised*) that you're back home. Oh, Harold, we did pray for you. And each Sunday Reverend Nelson...

Mr. Krebs (*interrupts with a yawn*): Folks...I'm goin' up. Welcome home, Harold.

(*Mr. Krebs extends his hand.*)

Harold: Night, Dad...It was a fine dinner...Guess I'll go on up, too. (*He starts to follow Mr. Krebs out.*)

Interior. Hallway at foot of stairs.

Mrs. Krebs (*to Harold at the foot of the stairs*): Son...Marjorie and I could fix up a special breakfast. Serve it to you in bed. Remember when you had those and awful winter coughs and...

Harold: Not tomorrow, Mom...I'll want to get up early, and...

Mrs. Krebs: Hare?

Harold: Mom?

Mrs. Krebs (*moves to hug him*): Sleep well.

Harold (*stiffens, hugs her back*): I will...thanks...for everything.

Exterior. Bright morning.

Harold walking to town. Is stopped by a prim old man.

Man: Mornin', young Krebs. Welcome home. How long you back now?

Harold: It's two weeks, today.

Man: Your folks said you had some very difficult times over there?

Harold: No...not that bad.

Man: Anyhow, you must be glad to be home...Are you planning to go back to school?

Harold: No.

Man: You going to be selling farm land with Dad? At the bank? It's a blessing when a man and his son can...

Harold (*edging away*): 'Scuse me.

Unit Four Character
Chapter 7 Soldier's Home

(*Harold walks on down street.*)

Man: Well, I'll be! You'd think he'd killed the Kaiser. Even as a young boy...

(*They exit; their voices trail.*)

Exterior. Day.

Harold walks on to town. Nods back to few passersby who seem to remember him. Harold notices the young girls in town. He sees one through shop windows. He notices their pretty faces and the patterns that they make.

Narrator (*off camera*): Nothing was changed in the town except that the young girls had grown up. There were so many good-looking young girls.

Exterior. Day.

Harold stops in front of bank where Mr. Krebs works as land agent.

Narrator (*off camera*): Before Krebs went away to the war he had never been allowed to drive the family motor car. The car always stood outside the First National Bank building where his father had an office. Now, after the war, it was still the same car.

Harold crosses the street, walks past the car to the window of his father's office. He looks in.

Reverse Angle of Mr. Krebs amiably chatting with young customers Harold's age. Offers cigar. Laughter and clapping of each other's shoulders. Harold stares for several seconds and then turns away, crossing the street quickly.

Exterior. Greek's soda shop. Day.

Car pulls up in front of soda shop with Krebs driving. Harold get out of car and looks in window. Sees the interior, decorated with décor of period. Marge and friends are having ice-cream sodas. They are exuberant as they "recreate" some incident from school (*in pantomime*).

Harold looks in, raps on window, and beckons Marge to come outside. She signals to Harold that she'll be out in one minute.

Bill Kenner (*off camera*): Hey, Krebs...Harold Krebs...

(*Bill Kenner: early 20s. Dressed flamboyantly with bohemian dash. Sports cane with golden handle. He limps perceptibly into frame.*)

Remember me? William Kenner. Your fellow sufferer in geometry and Latin. C'mere, my lovelies.

(*Kenner waves to two teenagers, who obediently follow.*)

Harold: Sure...Bill Kenner. I remember you. You all right?

Bill Kenner (*with bravura*): Sure...if losing a chunk of your knee on a mine is all right, then I'm just fine.

Harold (*embarrassed for the girls*): That's...that's too bad. You seem to be doin' well though.

Kenner: Well...with lovelies like these, *pourquoi s'en faire*?...Am I right?

Harold (*edgy*): I guess.

Kenner: You guess. Aren't we lucky to be alive? You know this little town had three killed? Lots of injured, too. In our graduating class alone...

Harold (*spot Marge*): Here...Right here, Marge.

Kenner: Is that lovely mademoiselle a Krebs?

(*bows.*)

May I introduce myself?

Marge: Let's go, Hare...

Harold: Well...goodbye, Bill.

Kenner (*not dissuaded*): That your car?

Harold: My dad's.

Kenner: Splen-did work of art.

Harold: Thanks.

Kenner: Can you get it nights?

Marge (*impatient*): Har-old!

Harold: I guess so. Why?

Kenner: You busy this Friday?

Harold: Well...I'm not sure. Let me think about it....

Kenner: Think about it! About what? Let's you and I live it up, my friend. (*Girls giggle.*) There's a dance at the Y. I might even have some gen-u-ine cognac. Come by at 8:00.

Harold: All right...I'll try.

Kenner: I'll *expect* you. (*Winks.*) Bye now.

(*To Marge*): Bye, lovely. See you on the Champs Elysees.

(*Tips his hat and limps away dramatically. Harold and Marge drive away.*)

Interior. Hallway.

Cases filled with trophies. Pictures of austere town philanthropist.

Roselle: Harold? Harold Krebs. (*For her, all conversation is a flirtation.*)

Harold: It's me.

Roselle: I'm Roselle, Roselle Simmons.

Harold: Charlie's sister...right?

Roselle: Why...heavens...have I changed all that much in two years?

Harold: Three years...actually.

Roselle: You don't seem to be having much fun at all....You haven't danced once. I've been spying on you.

Harold: Well, I'm not up to the steps...or all the chatter...

Roselle: You need to be taught....Didn't your little sister Marge ever try? There are lots of new steps...I could teach you...It's my war effort...Trade for a smoke?

Harold (*doesn't offer her a cigarette*): It's a waste of time. I never could get my feet straight...

Roselle: Silly...the feet are the easy part...it's the rest of your body...the way you lead...the way you hold your partner...I'll bet you like to command a girl...

Harold (*surprised*): Command a girl...Why?

Roselle (*she leads to music*): Command me, Mr. Harold Krebs...

Harold (*he responds slowly*): Like this?

(*These scenes should be played slowly—moving from awkwardness to Harold's own arousal and assertion.*)

Roselle (*Gently circling his arms around her. Emphasize physical aspects of their dancing*): Just move one, two, three, four...get closer...Did you ever dance like this, with those foreign women?

(*Cuts to Harold dancing closer. Stroking her as he would the women he has known in Europe. The music stops, and Harold continues to caress her with sureness.*)

Roselle (*scared now*): Don't...I've got to freshen up...I won't be long...All right? Wait out here...Don't!

Harold (*confused*): Hey...Where're you going? C'mon back here, Roselle.

Roselle (*vampishly over her shoulder*): Silly...

(*Roselle leaves. Harold continues to wait. The music begins. He is filled with a crushing sadness, a new confusion, a feeling of betrayed.*)

Discussion Questions:

1. What war does Harold go to fight for? Why does he come home so late?
2. Harold can't find himself fit in anymore. Has he or the community changed? Or both have changed?
3. Where does the pressure come from? What's the conflict between his mother and him?
4. Harold has to make a decision for his future. What kind of life is waiting for the homecoming soldier?
5. The author thinks that the hardest part of the war is coming home. Do you agree with that or not?

Further Reading and Watching:

The Snows of Kilimanjaro

Chapter 8

The Jilting of Granny Weatherall

Katherine Anne Porter

Author Introduction:

Katherine Anne Porter (1890—1980) was born in Indian Creek, Texas, and was educated at a Catholic convent and a series of private schools in Texas and Louisiana. Her mother died when she was two, and Porter was raised by a grandmother who surrounded the growing girl with books. Though she began to write stories as soon as she could form letters on paper, she made no attempt to publish until she was past 30 years old, and she associated with no literary people until she had become something of a celebrity with the publication of her first book of stories, *Flowering Judas* (1930). An expanded edition of this collection was published in 1935 and received such critical acclaim that it alone virtually assured her place in American literature. Yet, before and after that date she earned a meager living by journalism, traveling from city to city with little baggage except her manuscripts. She lived for a time in Mexico, which provided material for some of her most famous stories, and her nomadic career also took her to Europe to live some of her later years. Porter's only novel *Ship of Fools*, based on her reminiscences of a 1931 ocean cruise she had taken from Vera Cruz, Mexico, to Germany, was begun during the 1930s, but not finished for more than two decades. It was at last published in 1962, which received harsh critical notices, but proved a commercial success. Made into a movie, it ended Porter's lifelong struggle to earn a living. Her shorter works have also been collected in *Hacienda: A Story of Mexico* (1934), *Pale Horse, Pale Rider* (1939), and *The Leaning Tower and Other Stories* (1944). *The Collected Stories of Katherine Anne Porter* appeared in 1965, winning the Pulitzer Prize and the National Book Award.

Unit Four　Character

Chapter 8　The Jilting of Granny Weatherall

Story Summary:

Granny Weatherall is spunky, 80, and bosses her doctors and children. On her death bed she realizes that all her accomplishments in life and matriarchal control cannot compensate for the day that George Heatherton left her standing at the altar. Many decades ago she donned her white veil, set out her cake and waited in the house with the priest for tall handsome George to arrive. He never came. She snaps to her daughter, "Go and find him. Tell him I forgot him years ago." Something has been held back in Granny Weatherall. She waits for life to claim her rather than seeking out life for herself.

Key Terms:

Stream of Consciousness, Feminist, Tension, Conventional Society, Personal Freedom, Identity, Psychological Repression

The Jilting of Granny Weatherall[1]

She flicked her wrist neatly out of Doctor Harry's pudgy careful fingers and pulled the sheet up to her chin. The brat ought to be in knee breeches[2]. Doctoring around the country with spectacles on his nose! "Get along now, take your schoolbooks and go. There's nothing wrong with me."

Doctor Harry spread a warn paw like a cushion on her forehead where the forked green vein danced and made her eyelids twitch. "Now, now, be a good girl, and we'll have you up in no time."

"That's no way to speak to a woman nearly eighty years old just because she's down. I'd have you respect your elders, young man."

"Well, Missy, excuse me." Doctor Harry patted her cheek. "But I've got to warn you, haven't I? You're a marvel, but you must be careful or you're going to be good and sorry."

"Don't tell me what I'm going to be. I'm on my feet now, morally speaking. It's Cornelia. I had to go to bed to get rid of her."

Her bones felt loose, and floated around in her skin, and Doctor Harry floated like a balloon around the foot of the bed. He floated and pulled down his waistcoat and swung his glasses on a cord. "Well, stay where you are, it certainly can't hurt you."

"Get along and doctor your sick," said Granny Weatherall. "Leave a well woman alone. I'll call for you when I want you....Where were you forty years ago when I pulled through milk-leg[3] and double pneumonia? You weren't even born. Don't let Cornelia lead you on," she shouted, because Doctor Harry appeared to float up to the ceiling and out. "I pay my own bills, and I don't

---

[1] First published in *Flowering Judas and Other Stories*, 1930.
[2] Trousers extending down to or just below the knee.
[3] A swelling that occasionally follows pregnancy.

throw my money away on nonsense!"

She meant to wave good-bye, but it was too much trouble. Her eyes closed of themselves, it was like a dark curtain drawn around the bed. The pillow rose and floated under her, pleasant as a hammock in a light wind. She listened to the leaves rustling outside the window. No, somebody was swishing newspapers: no, Cornelia and Doctor Harry were whispering together. She leaped broad awake, thinking they whispered in her ear.

"She was never like this, *never* like this!" "Well, what can we expect?" "Yes, eighty years old...."

Well, and what if she was? She still had ears. It was like Cornelia to whisper around doors. She always kept things secret in such a public way. She was always being tactful and kind. Cornelia was dutiful; that was the trouble with her. Dutiful and good: "So good and dutiful," said Granny, "that I'd like to spank her." She saw herself spanking Cornelia and making a fine job of it.

"What'd you say, Mother?"

Granny felt her face tying up in hard knots.

"Can't a body think, I'd like to know?"

"I thought you might want something."

"I do. I want a lot of things. First off, go away and don't whisper."

She lay and drowsed, hoping in her sleep that the children would keep out and let her rest a minute. It had been a long day. Not that she was tired. It was always pleasant to snatch a minute now and then. There was always so much to be done, let me see: tomorrow.

Tomorrow was far away and there was nothing to trouble about. Things were finished somehow when the time came; thank God there was always a little margin over for peace: then a person could spread out the plan of life and tuck in the edges orderly. It was good to have everything clean and folded away, with the hair brushes and tonic bottles sitting straight on the white embroidered linen: the day started without fuss and the pantry shelves laid out with rows of jelly glasses and brown jugs and white stone-china jars with blue whirligigs and words painted on them: coffee, tea, sugar, ginger, cinnamon, allspice: and the bronze clock with the lion on top nicely dusted off. The dust that lion could collect in twenty-four hours! The box in the attic with all those letters tied up, well, she'd have to go through that tomorrow. All those letters—George's letters and John's letters and her letters to them both—lying around for the children to find afterwards made her uneasy. Yes, that would be tomorrow's business. No use to let them know how silly she had been once.

While she was rummaging around she found death in her mind and it felt clammy and unfamiliar. She had spent so much time preparing for death there was no need for bringing it up again. Let it take care of itself now. When she was sixty she had felt very old, finished, and went around making farewell trips to see her children and grandchildren, with a secret in her mind: This is the very last of your mother, children! Then she made her will and came down with a

Unit Four Character

Chapter 8 The Jilting of Granny Weatherall

long fever. That was all just a notion like a lot of other things, but it was lucky too, for she had once for all① got over the idea of dying for a long time. Now she couldn't be worried. She hoped she had better sense now. Her father had lived to be one hundred and two years old and had drunk a noggin② of strong hot toddy③ on his last birthday. He told the reporters it was his daily habit, and he owed his long life to that. He had made quite a scandal and was very pleased about it. She believed she'd just plague Cornelia a little.

"Cornelia! Cornelia!" No footsteps, but a sudden hand on her cheek. "Bless you, where have you been?"

"Here, Mother."

"Well, Cornelia, I want a noggin of hot toddy."

"Are you cold, darling?"

"I'm chilly, Cornelia. Lying in bed stops the circulation. I must have told you that a thousand times."

Well, she could just hear Cornelia telling her husband that Mother was getting a little childish and they'd have to humor her. The thing that most annoyed her was that Cornelia thought she was deaf, dumb, and blind. Little hasty glances and tiny gestures tossed around her and over her head saying, "Don't cross her, let her have her way, she's eighty years old," and she sitting there as if she lived in a thin glass cage. Sometimes Granny almost made up her mind to pack up and move back to her own house where nobody could remind her every minute that she was old. Wait, wait, Cornelia, till your own children whisper behind your back!

In her day she had kept a better house and had got more work done. She wasn't too old yet for Lydia to be driving eighty miles for advice when one of the children jumped the track, and Jimmy still dropped in and talked things over: "Now, Mammy, you've a good business head, I want to know what you think of this?..." Old. Cornelia couldn't change the furniture around without asking. Little things, little things! They had been so sweet when they were little. Granny wished the old days were back again with the children young and everything to be done over. It had been a hard pull, but not too much for her. When she thought of all the food she had cooked, and all the clothes she had cut and sewed, and all the gardens she had made—well, the children showed it. There they were, made out of her, and they couldn't get away from that. Sometimes she wanted to see John again and point to them and say, Well, I didn't do so badly, did I? But that would have to wait. That was for tomorrow. She used to think of him as a man, but now all the children were older than their father, and he would be a child beside her if she saw him now. It seemed strange and there was something wrong in the idea. Why, he couldn't possibly recognize her. She had fenced in a hundred acres once, digging the post holes herself and clamping the wires with just a negro boy to help. That changed a woman. John would be looking for a young

---

① Sometimes "once and for all" means "certainly" or "definitely."
② A small cup containing about four ounces.
③ A drink of liquor, hot water, sugar, and spices.

woman with the peaked Spanish comb in her hair and the painted fan. Digging post holes changed a woman. Riding country roads in the winter when women had their babies was another thing: sitting up nights with sick horses and sick negroes and sick children and hardly ever losing one. John, I hardly ever lost one of them! John would see that in a minute, that would be something he could understand, she wouldn't have to explain anything.

It made her feel like rolling up her sleeves and putting the whole place to rights again. No matter if Cornelia was determined to be everywhere at once, there were a great many things left undone on this place. She would start tomorrow and do them. It was good to be strong enough for everything, even if all you made melted and changed and slopped under your hands, so that by the time you finished you almost forgot what you were working for. What was it I set out to do? She asked herself intently, but she could not remember. A fog rose over the valley, she saw it marching across the creek swallowing the trees and moving up the hill like an army of ghosts. Soon it would be at the near edge of the orchard, and then it was time to go in and light the lamps. Come in, children, don't stay out in the night air.

Lighting the lamps had been beautiful. The children huddled up to her and breathed like little calves waiting at the bars in the twilight. Their eyes followed the match and watched the flame rise and settle in a blue curve, then they moved away from her. The lamp was lit, they didn't have to be scared and hang on to mother any more. Never, never, never more. God, for all my life I thank Thee. Without Thee, my God, I could never have done it. Hail, Mary[①], full of grace.

I want you to pick all the fruit this year and see that nothing is wasted. There's always someone who can use it. Don't let good things rot for want of using. You waste life when you waste good food. Don't let things get lost. It's bitter to lose things. Now, don't let me get to thinking, not when I am tired and taking a little nap before supper....

The pillow rose about her shoulders and pressed against her heart and the memory was being squeezed out of it: oh, push down the pillow, somebody: it would smother her if she tried to hold it. Such a fresh breeze blowing and such a green day with no threats in it. But he had not come, just the same. What does a woman do when she has put on the white veil and set out the white cake for a man and he doesn't come? She tried to remember. No, I swear he never harmed me but in that. He never harmed me but in that...and what if he did? There was the day, the day, but a whirl of dark smoke rose and covered it, crept up and over into the bright field where everything was planted so carefully in orderly rows. That was hell, she knew hell when she saw it. For sixty years she had prayed against remembering him and against losing her soul in the deep pit of hell, and now the two things were mingled in one and the thought of him was a smoky cloud from hell that moved and crept in her head when she had just got rid of Doctor Harry and was trying to rest a minute. Wounded vanity, Ellen, said a sharp voice in the top of her mind. Don't

---

① In the New Testament, the mother of Jesus and the principal saint of many Christian churches.

Unit Four Character

Chapter 8 *The Jilting of Granny Weatherall*

let your wounded vanity get the upper hand of you. Plenty of girls get jilted①. You were jilted, weren't you? Then stand up to it. Her eyelids wavered and let in streamers of blue-gray light like tissue paper over her eyes. She must get up and pull the shades down or she'd never sleep. She was in bed again and the shades were not down. How could that happen? Better turn over, hide from the light, sleeping in the light gave you nightmares. "Mother, how do you feel now?" and a stinging wetness on her forehead. But I don't like having my face washed in cold water!

Hapsy? George? Lydia? Jimmy? No, Cornelia, and her features were swollen and full of little puddles. "They're coming, darling, they'll all be here soon." Go wash your face, child, you look funny.

Instead of obeying, Cornelia knelt down and put her head on the pillow. She seemed to be talking but there was so sound. "Well, are you tongue-tied? Whose birthday is it? Are you going to give a party?"

Cornelia's mouth moved urgently in strange shapes. "Don't do that, you bother me, daughter."

"Oh, no, Mother. Oh, no...."

Nonsense. It was strange about children. They disputed your every word. "No what, Cornelia?"

"Here's Doctor Harry."

"I won't see that boy again. He just left five minutes ago."

"That was this morning, Mother. It's night now. Here's the nurse."

"This is Doctor Harry, Mrs. Weatherall. I never saw you look so young and happy!"

"I'll never be young again—but I'd be happy if they'd let me lie in peace and get rested."

She thought she spoke up loudly, but no one answered. A warm weight on her forehead, a warm bracelet on her wrist, and a breeze went on whispering, trying to tell her something. A shuffle of leaves in the everlasting hand of God, He blew on them and they danced and rattled. "Mother, don't mind, we're going to give you a little hypodermic②." "Look here, daughter, how do ants get in this bed? I saw sugar ants yesterday." Did you send for Hapsy too?

It was Hapsy she really wanted. She had to go a long way back through a great many rooms to find Hapsy standing with a baby on her arm. She seemed to herself to be Hapsy also, and the baby on Hapsy's arm was Hapsy and himself and herself, all at once, and there was no surprise in the meeting. Then Hapsy melted from within and turned flimsy as gray gauze and the baby was a gauzy shadow, and Hapsy came up close and said, "I thought you'd never come," and looked at her very searchingly and said, "You haven't changed a bit!" They leaned forward to kiss, when Cornelia began whispering from a long way off, "Oh, is there anything you want to tell me? Is there anything I can do for you?"

Yes, she had changed her mind after sixty years and she would like to see George. I want

---

① Deceived or dropped suddenly or callously.
② Injected beneath the skin.

you to find George. Find him and be sure to tell him I forgot him. I want him to know I had my husband just the same and my children and my house like any other woman. A good house too and a good husband that I loved and fine children out of him. Better than I hoped for even. Tell him I was given back everything he took away and more. Oh, no, oh, God, no, there was something else besides the house and the man and the children. Oh, surely they were not all? What was it? Something not given back....Her breath crowded down under her ribs and grew into a monstrous frightening shape with cutting edges; it bored up into her head, and the agony was unbelievable: Yes, John, get the Doctor now, no more talk, my time has come.

When this one was born it should be the last. The last. It should have been born first, for it was the one she had truly wanted. Everything came in good time. Nothing left out, left over. She was strong, in three days she would be as well as ever. Better. A woman needed milk in her to have her full health.

"Mother, do you hear me?"

"I've been telling you—"

"Mother, Father Connolly's here."

"I went to Holy Communion① only last week. Tell him I'm not so sinful as all that."

"Father just wants to speak to you."

He could speak as much as he pleased. It was like him to drop in and inquire about her soul as if it were a teething baby, and then stay on for a cup of tea and a round of cards and gossip. He always had a funny story of some sort, usually about an Irishman who made his little mistakes and confessed them, and the point lay in some absurd thing he would blurt out in the confessional showing his struggles between native piety and original sin. Granny felt easy about her soul. Cornelia, where are your manners? Give Father Connolly a chair. She had her secret comfortable understanding with a few favorite saints who cleared a straight road to God for her. All as surely signed and sealed as the papers for the new Forty Acres. Forever...heirs and assigns forever. Since the day the wedding cake was not cut, but thrown out and wasted. The whole bottom dropped out of the world, and there she was blind and sweating with nothing under her feet and the walls falling away. His hand had caught her under the breast, she had not fallen, there was the freshly polished floor with the green rug on it, just as before. He had cursed like a sailor's parrot and said, "I'll kill him for you." Don't lay a hand on him, for my sake leave something to God. "Now, Ellen, you must believe what I tell you...."

So there was nothing, nothing to worry about any more, except sometimes in the night one of the children screamed in a nightmare, and they both hustled out shaking and hunting for the matches and calling, "There, wait a minute, here we are!" John, get the doctor now, Hapsy's time has come. But there was Hapsy standing by the bed in a white cap. "Cornelia, tell Hapsy to take off her cap. I can't see her plain."

---

① The sacrament of the Eucharist received by a congregation.

Unit Four Character

Chapter 8 The Jilting of Granny Weatherall

Her eyes opened very wide and the room stood out like a picture she had seen somewhere. Dark colors with the shadows rising towards the ceiling in long angles. The tall black dresser gleamed with nothing on it but John's picture, enlarged from a little one, with John's eyes very black when they should have been blue. You never saw him, so how do you know how he looked? But the man insisted the copy was perfect, it was very rich and handsome. For a picture, yes, but it's not my husband. The table by the bed had a linen cover and a candle and a crucifix. The light was blue from Cornelia's silk lampshades. No sort of light at all, just frippery. You had to live forty years with kerosene lamps to appreciate honest electricity. She felt very strong and she saw Doctor Harry with a rosy nimbus① around him.

"You look like a saint, Doctor Harry, and I vow that's as near as you'll ever come to it."

"She's saying something."

"I heard you, Cornelia. What's all this carrying-on?"

"Father Connolly's saying—"

Cornelia's voice staggered and bumped like a cart in a bad road. It rounded corners and turned back again and arrived nowhere. Granny stepped up in the cart very lightly and reached for the reins, but a man sat beside her and she knew him by his hands, driving the cart. She did not look in his face, for she knew without seeing, but looked instead down the road where the trees leaned over and bowed to each other and a thousand birds were singing a Mass②. She felt like singing too, but she put her hand in the bosom of her dress and pulled out a rosary③, and Father Connolly murmured Latin in a very solemn voice and tickled her feet.④ My God, will you stop that nonsense? I'm a married woman. What if he did run away and leave me to face the priest by myself? I found another a whole world better. I wouldn't have exchanged my husband for anybody except St. Michael himself, and you may tell him that for me with a thank you in the bargain.

Light flashed on her closed eyelids, and a deep roaring shook her. Cornelia, is that lightning? I hear thunder. There's going to be a storm. Close all the windows. Call the children in.... "Mother, here we are, all of us." "Is that you, Hapsy?" "Oh, no, I'm Lydia. We drove as fast as we could." Their faces drifted above her, drifted away. The rosary fell out of her hands and Lydia put it back. Jimmy tried to help, their hands fumbled together, and Granny closed two fingers around Jimmy's thumb. Beads wouldn't do, it must be something alive. She was so amazed her thoughts ran round and round. So, my dear Lord, this is my death and I wasn't even thinking about it. My children have come to see me die. But I can't, it's not time. Oh, I always hated surprises. I wanted to give Cornelia the amethyst set—Cornelia, you're to have the amethyst set, but Hapsy's to wear it when she wants, and, Doctor Harry, do shut up. Nobody sent for you. Oh,

---

① A radiant light that appears usually in the form of a circle or halo about or over the head in the representation of a god, demigod, saint, or sacred person such as a king or an emperor.

② A musical setting of certain parts of the Mass.

③ A string of beads of 5 or 15 decades on which the prayers are counted.

④ As part of the sacrament for the dying, the priest anoints the feet with oil.

my dear Lord, do wait a minute. I meant to do something about the Forty Acres, Jimmy doesn't need it and Lydia will later on, with that worthless husband of hers. I meant to finish the altar cloth and send six bottles of wine to Sister Borgia, Father Connolly, now don't let me forget.

Cornelia's voice made short turns and tilted over and crashed. "Oh, Mother, oh, Mother, oh, Mother...."

"I'm not going, Cornelia. I'm taken by surprise. I can't go."

You'll see Hapsy again. What about her? "I thought you'd never come." Granny made a long journey outward, looking for Hapsy. What if I don't find her? What then? Her heart sank down and down, there was no bottom to death, she couldn't come to the end of it. The blue light from Cornelia's lampshade drew into a tiny point in the center of her brain, it flickered and winked like an eye, quietly it fluttered and dwindled. Granny lay curled down within herself, amazed and watchful, staring at the point of light that was herself; her body was now only a deeper mass of shadow in an endless darkness and this darkness would curl around the light and swallow it up. God, give a sign.

For the second time there was no sign. Again no bridegroom and the priest in the house.[①] She could not remember any other sorrow because this grief wiped them all away. Oh, no, there's nothing more cruel than this—I'll never forgive it. She stretched herself with a deep breath and blew out the light.

Film Comment:

Katherine Anne Porter's *The Jilting of Granny Weatherall*: 57 minutes, color

Starring: Geraldine Fitzgerald

Screenplay by: Corinne Jacker

Directed by: Randa Haines

Granny Weatherall (Geraldine Fitzgerald) is a spunky old lady of eighty who bosses her doctor and her children. She seems so strong and in control. Yet she has never had the upper hand in her destiny.

One morning, a flood of long-forgotten memories bring her to the realization that of all her accomplishments, she cannot console herself for the shame-filled day she was left standing at the altar. Still, her indomitable will to live and act independently infuses the last day of her life.

Adapted from the short story by acclaimed writer Katherine Anne Porter, "The Jilting of Granny Weatherall" reminds us of the plight of many women who wait for life to claim them, rather than seek life out for themselves.

---

① Cf. Christ's parable of the bridegroom (Matthew xxv: 1-13).

Unit Four   Character

Chapter 8   *The Jilting of Granny Weatherall*

Film Scenes:

Scene 1: Granny Weatherall
Scene 2: Memories
Scene 3: Baking a white cake
Scene 4: Is it time to go?
Scene 5: The priest

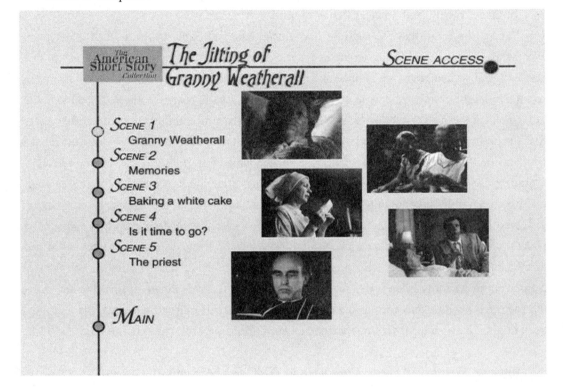

Script Excerpts:

Exterior. Weatherall farm. Day.

It is just daybreak on a morning in early May. The Weatherall farm has been lived in for several generations, and is still in good repair. It is a matter-of-fact sort of place, gray, unpainted clapboard, square window openings; no fancy gingerbread molding or imitation Georgian columns try to make the place look like anything more than it is. Seen from a distance, as the sun begins to pick it out, making shadow and light where only shadow was before, the farmyard, where the roosters and chickens are already out, and the stables, the barn, the fenced-in vegetable garden—all show the same signs of no-nonsense care.

Under credits.

While the camera is still viewing the exterior of the farm, we hear,

Sound: off-camera alarm clock

This is one of those twenties or thirties clocks with the bell that rings so harshly and insistently. Whether it is by intent or accident, the alarm is echoed by a rooster call, and then another, and then several more.

At the same time, a beam of sunlight strikes the house, illuminates one of the windows, which is still unwashed from the winter winds and snows and reflects the light back out at nature.

Interior. Weatherall house. Ellen's room. Daybreak.

This is the room that the sunlight has struck first. The light strikes the bed and Granny Weatherall (Ellen), who is lying on the bed, her eyes wide open, her arms motionless at her side. She is an old woman, her face is lined and worn with years of hard living, and as she lies there, so immobile, she could be a corpse, laid out for viewing. As she hears the alarm, she turns in disgust, looks at the wall through which the sound of the alarm is coming, the bedroom next door. She sits up in bed, turns to the night table next to her bed, and turns on the light. The table has a Bible, a crucifix, her rosary, and a small, rose-shaded lamp on it. It also has a wedding picture of a time of fifty or so years ago, with a young teen-aged bride, plump cheeked, smiling, hopeful; the groom, an older man, plump, balding, but cheerful, is more serious. He has his eyes on the girl, who looks straight into the camera, as though the joke that made her smile is there. Ellen picks it up, looks at it, as she does every morning of her life, puts it down, and gets out of bed. The flannel nightgown she is wearing has become too big for her shrunken frame, and it is old from years of wearing. Ellen walks to the window, pulls the shade down, to keep the sun out of the room for a while, and goes to the closet for her clothes. During all this time, the alarm has been ringing. Now suddenly it stops and she looks at that same wall with satisfaction.

Interior. Weatherall house. Cornelia and William's bedroom. Daybreak.

Cornelia and William lie in bed, a bed that is almost an exact duplicate of Ellen's. William has his hand on the alarm, having just turned it off. Cornelia is still asleep, and she does not stir when William, in his long johns, gets out of the bed and goes over to the chair where his clothes are laid out and ready for the morning. William is not a young man, but he is a determined one. His body, a little thick with some added weight, since he is in his forties, is nevertheless in good shape. He begins to do some exercises, hands out in front of him, going down on his haunches, and back up again, breathing healthily and deeply. It is just possible to hear him muttering a slogan to himself, although the words are inaudible. The slogan is "Every day in every way, I'm getting better and better." A sunbeam comes into this room as well, striking Cornelia on the face with its bright, hot light. Cornelia, also in her forties, responds by pulling the sheet over her head and turning over. William, too, is illuminated by the sun, almost a silhouette against the window, as he goes back to his knee-bends. Near him, on the dresser, are more framed photos. The same wedding picture that was in Ellen's room, and another, more modern wedding of perhaps fifteen years ago—Cornelia and William. After a moment William hears sounds from the other side of

Unit Four Character
Chapter 8 The Jilting of Granny Weatherall

the wall, Ellen's bedroom.

William: She's up!...Cornelia....Wake up!...I said your mother's awake and stirring!

At last, the reluctant Cornelia rises from the bed, makes her way toward the bathroom, nodding a greeting to William as she passes him.

Interior. Ellen's room. Day.

Ellen is fully dressed, sitting in her straight-backed chair and looking out the window. The shade is up and a really strong sun strikes her. She has a comb and brush, both of them old, but still functioning, and as she looks out the window at the farmland and the surrounding countryside, she is brushing her still strong and thick hair. Something outside strikes her attention and she gets up suddenly, dropping the comb as she does so.

Exterior. Road leading to the Weatherall farm. Day.
POV Ellen.

In the long view Ellen has from her window, a rider, wearing a dark jacket, and mounted on a sorrel horse and galloping at full speed, is riding away from the farm.

Interior. Ellen's bedroom. Day.

She can no longer see the rider; she turns back to the room, having forgotten for a moment what she was doing, sees the brush and comb on the floor, stoops down, gets the brush, and is furious to see that the tomb, a loved old treasure, has broken in half. As she picks it up, a twinge of pain strikes her in the breast, and then on her upper right arm. She puts her hand on the arm, rubs it, and busily sets about pinning up her hair. She looks over at the wedding picture, talks to the man in it, as she has grown accustomed to doing.

Ellen: Thing to do it—if it's arthritis—is ignore it!
End of Credits.

Interior. Weatherall kitchen. Day.

It is about half an hour later. Connelia is at the stove, making eggs and bacon. On top of the stove is a pot of coffee, steaming and hot. Every few moments Cornelia stops tending to the breakfast, and steals a gulp from a mug of coffee that sits next to her pans. William is at the breakfast table, drinking coffee, and fiddling with a radio, trying to bring in something other than the annoying static that fills the room. Ellen is sitting, her coffee untouched, poring through several scrapbooks filled with old handwritten recipes on cards, paper, backs of envelopes, but carefully preserved.

Cornelia serves up eggs and bacon to both William and Ellen.

Cornelia (*to William*): Take it back! Nothing but that noise! They promised singing and comedies—

William: It came in clear enough last night.

Cornelia: And this is this morning.

William: And I need to know the weather. Galton's got planting to do.

Cornelia (*to Ellen*): Mama—you aren't eating your eggs.

Ellen: They're too hard. Eggs ought to be soft.

Cornelia: I'll make you fresh.

She makes a move for the plate, Ellen stops her.

William: What 'cha looking for, Grannie?

Ellen: Recipe.

William: I can see that....Which one?

Ellen looks at him, doesn't answer, instead takes a forkful of bacon and eggs.

Ellen (*to Cornelia*): Bacon's almost burnt.

She gets up, goes to the outside door where a small basket is sitting. Ellen picks up the basket and is about to leave.

William: Where are you off to at the crack of dawn?

Ellen: Working.

Cornelia: You don't have to work so hard, Mama. I can do whatever it is. You sit down. You look pale.

Ellen (*to William*): You never should buy anything from Ben Wolf. It always turns bad.

And she is out the door.

Cornelia: She won't forget that one bad saddle Ben's father sold her, and that was forty-five years ago!

Exterior. Weatherall barn. Day.

POV Ellen.

A carriage is just turning the corner at the barn, going out toward the town road. It is moving fast, and can barely be seen, just the last little bit of it visible, and the sound of it moving.

Ellen (OS): George?

Exterior. Weatherall house. Porch. Day.

Ellen is on the porch, still holding her egg basket. A form moves out of the shadows around the barn. It is a man, not quite as yet recognizable as he moves with the morning light behind him.

Ellen: Who's there?

Galton: It's me.

Ellen: Galton?

At that moment the house door opens and Cornelia comes out with a sweater for Ellen, puts it over her shoulders.

Cornelia: You'll freeze to death in that flimsy dress. Mama, you have to start taking care.

Ellen (*to Galton*): She means I'm old now. (*To Cornelia*) Haven't you noticed? I've been an old lady for more than ten years.

Cornelia pops inside the house, having noticed Galton on the porch.

Discussion Questions:

1. Who is George? What happened between George and Granny Weatherall?
2. During the last day of her life, what comes into her mind? Can you infer what kind of person she is?
3. How does Granny compare the experience of being jilted with the experience of death? What will she "never forgive"?
4. What's the attitude of Granny Weatherall toward life and death? Is she afraid of death?
5. The narrative perspective of this story is quite special. How do the comments of the doctor, the priest, and Cornelia help establish the restricted focus of Granny's point of view?

Further Reading and Watching:

Theft

Unit Five

Tone and Style

Chapter 9

The Greatest Man in the World

James Thurber

Author Introduction:

James Thurber (1894—1961) was born in Columbus, Ohio, and attended Ohio State University. The accidental loss of an eye in boyhood kept him from military service in the First World War, but he worked briefly for the Department of State as a code clerk, first in Washington, D.C., and then at the Embassy of the United States, Paris, France. After the war, he returned home to write for the *Columbus Dispatch*, and to compose and direct musical comedies for a theatrical group at Ohio State University. In 1924, he traveled to Paris as a correspondent to sample the world of the expatriates, where he wrote for the *Chicago Tribune* and other newspapers. Thurber was back in New York, by 1926, submitting his humorous pieces to *The New Yorker* in its early days. With the help of E. B. White, his friend and fellow *New Yorker* contributor, he worked briefly as its managing editor and then contributed regularly to its "Talk of the Town" department until the 1950s. Thurber had drawn before he began to write, and *The New Yorker* printed several series of his cartoons as well as fables, essays, comment, and short stories through the many years of his association with the magazine. Many of his short stories are humorous fictional memoirs from his life, but he also wrote darker materials. Despite his failing eyesight, Thurber continues writing humor and satire until his death, including "The Secret Life of Walter Mitty," which is regarded as one of the best short stories written in the 20th century. His carefully wrought style faithfully embodies the richness of the American vernacular. Most of his books contain mixed offerings of stories, essays, fables, and cartoons. Among them are *Fables for Our Time* (1940), *My World—And Welcome to It* (1942), *The Thurber Carnival* (1945), and *Thurber Country* (1953).

The American Short Story Through Film

Story Summary:
It is 1937—Admiral Byrd has flown over the North and South Poles. Lucky Lindbergh has flown solo from New York to Paris. But what if our next aviation hero turns out to be a slob, author James Thurber wonders. Enter Pal Smurch, a foul-mouthed, gin-guzzling mechanic who becomes the first man to fly solo around the world. Here is a hero in a new mold who the press and even the President try to make into the Byrd-Lindbergh model. It doesn't work. Smurch scratches himself and bellows, "When do the parties start? Where's the broad? Where's the dough?" Smurch has to go. He simply can't be allowed to besmirch his officially created public image.

Key Terms:
Truth, Politics and the Media, Image, Satire, Hero

The Greatest Man in the World[1]

Looking back on it now, from the vantage point of 1950, one can only marvel that it hadn't happened long before it did. The United States of America had been, ever since Kitty Hawk[2], blindly constructing the elaborate petard[3] by which, sooner or later, it must be hoist. It was inevitable that some day there would come roaring out of the skies a national hero of insufficient intelligence, background, and character successfully to endure the mounting orgies of glory prepared for aviators who stayed up a long time or flew a great distance. Both Lindbergh[4] and Byrd[5], fortunately for national decorum and international amity, had been gentlemen; so had our other famous aviators. They wore their laurels gracefully, withstood the awful weather of publicity, married excellent women, usually of fine family, and quietly retired to private life and the enjoyment of their varying fortunes. No untoward incidents, on a world-wide scale, marred the perfection of their conductor on the perilous heights of fame. The exception to the rule was, however, bound to occur and it did, in July, 1937, when Jack ("Pal") Smurch, erstwhile mechanic's helper in a small garage in Westfield, Iowa, flew a second-hand, single-motored Bresthaven Dragon-Fly III monoplane all the way around the world, without stopping.

Never before in the history of aviation had such a flight as Smurch's ever been dreamed of. No one had even taken seriously the weird floating auxiliary gas tanks, invention of the mad New Hampshire professor of astronomy, Dr. Charles Lewis Gresham, upon which Smurch

---

[1] First published in *The Middle-Aged Man on the Flying Trapeze* (1931).
[2] The site of the first sustained airplane flights, in 1903 by Orville and Wilbur Wright.
[3] A case containing explosives to break down a door, gate, or wall. Thurber alludes to the expression "Hoist with one's own petard," which means to get caught in one's own trap.
[4] American aviator Charles Augustus Lindbergh (1902—1974) made the first solo, nonstop transatlantic flight.
[5] American explorer Richard Evelyn Byrd (1888—1957) and Floyd Bennett were the first men to fly over the North Pole in 1926.

Unit Five   Tone and Style
Chapter 9   The Greatest Man in the World

placed full reliance. When the garage worker, a slightly built, surly, unprepossessing young man of twenty-two, appeared at Roosevelt Field in early July, 1937, slowly chewing a great quid of scrap tobacco, and announced, "Nobody ain't seen no flyin' yet," the newspapers touched briefly and satirically upon his projected twenty-five-thousand-mile flight. Aeronautical and automotive experts dismissed the idea curtly, implying that it was a hoax, a publicity stunt. The rusty, battered, second-hand plane wouldn't go. The Gresham auxiliary tanks wouldn't work. It was simply a cheap joke.

Smurch, however, after calling on a girl in Brooklyn who worked in the flap-folding department of a large paper-box factory, a girl whom he later described as his "sweet patootie," climbed nonchalantly into his ridiculous plane at dawn of the memorable seventh of July, 1937, spit a curve of tobacco juice into the still air, and took off, carrying with him only a gallon of bootleg[①] gin and six pounds of salami.

When the garage boy thundered out over the ocean the papers were forced to record, in all seriousness, that a mad, unknown young man—his name was variously misspelled—had actually set out upon a preposterous attempt to span the world in a rickety, one-engined contraption, trusting to the long-distance refueling device of a crazy schoolmaster. When, nine days later, without having stopped once, the tiny plane appeared above San Francisco Bay, headed for New York, spluttering and choking, to be sure, but still magnificently and miraculously aloft, the headlines, which long since had crowded everything else off the front page—even the shooting of the Governor of Illinois by the Vileti gang—swelled to unprecedented size, and the news stories began to run to twenty-five and thirty columns. It was noticeable, however, that the accounts of the epoch-making flight touched rather lightly upon the aviator himself. This was not because facts about the hero as a man were too meager, but because they were too complete.

Reporters, who had been rushed out to Iowa when Smurch's plane was first sighted over the little French coast town of Serly-le-Mer, to dig up the story of the great man's life, had promptly discovered that the story of his life could not be printed. His mother, a sullen short-order cook in a shack restaurant on the edge of a tourists' camping ground near Westfield, met all inquiries as to her son with an angry "Ah, the hell with him; I hope he drowns." His father appeared to be in jail somewhere for stealing spotlights and lap robes from tourists' automobiles; his young brother, a weak-minded lad, had but recently escaped from the Preston, Iowa, Reformatory[②] and was already wanted in several Western towns for the theft of money-order blanks from post offices. These alarming discoveries were still piling up at the very time that Pal Smurch, the greatest hero of the twentieth century, blear-eyed, dead for sleep, half-starved, was piloting his crazy junk-heap high above the region in which the lamentable story of his private life was being unearthed, headed for New York and a greater glory than any

---

① Produced, sold, or transported illegally.
② A penal institution for the discipline, reformation, and training of young or first offenders.

man of his time had ever known.

The necessity for printing some account in the papers of the young man's career and personality had led to a remarkable predicament. It was of course impossible to reveal the facts, for a tremendous popular feeling in favor of the young hero had sprung up, like a grass fire, when he was halfway across Europe on his flight around the globe. He was, therefore, described as a modest chap, taciturn, blond, popular with his friends, popular with girls. The only available snapshot of Smurch, taken at the wheels of a phony automobile in a cheap photo studio at an amusement park, was touched up so that the little vulgarian looked quite handsome. His twisted leer① was smoothed into a pleasant smile. The truth was, in this way, kept from the youth's ecstatic compatriots; they did not dream that the Smurch family was despised and feared by its neighbors in the obscure Iowa town, nor that the hero himself, because of numerous unsavory exploits, had come to be regarded in Westfield as a nuisance and a menace. He had, the reporters discovered, once knifed the principal of his high school—not mortally, to be sure, but he had knifed him; and on another occasion, surprised in the act of stealing an altar-cloth from a church, he had bashed the sacristan② over the head with a pot of Easter lilies; for each of these offences he had served a sentence in the reformatory.

Inwardly, the authorities, both in New York and in Washington, prayed that an understanding Providence might, however awful such a thing seemed, bring disaster to the rusty, battered plane and its illustrious pilot, whose unheard-of flight had aroused the civilized world to hosannas③ of hysterical praise. The authorities were convinced that the character of the renowned aviator was such that the limelight of adulation was bound to reveal him to all the world as a congenital hooligan mentally and morally unequipped to cope with his own prodigious fame. "I trust," said the Secretary of State, at one of many secret Cabinet meetings called to consider the national dilemma, "I trust that his mother's prayer will be answered," by which he referred to Mrs. Emma Smurch's wish that her son might be drowned. It was, however, too late for that—Smurch had leaped the Atlantic and then the Pacific as if they were millponds. At three minutes after two o'clock on the afternoon of July 17, 1937, the garage boy brought his idiotic plane into Roosevelt Field for a perfect three-point landing.

It had, of course, been out of the question to arrange a modest little reception for the greatest flier in the history of the world. He was received at Roosevelt Field with such elaborate and pretentious ceremonies as rocked the world. Fortunately, however, the worn and spent hero promptly swooned④, had to be removed bodily from his plane, and was spirited from the field without having opened his mouth once. Thus he did not jeopardize the dignity of this first recep-

---

① A desirous, sly, or knowing look.
② Person in charge of the ceremonial equipment in a church.
③ A shout of fervent and worshipful praise, often used to express praise or adoration to God.
④ Fainted.

Unit Five Tone and Style
Chapter 9 The Greatest Man in the World

tion, a reception illumined by the presence of the Secretaries of War and the Navy, Mayor Michael J. Moriarity of New York, the Premier of Canada, governors Fanniman, Groves, McFeely, and Critchfield, and a brilliant array of European diplomats. Smurch did not, in fact, come to in time to take part in the gigantic hullabaloo arranged at City Hall for the next day. He was rushed to a secluded nursing home and confined to bed. It was nine days before he was able to get up, or to be more exact, before he was permitted to get up. Meanwhile the greatest minds in the country, in solemn assembly, had arranged a secret conference of city, state, and government officials, which Smurch was to attend for the purpose of being instructed in the ethics and behavior of heroism.

On the day that the little mechanic was finally allowed to get up and dress and, for the first time in two weeks, took a great chew of tobacco, he was permitted to receive the newspapermen—this by way of testing him out. Smurch did not wait for questions. "Youse guys," he said—and the *Times* man winced—"youse guys can tell the cock-eyed world dat I put it over on Lindbergh, see? Yeh—an' made an ass o' them two frogs." The "two frogs" was a reference to a pair of gallant French fliers who, in attempting a flight only halfway round the world, had, two weeks before, unhappily been lost at sea. The *Times* man was bold enough, at this point to sketch out for Smurch the accepted formula for interviews in cases of this kind; he explained that there should be no arrogant statements belittling the achievements of other heroes, particularly heroes of foreign nations. "Ah, the hell with that," said Smurch. "I did it, see? I did it, an' I'm talkin' about it." And he did talk about it.

None of this extraordinary interview was, of course, printed. On the contrary, the newspapers, already under the disciplined direction of a secret directorate created for the occasion and composed of statesmen and editors, gave out to a panting and restless world that "Jacky," as he had been arbitrarily nicknamed, would consent to say only that he was very happy and that anyone could have done what he did. "My achievement has been, I fear, slightly exaggerated," the *Times* man's article had him protest, with a modest smile. These newspaper stories were kept from the hero, a restriction which did not serve to abate the rising malevolence of his temper. The situation was, indeed, extremely grave, for Pal Smurch was, as he kept insisting, "rarin' to go." He could not much longer be kept from a nation clamorous to lionize him. It was the most desperate crisis the United States of America had faced since the sinking of the *Lusitania*[①].

On the afternoon of the twenty-seventh of July, Smurch was spirited away to a conference-room in which were gathered mayors, governors, government officials, behaviorist psychologists, and editors. He gave them each a limp, moist paw and a brief unlovely grin. "Hah ya?" he said. When Smurch was seated, the Mayor of New York arose and, with obvious pessimism, attempted to explain what he must say and how he must act when presented to the world, ending his talk with a high tribute to the hero's courage and integrity. The Mayor was followed by Gov-

---

① British luxury liner that was bombed by a German submarine on May 7, 1915. Of the 1,195 people who died, 128 were Americans.

ernor Fanniman of New York, who after a touching declaration of faith, introduced Cameron Spottiswood, Second Secretary of the American Embassy in Paris, the gentleman selected to coach Smurch in the amenities① of public ceremonies. Sitting in a chair, with a soiled yellow tie in his hand and his shirt open at the throat, unshaved, smoking a rolled cigarette, Jack Smurch listened with a leer on his lips. "I get ya, I get ya," he cut in, nastily. "Ya want me to ack like a softy, huh? Ya want me to ack like that—baby-faced Lindbergh, huh? Well, nuts to that, see?" Everyone took in his breath sharply; it was a sigh and a hiss. "Mr. Lindbergh," began a United States Senator, purple with rage, "and Mr. Byrd—" Smurch, who was paring his nails with a jackknife, cut in again. "Byrd!" he exclaimed. "Aw fa God's sake, dat big—" Somebody shut off his blasphemies with a sharp word. A newcomer had entered the room. Everyone stood up, except Smurch, who, still busy with his nails, did not even glance up. "Mr. Smurch," said someone sternly, "the President of the United States!" It had been thought that the presence of the Chief Executive might have a chastening effect upon the young hero, and the former had been, thanks to the remarkable cooperation of the press, secretly brought to the obscure conference-room.

A great, painful silence fell. Smurch looked up, waved a hand at the President. "How ya comin'?" he asked, and began rolling a fresh cigarette. The silence deepened. Someone coughed in a strained way. "Geez, it's hot, ain't it?" said Smurch. He loosened two more shirt buttons, revealing a hairy chest and the tattooed word "Sadie" enclosed in a stenciled heart. The great and important men in the room, faced by the most serious crisis in recent American history, exchanged worried frowns. Nobody seemed to know how to proceed. "Come awn, come awn," said Smurch. "Let's get the hell out here! When do I start cuttin' in on de parties, huh? And what's they goin' to be *in* it?" he rubbed a thumb and forefinger together meaningly. "Money!" exclaimed a state senator, shocked, pale. "Yeh, money," said Pal, flipping his cigarette out of a window. "An' big money." He began rolling a fresh cigarette. "Big money," he repeated, frowning over the rice paper. He titled back in his chair, and leered at each gentleman, separately, the leer of an animal that knows its power, the leer of a leopard loose in a bird-and-god shop. "Aw fa God's sake, let's get some place where it's cooler," he said. "I have cooped up plenty for three weeks!"

Smurch stood up and walked over to an open window, where he stood staring down into the street, nine floors below. The faint shouting of newsboys floated up to him. He made out his name. "Hot dog!" he cried, grinning, ecstatic. He leaned out over the sill. "You tell 'em, babies!" he shouted down. "Hot diggity dog!" In the tense little knot of men standing behind him, a quick, mad impulse flared up. An unspoken word of appeal, of command, seemed to ring through the room. Yet it was deadly silent. Charles K. L. Brand, secretary to the Mayor of New York City, happened to be standing nearest Smurch; he looked inquiringly at the President of the

---

① Social courtesies; pleasantries.

Unit Five　Tone and Style
Chapter 9　The Greatest Man in the World

United States. The President, pale, grim, nodded shortly. Brand, a tall, powerfully built man, once a tackle① at Rutgers, stepped forward, seized the greatest man in the world by his left shoulder and the seat of his pants, and pushed him out the window.

"My God, he's fallen out the window!" cried a quick-witted editor.

"Get me out of here!" cried the President. Several men sprang to his side and he was hurriedly escorted out of a door toward a side-entrance of the building. The editor of the Associated Press took charge, being used to such things. Crisply he ordered certain men to leave, others to stay; quickly he outlined a story which all the papers were to agree on, sent two men to the street to handle that end of the tragedy, commanded a Senator to sob and two Congressmen to go to pieces nervously. In a word, he skillfully set the stage for the gigantic task that was to follow, the task of breaking to a grief-stricken world the sad story of the untimely, accidental death of its most illustrious and spectacular figure.

The funeral was, as you know, the most elaborate, the finest, the solemnest, and the saddest ever held in the United States of America. The monument in Arlington Cemetery②, with its clean white shaft of marble and the simple device of a tiny plane carved on its base, is a place for pilgrims, in deep reverence, to visit. The nations of the world paid lofty tributes to little Jacky Smurch, America's greatest hero. At a given hour there were two minutes of silence throughout the nation. Even the inhabitants of the small, bewildered town of Westfield, Iowa, observed this touching ceremony; agents of the Department of Justice saw to that. One of them was especially assigned to stand grimly in the doorway of a little shack restaurant on the edge of the tourists' camping ground just outside the town. There, under his stern scrutiny, Mrs. Emma Smurch bowed her head above two hamburger steaks sizzling on her grill—bowed her head and turned away, so that the Secret Service man could not see the twisted, strangely familiar, leer on her lips.

Film Comment:

James Thurber's *The Greatest Man in the World*: 51 minutes, color
Starring: Brad Davis & Carol Kane
Screenplay by: Jeff Wanshel
Directed by: Ralph Rosenblum

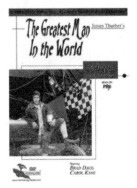

Only the off-beat humor of writing great, James Thurber could bring to life a "hero" like Jack Smurch, played by Brad Davis ("Midnight Express"). Fortified with only a gallon of gin and a salami, Smurch bests even Lindberg with the first non-stop, around the world flight. During the four days he's airborne, this unknown kid becomes a

---

① Either of the two line players on a team positioned between the guard and the end.
② Located in northern Virginia across the Potomac River from Washington, D.C.; it is the place where American war dead and other notables, including William Howard Taft and John F. Kennedy, are buried.

world hero. But, on the ground a young reporter, anxious to tell the world about their new idol, learns Smurch is bad news. An arrogant, illiterate lout with a police record, Smurch's only interests are "parties, broads and dough." But, the reporter is silenced and Smurch is locked up until the press and politicos can make him into their kind of American hero at any cost.

Film Scenes:

Scene 1: the flight
Scene 2: Jack's life
Scene 3: the lies
Scene 4: the cover up
Scene 5: the assassination

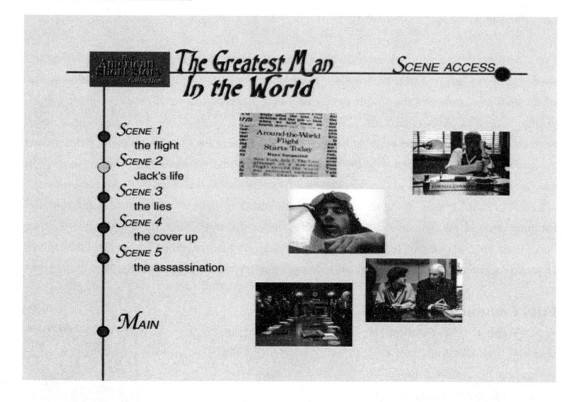

Script Excerpts:

Newspaper headline:

Governor of Illinois Shot by
Member of Vileti Gang
Gunman Escapes

The pages of the newspaper turn. Camera pans along the newsprint down to the bottom of a page and zooms in on a tiny article:

Unit Five Tone and Style
Chapter 9 The Greatest Man in the World

Around-the-World Flight Starts Today

Hoax Suspected

New York, July 7. The first attempt at a nonstop flight around the world was announced yesterday by Dr. Charles Lewis Gresham of the College of New Hampshire. An ex-mechanic from Iowa, Mr. Jack Smurch, will pilot. Aviation experts say the plane will not fly. "It's a hoax—or should be. The technology for such a flight simply does not exist at this time," a spokesman for the aviation industry...

Camera lingers long enough for the headline to be read, and the article begun; then a pen circles the article in red ink.

Slow dissolve.

Credits over:

Exterior. Country road. Day.

A windy July day, 1937. A sporty black coupe driving through fields. Inside, Ames Herbert (spiffily dressed, late forties or early fifties, medium to stocky build), whistling tunelessly. His point of view: fields passing, cows, a tractor, a diner. Suddenly a car, rushing up from behind, overtakes, passes, and cuts him off; veering to avoid it, Herbert piles into the ditch. He pauses expressionlessly while the dust settles. Herbert pulls back onto the road and resumes driving. He is no longer whistling. Up ahead, at a crossroads, the car which overtook him is idling by the roadside. As Herbert approaches, the other driver, Raymond Smidgeon (early twenties, thin to medium build), sticks his hand out the window and urgently waves him down. Herbert slows, stops, and rolls down his window to regard Smidgeon, who has a crumpled map in one hand.

Smidgeon: Where's Dismal Lane?

Herbert: In a hurry?

Smidgeon: I'm a reporter, mister—hot on the trail of a story—a *big* story. Where's Dismal Lane?

Herbert: What paper do you work for?

Smidgeon (*knowing it to be impressive*): Journal-Herald.

Herbert: The *Journal-Herald*? A continuing insult, the promiscuous breeding-ground of distortion and lies. If you work for the *Journal-Herald*—I never heard of Dismal Lane.

Smidgeon: We'll see, wise guy—

Smidgeon exits from his car, slams the door, and approaches Herbert menacingly. Herbert guns his motor and makes off, showering Smidgeon with dust.

Smidgeon (*continues, choking and spluttering*): Hey—come back here!

Exterior. Cowfield. Day.

Herbert's car, bouncing as it crosses dirt ruts. Herbert, looking through the window. His POV: a small, mad-looking plane; a mad-looking man, shouting and pointing at it; LOCALS, sitting nearby, watching. The car stops a good distance clear; Herbert exits, closes the door, and starts for the plane. The car driven by Smidgeon hurtles across the field, bouncing exaggeratedly, and stops by Herbert.

Smidgeon: Hey—you!

Herbert continues walking unhurriedly toward the plane. Smidgeon exits from the car, slams the door, and catches up to Herbert rapidly. They continue to move throughout the following dialogue.

Smidgeon (*continues*): I owe you a poke in the nose, buddy. What're you doing here?
Herbert: Press.
Smidgeon (*somewhat taken aback, then dubious*): What paper?
Herbert: *Journal-Herald*.
Smidgeon: You're Ames Herbert? Why didn't you say so?
Herbert: Did you ask?
Smidgeon: I'm Ray Smidgeon. It's my first assignment—I'm to tag along, and—
Herbert: I was forewarned.
Smidgeon: Sorry about—
Herbert: Forewarned is forearmed, Mr. Smidgeon.
Smidgeon: Do you really feel that way about the *Journal-Herald*?
Herbert: You can't interview me, Mr. Smidgeon; I never talk to the press.

By now, they're next to the plane. A number of awkward-looking "tanks" trail from the fuselage. By the plane are Dr. Charles Lewis Gresham (mad professor, mid-fifties) and Jack Smurch (undersized, insolent, early twenties). Gresham, having a fit, gesticulates wildly; Smurch, chewing tobacco, works on the plane with a wrench.

Interior. Westfield, Iowa, restaurant. Day.

Herbert and Smidgeon enter and sit at the counter. Behind it rests a small, plain woman who looks sixty but is probably no more than forty-five. She regards them silently.

Smidgeon: Two coffees, please.
Herbert: No dust in mine.

After a pause, the woman gets up, goes to a pot on a stove, and pours.

Smidgeon: Say—we're looking for somebody who's supposed to live here—Mrs. Emma Smurch.
The Woman: You the law?
Herbert: No—
The Woman: Bill collector?
Smidgeon: No, ma'am.
The Woman: You found her—

The woman slams the two cups down on the counter, onto which coffee liberally sloshes.

Unit Five Tone and Style
Chapter 9 The Greatest Man in the World

Smidgeon: *You're* Emma Smurch?

Emma Smurch: Ain't I just said so?

Smidgeon: Mrs. Smurch—we've come all the way from New York—because your son Jack is going to fly around the world—without stopping—

Emma Smurch: Nothing you could say about Jack Smurch could interest me.

Herbert: Is Jack's father around?

Emma Smurch: He don't live here no more.

Herbert: Know where we might find him?

Emma Smurch: Number two six five Main Street, Preston. If you see him you tell him I said—he got what he had coming.

Emma Smurch favors us with a twisted leer.

Smidgeon: Mrs. Smurch—did Jack have any childhood toys he cherished—a sled, or something?

Emma Smurch: He had a motorcycle when he was thirteen—

Smidgeon: Would that still be around somewhere?

Emma Smurch: He drove it through a drugstore window drunk—didn't stick around to see how bad was the damage.

Herbert: Do you have any childhood pictures of Jack?

Emma Smurch rummages in a dusty cabinet and pulls out a photograph, which she hands to Smidgeon.

Cut to:

Insert: cheap studio photo of young Smurch in a phony automobile at an amusement park, leering.

Cut back to:

Interior. Restaurant.

Emma Smurch: That's the only one.

Smidgeon: We'll give it right back—

Emma Smurch: You can keep it.

Herbert: Mrs. Smurch—as a mother—how does it feel to know that your boy may pass away any time in the next few days—may in fact already be dead?

Emma Smurch: To hell with him—I hope he drowns.

Reaction Shot: Smidgeon.

Interior. Government building. Conference hall.

Assembled dignitaries—governors, mayors, diplomats, officials—sitting in an unconvivial manner, hot, solemn, tight-lipped.

Interior. Government building.

Smurch walking flunked by guards and preceded by Charles K. L. Brand. Ominous Music.

Smurch (*referring to Brand*): Who's the big deadhead?

Guard: That's Mr. Charles K. L. Brand, aide to Secretary Codd—your personal bodyguard. Mr. Brand was an All-American tackle at Rutgers.

Smurch: You must have been a tough guy, huh? Before you got flabby—and they stuffed you in that suit. Should have stayed like you were, Brand—a helmet would have kept your face hid.

Interior. Conference hall.

The entourage enters. Standing ovation. Smurch does not acknowledge. All sit except Brand. On the dais with Smurch, Codd, and officials.

Codd: Mr. Smurch, although we're aware that you're still suffering aftereffects from your flight—

Smurch rolls his eyes, shakes his head wearily, sighs, and leans on one elbow.

Codd (*continues*): —we have put together a schedule of appearances for you, with the cooperation of, among others, Governor Fanniman of New York...

Governor Fanniman of New York stands and shakes the hand of Smurch. Smurch does not get up.

Smurch: How are ya?

Codd: ...and Lord Snowcourt, British Ambassador.

Lord Snowcourt, British ambassador, stands and shakes the hand of Smurch. Smurch does not get up.

Smurch: How are ya?

Codd: To begin with, next Sunday, at Arlington Cemetery, you will place a wreath on the Tomb of the Unknown Soldier. On that solemn occasion—wearing a custom-tailored suit—you will deliver an address written for you by Mr. Cameron Spottiswood of the American Embassy in Paris, who has generously offered to assist as vocal coach. Then, on Tuesday, you will address the Veterans Association—

Smurch: I get ya, I get ya. Ya want me to act like that baby-face Lindbergh. Well nuts to that, see? I ain't putting pansies on nobody's tomb, I ain't slobbering over no veterans, and I ain't gonna kiss nobody on the cheek. Sure I want out—to get what I got coming to me. When do the parties start? (*Pumping his fist.*) Where's the broads? (Rubbing thumb and forefinger *together.*) Where's the dough? When you tell me that—then we got something to talk about.

Murmuring, shifting back and forth of seats. Reaction Shots to this and the following may include:

(1) Diplomat: Prince-nez falling from eye

(2) Line of senators mopping their brows in unison

(3) Elderly senator: his eyes roll back—he slides from his chair

(4) General: Unpinning medal from chest—regarding it—dropping it to floor

Unit Five Tone and Style
Chapter 9 The Greatest Man in the World

(5) AD LIB.

Smurch takes out his jackknife and begins paring his nails. Codd nods. Brand opens a door. Enter the President of the United States, late fifties or early sixties, clean cut.

Codd: Gentlemen—the President of the United Sates.

All stand except Smurch, who continues paring his nails.

Codd (*continues*): Mr. Smurch—*the President of the United States*!

Smurch does not stand. He waves at the Chief Executive.

Smurch: How ya doing, bigshot?

Reaction Shots: the president. **Camera pans** among the officials for **Reaction Shots**.

Smurch: Jeez, it's hot, ain't it?

Smurch undoes two buttons on his shirt until it hangs open loosely, and scratches his chest. **Camera zooms** in for **Extreme close-up** of the Smurch breastbone, upon which is tattooed the word "SADIE" enclosed in a heart.

Reaction Shots. Camera pans among the assembly—some of them similarly scratching—all of whose jaws scrape their chests.

Smurch: Come on, come on—let's get the hell out of here—it's stifling—

Smurch gets up and walks toward an open window. Brand is in his path.

Smurch (*continues*): Out of my way—I want some fresh air—*move*, ya big palooka—

Brand moves. Smurch goes to the window and looks out. Brand follows and stands behind him. Ominous Music.

Smurch POV Shot: The street, deserted except for scattered pedestrians and a teen-aged newsboy.

Exterior. Street.

Newsboy: Pro-Smurch parade today on Fifth Avenue!

Camera pans all the way up the building to the window and zooms in on Smurch for a **Reaction Shot**.

Interior. Conference Hall.

Smurch (*to the room*): Hear that? "Smurch!"

Smurch moves away from the window and begins to pace agitatedly.

Smurch (*continues*): Listen—think I'm gonna stick around to learn my p's and q's and how to hold my fork? In a pig's eye—to hell with that and to hell with you! I'm gonna shove off and clear out of here—I busted out once—I can do it again.

Codd (*to the President*): He may have a point, you know—he escaped from reform school six times.

Reaction Shots. Much gripping of armchairs and clenching of knuckles.

Smurch returns to the window.

Exterior. Street.

Newsboy: Japan and Russia invite Smurch to visit—read all about it!

Interior. Conference Hall.

Smurch: Hot dog! I'm on my way, babies!

Reaction Shots. Much balling of fists and mangling of ties.

Exterior. Street.

Newsboy: Pro-Smurch parade expected to draw huge crowd!

Interior. Conference Hall.

Smurch: Hot diggity dog! (*To Brand.*) Don't crowd me—don't crowd me, ya dumb cluck! (*To newsboy.*) Here I am—up here—rairin' to go!

Ominous Music: Punch.

Reaction Shot: Boiling point. **Camera cuts** rapidly among tight-lipped, livid faces.

Brand fires a glance at Secretary Codd. Codd looks at the President. Infinitesimally, in **Extreme Close-up**, the President nods. Codd nods toward Brand.

Brand lifts Smurch bodily and throws him out the window.

Exterior. Air.

Slow motion: Fall of Jack Smurch.

Interior. Conference Hall.

Codd: My God—he's fallen out the window!

The President exits rapidly.

Discussion Questions:

1. What makes Pal Smurch a national hero, the greatest man in the world?
2. What are the differences between Smurch and the other flying heroes, such as Byrd and Lindbergh?
3. How is Smurch's story different from the reports of newspapers? What are the relations between media and politics?
4. Why cannot Smurch live in this world? What can we learn from his death?
5. What do you think of Mrs. Smurch? Did she finally realize something about her son's death?

Further Reading and Watching:

The Secret Life of Walter Mitty

Chapter 10

Barn Burning

William Faulkner

Author Introduction:

William Faulkner (1897—1962) was born in New Albany, but soon moved to Oxford, Mississippi. He attended the University of Mississippi in Oxford before and after his service in the Royal Canadian Air Force in the First World War. Thereafter he lived in Oxford most of his life, though he had to write Hollywood scripts and teach at the University of Virginia to support himself. It was in New Orleans that his literary career began, and there he became acquainted with various members of the literary community, most notably Sherwood Anderson, who encouraged him to turn from poetry to fiction and helped him get  his first novel published. Beginning with *Sartoris* (1929), most of his novels and short stories were set in the fictional Yoknapatawpha County, which was based on, and nearly geographically identical to, Lafayette County, of which his hometown Oxford is the county seat. Faulkner traced the fortunes of several families in this fictional county, including the aristocratic Compsons and Sartorises and the white-trash, dollar-grabbing Snopeses, from the civil war to modern times. Faulkner made frequent use of "stream of consciousness" in his writing, whose influence on the fellow Southern writers has been profound, and in 1949 he was awarded the Nobel Prize for literature. His major novels include *The Sound and the Fury* (1929), *As I Lay Dying* (1930), *Sanctuary* (1931), *Light in August* (1932), *Absalom, Absalom!* (1936), *The Wild Palms* (1939), and *The Hamlet* (1940). His books of short stories include *These Thirteen* (1931), *Go Down, Moses* (1942), and *Collected Stories of William Faulkner* (1950).

Story Summary:

Abner Snopes, a proud, poor Southern tenant farmer in the late 19th century believes his employer has treated him unfairly. Abner will get revenge by burning his employer's barn. Abner's son, Sarty, wants his father's acceptance and love, but is horrified by the fire. Abner senses this and lectures his son on loyalty and the value of taking justice into your own hands. The burning can't be pinned on Snopes, but he and his family are told to move on. In a new job with a rich Major de Spain, Snopes once again is offended. So he tracks dirt on his employer's rug. The Major demands $100 compensation. Sarty sees the fire beginning to rage in his father's cold eyes. Sarty agonizes. He hesitates. Then he warns the Major to look after his barn and thus betrays his father.

Key Terms:
Authority, Revenge, Betrayal, Loyalty, Obligation, Sharecropper, Post Civil War South

Barn Burning[①]

The store in which the justice of the Peace's court was sitting smelled of cheese. The boy, crouched on his nail keg at the back of the crowded room, knew he smelled cheese, and more: from where he sat he could see the ranked shelves close-packed with the solid, squat, dynamic shapes of tin cans whose labels his stomach read, not from the lettering which meant nothing to his mind but from the scarlet devils and the silver curve of fish—this, the cheese which he knew he smelled and the hermetic meat[②] which his intestines believed he smelled coming in intermittent gusts momentary and brief between the other constant one, the smell and sense just a little of fear because mostly of despair and grief, the old fierce pull of blood. He could not see the table where the Justice sat and before which his father and his father's enemy (*our enemy* he thought in that despair; *ourn! mine and hisn both! He's my father!*) stood, but he could hear them, the two of them that is, because his father had said no word yet:

"But what proof have you, Mr. Harris?"

"I told you. The hog got into my corn. I caught it up and sent it back to him. He had no fence that would hold it. I told him so, warned him. The next time I put the hog in my pen.[③] When he came to get it I gave him enough wire to patch up his pen. The next time I put the hog up and kept it. I rode down to his house and saw the wire I gave him still rolled on to the spool in his yard. I told him he could have the hog when he paid me a dollar pound fee. That evening a nigger came with the dollar and got the hog. He was a strange nigger. He said, 'He say to tell you wood and hay kin burn.' I said, 'What?' 'That whut he say to tell you,' the nigger said. 'Wood and hay kin burn.' That night my barn burned. I got the stock out but I lost the barn."

"Where is the nigger? Have you got him?"

---

① First published in *Harper's Magazine* in 1939, later collected in Faulkner's *Collected Stories of William Faulkner* (1950) and reprinted in *Selected Short Stories* (1961).
② Canned meat.
③ A fenced enclosure for animals.

Unit Five Tone and Style
Chapter 10 Barn Burning

"He was a strange nigger, I tell you. I don't know what became of him."

"But that's not proof. Don't you see that's not proof?"

"Get that boy up here. He knows." For a moment the boy thought too that the man meant his older brother until Harris said, "Not him. The little one. The boy." and, crouching, small for his age, small and wiry like his father, in patched and faded jeans even too small for him, with straight, uncombed, brown hair and eyes gray and wild as storm scud, he saw the men between himself and the table part and become a lane of grim faces, at the end of which he saw the justice, a shabby, collarless, graying man in spectacles, beckoning him, he felt no floor under his bare feet; he seemed to walk beneath the palpable weight of the grim turning faces. His father, stiff in his black Sunday coat donned not for the trial but for the moving, did not even look at him. *He aims for me to lie*, he thought, again with that frantic grief and despair. *And I will have to do hit.*

"What's your name, boy?" the Justice said.

"Colonel Sartoris Snopes,"[①] the boy whispered.

"Hey?" the Justice said. "Talk louder. Colonel Sartoris? I reckon anybody named for Colonel Sartoris in this country can't help but tell the truth, can they?" The boy said nothing. *Enemy! Enemy!* he thought; for a moment he could not even see, could not see that the justice's face was kindly nor discern that his voice was troubled when he spoke to the man named Harris: "Do you want me to question this boy?" But he could hear, and during those subsequent long seconds while there was absolutely no sound in the crowded little room save that of quiet and intent breathing it was as if he had swung outward at the end of a grape vine, over a ravine, and at the top of the swing had been caught in a prolonged instant of mesmerized gravity, weightless in time.

"No!" Harris said violently, explosively. "Damnation! Send him out of here!" Now time, the fluid world, rushed beneath him again, the voices coming to him again through the smell of cheese and sealed meat, the fear and despair and the old grief of blood:

"This case is closed. I can't find against you, Snopes, but I can give you advice. Leave this county and don't come back to it."

His father spoke for the first time, his voice cold and harsh, level, without emphasis: "I aim to. I don't figure to stay in a country among people who..." he said something unprintable and vile, addressed to no one.

"That'll do," the justice said. "Take your wagon and get out of this county before dark. Case dismissed."

His father turned, and he followed the stiff black coat, the wiry figure walking a little stiffly from where a Confederate provost's man's[②] musket ball had taken him in the heel on a stolen

---

① The Snopes family figures in many Faulkner stories and novels; Colonel Sartoris is a major personage among Faulkner's fictional inhabitants of Yoknapatawpha County.

② Military policeman.

horse thirty years ago, followed the two backs now, since his older brother had appeared from somewhere in the crowd, no taller than the father but thicker, chewing tobacco steadily, between the two lines of grim-faced men and out of the store and across the worn gallery and down the sagging steps and among the dogs and half-grown boys in the mild May dust, where as he passed a voice hissed:

"Barn burner!"

Again he could not see, whirling; there was a face in a red haze, moonlike, bigger than the full moon, the owner of it half again his size, he leaping in the red haze toward the face, feeling no blow, feeling no shock when his head struck the earth, scrabbling up and leaping again, feeling no blow this time either and tasting no blood, scrabbling up to see the other boy in full flight and himself already leaping into pursuit as his father's hand jerked him back, the harsh, cold voice speaking above him: "Go get in the wagon."

It stood in a grove of locusts and mulberries across the road. His two hulking sisters in their Sunday dresses and his mother and her sister in calico and sunbonnets were already in it, sitting on and among the sorry residue① of the dozen and more movings which even the boy could remember—the battered stove, the broken beds and chairs, the clock inlaid with mother-of-pearl, which would not run, stopped at some fourteen minutes past two o'clock of a dead and forgotten day and time, which had been his mother's dowry. She was crying, though when she saw him she drew her sleeve across her face and began to descend from the wagon. "Get back," the father said.

"He's hurt. I got to get some water and wash his..."

"Get back in the wagon," his father said, he got in too, over the tail-gate. His father mounted to the seat where the older brother already sat and struck the gaunt mules two savage blows with the peeled willow, but without heat. It was not even sadistic; it was exactly that same quality which in later years would cause his descendants to over-run the engine before putting a motor car into motion, striking and reining back in the same movement. The wagon went on, the store with its quiet crowd of grimly watching men dropped behind; a curve in the road hid it. *Forever* he thought. *Maybe he's done satisfied now, now that he has* ... stopping himself, not to say it aloud even to himself. His mother's hand touched his shoulder.

"Does hit hurt?" she said.

"Naw," he said. "Hit don't hurt. Lemme be."

"Can't you wipe some of the blood off before hit dries?"

"I'll wash to-night," he said. "Lemme be, I tell you."

The wagon went on. He did not know where they were going. None of them ever did or ever asked, because it was always somewhere, always a house of sorts waiting for them a day or two days or even three days away. Likely, his father had already arranged to make a crop on

---

① The remainder of estate.

Unit Five Tone and Style
Chapter 10 Barn Burning

another farm before he... Again he had to stop himself. He (the father) always did. There was something about his wolflike independence and even courage, when the advantage was at least neutral, which impressed strangers, as if they got from his latent ravening① ferocity not so much a sense of dependability as a feeling that his ferocious conviction in the rightness of his own actions would be of advantage to all whose interest lay with his.

That night they camped, in a grove of oaks and beeches where a spring ran. The nights were still cool and they had a fire against it, of a rail lifted from a nearby fence and cut into lengths—a small fire, neat, niggard② almost, a shrewd fire; such fires were his father's habit and custom always, even in freezing weather. Older, the boy might have remarked this and wondered why not a big one; why should not a man who had not only seen the waste and extravagance of war, but who had in his blood an inherent voracious prodigality with material not his own, have burned everything in sight? Then he might have gone a step farther and thought that that was the reason: that niggard blaze was the living fruit of nights passed during those four years in the woods hiding from all men, blue or gray③, with his strings of horses (captured horses, he called them). And older still, he might have divined the true reason: that the element of fire spoke to some deep mainspring of his father's being, as the element of steel or of powder spoke to other men, as the one weapon for the preservation of integrity, else breath were not worth the breathing, and hence to be regarded with respect and used with discretion.

But, he did not think this now and he had seen those same niggard blazes all his life. He merely ate his supper beside it and was already half asleep over his iron plate when his father called him, and once more he followed the stiff back, the stiff and ruthless limp, up the slope and on to the starlit road where, turning, he could see his father against the stars but without face or depth—a shape black, flat, and bloodless as though cut from tin in the iron folds of the frockcoat which had not been made for him, the voice harsh like tin and without heat like tin:

"You were fixing to tell them. You would have told him." He didn't answer. His father struck him with the flat of his hand on the side of the head, hard but without heat, exactly as he had struck the two mules at the store, exactly as he would strike either of them with any stick in order to kill a horse fly, his voice still without heat or anger: "You're getting to be a man. You got to learn. You got to learn to stick to your own blood or you ain't going to have any blood to stick to you. Do you think either of them, any man there this morning, would? Don't you know all they wanted was a chance to get at me because they knew I had them beat? Eh?" Later, twenty years later, he was to tell himself, "If I had said they wanted only truth, justice, he would have hit me again." But now he said nothing. He was not crying. He just stood there. "Answer me," his father said.

"Yes," he whispered. His father turned.

---

① Greedily predacious; voracious or rapacious.
② Thrifty.
③ The color of Union and Confederate Civil War (1861—1865) uniforms, respectively.

"Get on to bed. We'll be there tomorrow."

Tomorrow they were there. In the early afternoon the wagon stopped before a paintless two-room house identical almost with the dozen others it had stopped before even in the boy's ten years, and again, as on the other dozen occasions, his mother and aunt got down and began to unload the wagon, although his two sisters and his father and brother had not moved.

"Likely hit ain't fitten for hawgs," one of the sisters said.

"Nevertheless, fit it will and you'll hog it and like it," his father said. "Get out of them chairs and help your Ma unload."

The two sisters got down, big, bovine, in a flutter of cheap ribbons; one of them drew from the jumbled wagon bed a battered lantern, the other a worn broom. His father handed the reins to the older son and began to climb stiffly over the wheel. "When they get unloaded, take the team to the barn and feed them." Then he said, and at first, the boy thought he was still speaking to his brother: "Come with me."

"Me?" he said.

"Yes," his father said. "You."

"Abner," his mother said. His father paused and looked back—the harsh level state beneath the shaggy, graying, irascible brows.

"I reckon I'll have a word with the man that aims to begin tomorrow owning me body and soul for the next eight months."

They went back up the road. A week ago—or before last night, that is—he would have asked where they were going, but not now. His father had struck him before last night but never before had he paused afterward to explain why, it was as if the blow and the following calm, outrageous voice still rang, repercussed, divulging nothing to him save the terrible handicap of being young, the light weight of his few years, just heavy enough to prevent his soaring free of the world as it seemed to be ordered but not heavy enough to keep him footed solid in it, to resist it and try to change the course of its events.

Presently he could see the grove of oaks and cedars and the other flowering trees and shrubs where the house would be, though not the house yet. They walked beside a fence massed with honeysuckle and Cherokee roses[①] and came to a gate swinging open between two brick pillars, and now, beyond a sweep of drive, he saw the house for the first time and at that instant he forgot his father and the terror and despair both, and even when he remembered his father again (who had not stopped) the terror and despair did not return. Because, for all the twelve movings, they had sojourned[②] until now in a poor country, a land of small farms and fields and houses, and he had never seen a house like this before. *Hit's big as a courthouse* he thought quietly, with a surge of peace and joy whose reason he could not have thought into words, being too young for

---

① A prickly, climbing, evergreen rose, native to China and naturalized in the southeast United States, having showy, white, fragrant flowers.

② To reside temporarily.

Unit Five   Tone and Style
Chapter 10   Barn Burning

that: *They are safe from him. People whose lives are a part of this peace and dignity are beyond his touch, he no more to them than a buzzing wasp: capable of stinging for a little moment but that's all; the spell of this peace and dignity rendering even the barns and stable and cribs which belong to it impervious to the puny flames he might contrive* ... this, the peace and joy, ebbing for an instant as he looked again at the stiff black back, the stiff and implacable limp of the figure which was not dwarfed by the house, for the reason that it had never looked big anywhere and which now, against the serene columned backdrop, had more than ever that impervious quality of something cut ruthlessly from tin, depthless, as though, sidewise to the sun, it would cast no shadow. Watching him, the boy remarked the absolutely undeviating course which his father held and saw the stiff foot come squarely down in a pile of fresh droppings① where a horse had stood in the drive and which his father could have avoided by a simple change of stride. But it ebbed only for a moment, though he could not have thought this into words either, walking on in the spell of the house, which he could ever want but without envy, without sorrow, certainly never with that ravening and jealous rage which unknown to him walked in the ironlike black coat before him: *Maybe he will feel it too, Maybe it will even change him now from what maybe he couldn't help but be.*

They crossed the portico. Now he could hear his father's stiff foot as it came down on the boards with clocklike finality, a sound out of all proportion to the displacement of the body it bore and which was not dwarfed either by the white door before it, as though it had attained to a sort of vicious and ravening minimum not to be dwarfed by anything—the flat, wide, black hat, the formal coat of broadcloth which had once been black but which had now that friction-glazed greenish cast of the bodies of old house flies, the lifted sleeve which was too large, the lifted hand like a curled claw. The door opened so promptly that the boy knew the Negro must have been watching them all the time, an old man with neat grizzled hair, in a linen jacket, who stood barring the door with his body, saying, "Wipe yo foots, white man, fo you come in here, Major ain't home nohow."

"Get out of my way, nigger," his father said, without heat too, flinging the door back and the Negro also and entering, his hat still on his head. And now the boy saw the prints of the stiff foot on the doorjamb and saw them appear on the pale rug behind the machinelike deliberation of the foot which seemed to bear (or transmit) twice the weight which the body compassed. The Negro was shouting "Miss Lula! Miss Lula!" somewhere behind them, then the boy, deluged as though by a warm wave by a suave turn of carpeted stair and a pendant glitter of chandeliers② and a mute gleam of gold frames, heard the swift feet and saw her too, a lady—perhaps he had never seen her like before either—in a gray, smooth gown with lace at the throat and an apron tied at the waist and the sleeves turned back, wiping cake or biscuit dough from her hands with a towel as she came up the hall, looking not at his father at all but at the tracks on the blond rug

---

① The excrement of animals.
② A branched, decorative lighting fixture that holds a number of bulbs or candles and is suspended from a ceiling.

with an expression of incredulous amazement.

"I tried," the Negro cried. "I tole him to . . ."

"Will you please go away?" she said in a shaking voice. "Major de Spain is not at home. Will you please go away?"

His father had not spoken again. He did not speak again. He did not even look at her. He just stood stiff in the center of the rug, in his hat, the shaggy iron-gray brows twitching slightly above the pebble-colored eyes as he appeared to examine the house with brief deliberation. Then with the same deliberation he turned; the boy watched him pivot on the good leg and saw the stiff foot drag round the arc of the turning, leaving a final long and fading smear. His father never looked at it, he never once looked down at the rug. The Negro held the door. It closed behind them, upon the hysteric and indistinguishable woman-wail. His father stopped at the top of the steps and scraped his boot clean on the edge of it. At the gate he stopped again. He stood for a moment, planted stiffly on the stiff foot, looking back at the house. "Pretty and white, ain't it?" he said. "That's sweat. Nigger sweat. Maybe it ain't white enough yet to suit him. Maybe he wants to mix some white sweat with it."

Two hours later the boy was chopping wood behind the house within which his mother and aunt and the two sisters (the mother and aunt, not the two girls, he knew that; even at this distance and muffled by walls the flat loud voices of the two girls emanated an incorrigible idle inertia) were setting up the stove to prepare a meal, when he heard the hooves and saw the linen-clad man on a fine sorrel[①] mare, whom he recognized even before he saw the rolled rug in front of the Negro youth following on a fat boy carriage horse—a suffused, angry face vanishing, still at full gallop, beyond the corner of the house where his father and brother were sitting in the two tilted chairs; and a moment later, almost before he could have put the axe down, he heard the hooves again and watched the sorrel mare go back out of the yard, already galloping again. Then his father began to shout one of the sisters' names, who presently emerged backward from the kitchen door dragging the rolled rug along the ground by one end while the other sister walked behind it.

"If you ain't going to tote, go on and set up the wash pot," the first said.

"You, Sarty!" the second shouted. "Set up the wash pot!" His father appeared at the door, framed against that shabbiness, as he had been against that other bland perfection, impervious to either, the mother's anxious face at his shoulder.

"Go on," the father said. "Pick it up." The two sisters stooped, broad, lethargic; stooping, they presented an incredible expanse of pale cloth and a flutter of tawdry ribbons.

"If I thought enough of a rug to have to git hit all the way from France I wouldn't keep hit where folks coming in would have to tromp on hit," the first said. They raised the rug.

"Abner," the mother said. "Let me do it."

---

① A brownish orange to light brown.

Unit Five Tone and Style
Chapter 10 Barn Burning

"You go back and git dinner," his father said. "I'll tend to this."

From the woodpile through the rest of the afternoon the boy watched them, the rug spread flat in the dust beside the bubbling wash-pot, the two sisters stooping over it with that profound and lethargic reluctance, while the father stood over them in turn, implacable and grim, driving them though never raising his voice again. He could smell the harsh homemade lye① they were using; he saw his mother come to the door once and look toward them with an expression not anxious now but very like despair; he saw his father turn, and he fell to with the axe and saw from the corner of his eye his father raise from the ground a flattish fragment of field stone and examine it and return to the pot, and this time his mother actually spoke: "Abner. Abner. Please don't. Please, Abner."

Then he was done too. It was dusk; the whippoorwills② had already begun. He could smell coffee from the room where they would presently eat the cold food remaining from the mid-afternoon meal, though when he entered the house he realized they were having coffee again probably because there was a fire on the hearth, before which the rug now lay spread over the backs of the two chairs. The tracks of his father's foot were gone. Where they had been were now long, water-cloudy scoriations resembling the sporadic course of a Lilliputian③ mowing machine.

It still hung there while they ate the cold food and then went to bed, scattered without order or claim up and down the two rooms, his mother in one bed, where his father would later lie, the older brother in the other, himself, the aunt, and the two sisters on pallets on the floor. But his father was not in bed yet. The last thing the boy remembered was the depthless, harsh silhouette of the hat and coat bending over the rug and it seemed to him that he had not even closed his eyes when the silhouette was standing over him, the fire almost dead behind it, the stiff foot prodding him awake. "Catch up the mule," his father said.

When he returned with the mule his father was standing in the black door, the rolled rug over his shoulder. "Ain't you going to ride?" he said.

"No, Give me your foot."

He bent his knee into his father's hand, the wiry, surprising power flowed smoothly, rising, he rising with it, on to the mule's bare back (they had owned a saddle once; the boy could remember it though not when or where) and with the same effortlessness his father swung the rug up in front of him. Now in the starlight they retraced the afternoon's path, up the dusty road rife with honeysuckle, through the gate and up the black tunnel of the drive to the lightless house, where he sat on the mule and felt the rough warp of the rug drag across his thighs and vanish.

"Don't you want me to help?" he whispered. His father did not answer and now he heard again that stiff foot striking the hollow portico with that wooden and clock like deliberation, that

---

① A caustic, unsuitable for cleaning fine fabrics.

② An insect-eating nocturnal North American bird of the goatsucker family, having spotted brown feathers that blend with its woodland habitat.

③ A very small person or being; after the Lilliputians, a people in *Gulliver's Travels* (1726) by Jonathan Swift.

outrageous overstatement of the weight it carried. The rug, hunched, not flung (the boy could tell that even in the darkness) from his father's shoulder struck the angle of wall and floor with a sound unbelievably loud, thunderous, then the foot again, unhurried and enormous; a light came on in the house and the boy sat, tense, breathing steadily and quietly and just a little fast, though the foot itself did not increase its beat at all, descending the steps now; now the boy could see him.

"Don't you want to ride now?" he whispered. "We kin both ride now," the light within the house altering now, flaring up and sinking. *He's coming down the stairs now*, he thought. He had already ridden the mule up beside the horse block; presently his father was up behind him and he doubled the reins over and slashed the mule across the neck, but before the animal could begin to trot the hard, thin arm came round him, the hard, knotted hand jerking the mule back to a walk.

In the first red rays of the sun they were in the lot, putting plow gear on the mules. This time the sorrel mare was in the lot before he heard it at all, the rider collarless and even bareheaded, trembling, speaking in a shaking voice as the woman in the house had done, his father merely looking up once before stooping again to the hame he was buckling, so that the man on the mare spoke to his stooping back:

"You must realize you have ruined that rug. Wasn't there anybody here, any of your women..." he ceased, shaking, the boy watching him, the older brother leaning now in the stable door, chewing, blinking slowly and steadily at nothing apparently. "It cost a hundred dollars. But you never had a hundred dollars. You never will. So I'm going to charge you twenty bushels of corn against your crop. I'll add it in your contract and when you come to the commissary you can sign it. That won't keep Mrs. de Spain quiet but maybe it will teach you to wipe your feet off before you enter her house again."

Then he was gone. The boy looked at his father, who still had not spoken or even looked up again, who was now adjusting the logger-head in the hame.

"Pap," he said. His father looked at him—the inscrutable① face, the shaggy brows beneath which the gray eyes glinted coldly. Suddenly the boy went toward him, fast, stopping also, suddenly. "You done the best you could!" he cried. "If he wanted hit done different why didn't he wait and tell you how? He won't git no twenty bushels! He won't git none! We'll gether hit and hide hit! I kin watch . . ."

"Did you put the cutter back in that straight stock like I told you?"

"No, sir," he said.

"Then go do it."

That was Wednesday. During the rest of that week he worked steadily, at what was within his scope and some which was beyond it, with an industry that did not need to be driven nor

---

① Hard to predict.

Unit Five　Tone and Style
Chapter 10　Barn Burning

even commanded twice; he had this from his mother, with the difference that some at least of what he did he liked to do, such as splitting wood with the half-size axe which his mother and aunt had earned; or saved money somehow, to present him with at Christmas. In company with the two older women (and on one afternoon, even one of the sisters), he built pens for the shoat① and the cow which were a part of his father's contract with the landlord, and one afternoon, his father being absent, gone somewhere on one of the mules, he went to the field.

They were running a middle buster② now, his brother holding the plow straight while he handled the reins, and walking beside the straining mule, the rich black sod shearing cool and damp against his bare ankles, he thought *Maybe this is the end of it. Maybe even that twenty bushels that seems hard to have to pay for just a rug will be a cheap price for him to stop forever and always from being what he used to be*; thinking, dreaming now, so that his brother had to speak sharply to him to mind the mule: *Maybe he even won't collect the twenty bushels. Maybe it will all add up and balance and vanish—corn, rug, fire; the terror and grief the being pulled two ways like between two teams of horses—gone, done with for ever and ever.*

Then it was Saturday; he looked up from beneath the mule he was harnessing and saw his father in the black coat and hat. "Not that," his father said. "The wagon gear." And then, two hours later, sitting in the wagon bed behind his father and brother on the seat, the wagon accomplished a final curve, and he saw the weathered paintless store with its tattered tobacco- and patent-medicine posters and the tethered wagons and saddle animals below the gallery. He mounted the gnawed steps behind his father and brother, and there again was the lane of quiet, watching faces for the three of them to walk through. He saw the man in spectacles sitting at the plank table and he did not need to be told this was a Justice of the Peace; he sent one glare of fierce, exultant, partisan defiance at the man in collar and cravat now, whom he had seen but twice before in his life, and that on a galloping horse, who now wore on his face an expression riot of rage but of amazed unbelief which the boy could not have known was at the incredible circumstance of being sued by one of his own tenants, and came and stood against his father and cried at the Justice: "He ain't done it! He ain't burnt ..."

"Go back to the wagon," his father said.

"Burnt?" the Justice said. "Do I understand this rug was burned too?"

"Does anybody here claim it was?" his father said. "Go back to the wagon." But he did not, he merely retreated to the rear of the room, crowded as that other had been, but not to sit down this time, instead, to stand pressing among the motionless bodies, listening to the voices:

"And you claim twenty bushels of corn is too high for the damage you did to the rug?"

"He brought the rug to me and said he wanted the tracks washed out of it. I washed the tracks out and took the rug back to him."

"But you didn't carry the rug back to him in the same condition it was in before you made

---

① A young pig just after weaning.
② A double moldboard plow that throws a ridge of earth both ways.

the tracks on it."

His father did not answer, and now for perhaps half a minute there was no sound at all save that of breathing, the faint, steady suspiration of complete and intent listening.

"You decline to answer that, Mr. Snopes?" Again his father did not answer. "I'm going to find against you, Mr. Snopes. I'm going to find that you were responsible for the injury to Major de Spain's rug and hold you liable for it. But twenty bushels of corn seems a little high for a man in your circumstances to have to pay. Major de Spain claims it cost a hundred dollars. October corn will be worth about fifty cents. I figure that if Major de Spain can stand a ninety-five dollar loss on something he paid cash for, you can stand a five-dollar loss you haven't earned yet. I hold you in damages to Major de Spain to the amount of ten bushels of corn over and above your contract with him, to be paid to him out of your crop at gathering time. Court adjourned①."

It had taken no time hardly, the morning was but half begun. He thought they would return home and perhaps back to the field, since they were late, far behind all other farmers. But instead his father passed on behind the wagon, merely indicating with his hand for the older brother to follow with it, and crossed the road toward the blacksmith shop opposite, pressing on after his father, overtaking him, speaking, whispering up at the harsh, calm face beneath the weathered hat: "He won't git no ten bushels neither. He won't git one. We'll ..." until his father glanced for an instant down at him, the face absolutely calm, the grizzled eyebrows tangled above the cold eyes, the voice almost pleasant, almost gentle:

"You think so? Well, we'll wait till October anyway."

The matter of the wagon—the setting of a spoke or two and the tightening of the tires—did not take long either, the business of the tires accomplished by driving the wagon into the spring branch behind the shop and letting it stand there, the mules nuzzling into the water from time to time, and the boy on the seat with the idle reins, looking up the slope and through the sooty tunnel of the shed where the slow hammer rang and where his father sat on an upended cypress bolt, easily, either talking or listening, still sitting there when the boy brought the dripping wagon up out of the branch and halted it before the door.

"Take them on to the shade and hitch," his father said. He did so and returned. His father and the smith and a third man squatting on his heels inside the door were talking, about crops and animals; the boy, squatting too in the ammoniac dust and hoof parings and scales of rust, heard his father tell a long and unhurried story out of the time before the birth of the older brother even when he had been a professional horsetrader. And then his father came up beside him where he stood before a tattered last year's circus poster on the other side of the store, gazing rapt and quiet it the scarlet horses, the incredible poisings and convolutions of tulle and tights and painted leers of comedians, and said, "It's time to eat."

---

① Ended.

Unit Five   Tone and Style
Chapter 10   Barn Burning

But not at home. Squatting beside his brother against the front wall, he watched his father emerge from the store and produce from a paper sack a segment of cheese and divide it carefully and deliberately into three with his pocket knife and produce crackers from the same sack. They all three squatted on the gallery and ate, slowly, without talking; then in the store again, they drank from a tin dipper tepid water smelling of the cedar bucket and of living beech trees. And still they did not go home. It was as a horse lot this time, a tall rail fence upon and along which men stood and sat and out of which one by one horses were led, to be walked and trotted and then cantered back and forth along the road while the slow swapping and buying went on and the sun began to slant westward, they—the three of them—watching and listening, the older brother with his muddy eyes and his steady, inevitable tobacco, the father commenting now and then on certain of the animals, to no one in particular.

It was after sundown when they reached home. They ate supper by lamplight, then, sitting on the doorstep, the boy watched the night fully accomplish, listening to the whippoorwills and the frogs, when he heard his mother's voice: "Abner! No! No! Oh, God. Oh, God. Abner!" and he rose, whirled, and saw the altered light through the door where a candle stub now burned in a bottle neck on the table and his father, still in the hat and coat, at once formal and burlesque as though dressed carefully for some shabby and ceremonial violence, emptying the reservoir of the lamp back into the five-gallon kerosene can from which it had been filled, while the mother tugged at his arm until he shifted the lamp to the other hand and flung her back, not savagely or viciously, just hard, into the wall, her hands flung out against the wall for balance, her mouth open and in her face the same quality of hopeless despair as had been in her voice. Then his father saw him standing in the door. "Go to the barn and get that can of oil we were oiling the wagon with," he said. The boy did not move. Then he could speak.

"What ..." he cried. "What are you ..."

"Go get that oil," his father said. "Go."

Then he was moving, running, outside the house, toward the stable: this the old habit, the old blood which he had not been permitted to choose for himself, which had been bequeathed him willy nilly and which had run for so long (and who knew where, battening on what of outrage and savagery and lust) before it came to him. *I could keep on*, he thought. *I could run on and on and never look back, never need to see his face again. Only I can't, I can't*, the rusted can in his hand now, the liquid sploshing in it as he ran back to the house and into it, into the sound of his mother's weeping in the next room, and handed the can to his father.

"Ain't you going to even send a nigger?" he cried. "At least you sent a nigger before!"

This time his father didn't strike him. The hand came even faster than the blow had, the same hand which had set the can on the table with almost excruciating① care flashing from the can toward him too quick for him to follow it, gripping him by the back of his shirt and on to tip-

---

① Intensely painful; agonizing.

toe before he had seen it quit the can, the face stooping at him in breathless and frozen ferocity, the cold, dead voice speaking over him to the older brother who leaned against the table, chewing with that steady, curious, sidewise motion of cows:

"Empty the can into the big one and go on. I'll catch up with you."

"Better tie him up to the bedpost," the brother said.

"Do like I told you," the father said. Then the boy was moving, his bunched shirt and the hard, bony hand between his shoulder-blades, his toes just touching the floor, across the room and into the other one, past the sisters sitting with spread heavy thighs in the two chairs over the cold hearth, and to where his mother and aunt sat side by side on the bed, the aunt's arms about his mother's shoulders.

"Hold him," the father said. The aunt made a startled movement. "Not you," the father said. "Lennie. Take hold of him. I want to see you do it." His mother took him by the wrist. "You'll hold him better than that. If he gets loose don't you know what he is going to do? He will go up yonder." He jerked his head toward the road. "Maybe I'd better tie him."

"I'll hold him," his mother whispered.

"See you do then." Then his father was gone, the stiff foot heavy and measured upon the boards, ceasing at last.

Then he began to struggle. His mother caught him in both arms, he jerking and wrenching at them. He would be stronger in the end, he knew that. But he had no time to wait for it. "Lemme go!" he cried. "I don't want to have to hit you!"

"Let him go!" the aunt said. "If he don't go, before God, I am going up there myself!"

"Don't you see I can't?" his mother cried. "Sarty! Sarty! No! No! Help me, Lizzie!"

Then he was free. His aunt grasped at him but it was too late. He whirled, running, his mother stumbled forward on to her knees behind him, crying to the nearer sister: "Catch him, Net! Catch him!" But that was too late too, the sister (the sisters were twins, born at the same time, yet either of them now gave the impression of being, encompassing as much living meat and volume and weight as any other two of the family) not yet having begun to rise from the chair, her head, face, alone merely turned, presenting to him in the flying instant an astonishing expanse of young female features untroubled by any surprise even, wearing only an expression of bovine interest. Then he was out of the room, out of the house, in the mild dust of the starlit road and the heavy rifeness of honeysuckle, the pale ribbon unspooling with terrific slowness under his running feet, reaching the gate at last and turning in, running, his heart and lungs drumming, on up the drive toward the lighted house, the lighted door. He did not knock, he burst in, sobbing for breath, incapable for the moment of speech; he saw the astonished face of the Negro in the linen jacket without knowing when the Negro had appeared.

"De Spain!" he cried, panted. "Where's ..." then he saw the white man too emerging from a white door down the hall. "Barn!" he cried. "Barn!"

"What?" the white man said. "Barn?"

Unit Five   Tone and Style
Chapter 10   Barn Burning

"Yes!" the boy cried. "Barn!"

"Catch him!" the white man shouted.

But it was too late this time too. The Negro grasped his shirt, but the entire sleeve, rotten with washing, carried away, and he was out that door too and in the drive again, and had actually never ceased to run even while he was screaming into the white man's face.

Behind him the white man was shouting, "My horse! Fetch my horse!" and he thought for an instant of cutting across the park and climbing the fence into the road, but he did not know the park nor how high the vine-massed fence might be and he dared not risk it. So he ran on down the drive, blood and breath roaring; presently he was in the road again though he could not see it. He could not hear either: the galloping mare was almost upon him before he heard her, and even then he held his course, as if the very urgency of his wild grief and need must in a moment more find him wings, waiting until the ultimate instant to hurl himself aside and into the weed-choked roadside ditch as the horse thundered past and on, for an instant in furious silhouette against the stars, the tranquil early summer night sky which, even before the shape of the horse and rider vanished, stained abruptly and violently upward: a long, swirling roar incredible and soundless, blotting the stars, and he springing up and into the road again, running again, knowing it was too late yet still running even after he heard the shot and, an instant later, two shots, pausing now without knowing he had ceased to run, crying "Pap! Pap!", running again before he knew he had begun to run, stumbling, tripping over something and scrabbling up again without ceasing to run, looking backward over his shoulder at the glare as he got up, running on among the invisible trees, panting, sobbing, "Father! Father!"

At midnight he was sitting on the crest of a hill. He did not know it was midnight and he did not know how far he had come. But there was no glare behind him now and he sat now, his back toward what he had called home for four days anyhow, his face toward the dark woods which he would enter when breath was strong again, small, shaking steadily in the chill darkness, hugging himself into the remainder of his thin, rotten shirt, the grief and despair now no longer terror and fear but just grief and despair. *Father. My father*, he thought. "He was brave!" he cried suddenly, aloud but not loud, no more than a whisper: "He was! He was in the war! He was in Colonel Sartoris' cav'ry!" not knowing that his father had gone to that war a private in the fine old European sense, wearing no uniform, admitting the authority of and giving fidelity to no man or army or flag, going to war as Malbrouck① himself did; for booty—it meant nothing and less than nothing to him if it were enemy booty or his own.

The slow constellations wheeled on. It would be dawn and then sun-up after a while and he would be hungry. But that would be to-morrow and now he was only cold, and walking would cure that. His breathing was easier now, and he decided to get up and go on, and then he found

---

① The reference is to the chief character in a popular and pervasive 18th-century nursery ditty about a legendary warrior. Originally this warrior figure may have derived from the character and exploits of John Churchill, duke of Marlborough (1650—1722).

that he had been asleep because he knew it was almost dawn, the night almost over. He could tell that from the whippoorwills. They were everywhere now among the dark trees below him, constant and inflectioned and ceaseless, so that, as the instant for giving over to the day birds drew nearer and nearer, there was no interval at all between them. He got up. He was a little stiff, but walking would cure that too as it would the cold, and soon there would be the sun. He went on down the hill, toward the dark woods within which the liquid silver voices of the birds, called unceasing—the rapid and urgent beating of the urgent and quiring heart of the late spring night. He did not look back.

Film Comment:

William Faulkner's *Barn Burning*: 41 minutes, color

Starring: Tommy Lee Jones & Diane Kagan

Screenplay by: Horton Foote

Directed by: Peter Werner

Abner Snopes (Tommy Lee Jones, Academy Award Winner) is a Southern tenant farmer whose unrelenting and violent nature proves to be his undoing in William Faulkner's "Barn Burning."

Snopes sets his employer's barn on fire when he thinks he's been treated unfairly. His son, Sarty, is horrified. Snopes escapes justice for lack of proof, but he and his family are told to move on. No sooner do they move than Snopes is offended by his new rich employer. Torn between trying to win his father's acceptance and his aversion to what his father will do, Sarty must make a decision and act quickly.

Adapted by Academy Award winning screenwriter Horton Foote, Faulkner's complex world of class divisions and hostile family relationships comes to life through a boy's attempt to liberate himself from hatred and poverty.

Film Scenes:

Scene 1: departure
Scene 2: the rug
Scene 3: the hearing
Scene 4: barn burning

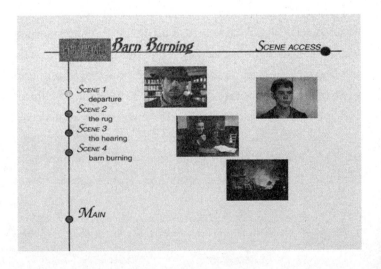

Unit Five Tone and Style
Chapter 10 Barn Burning

Script Excerpts:

During a country-store trial in which Abner Snopes is accused of burning down his employer's barn, his twelve-year-old son, Sarty, is called to the witness stand. Only the judge's compassion keeps him from being required to testify against his father. When the case is dismissed for lack of evidence and the father and his sons leave the store, Sarty hits an older boy who calls his father a barn burner. Immediately after Abner Snopes separates the two fighting youngsters and heads across the road, the following scenes begin.

Exterior. Grove of trees. Locusts and mulberry.
Across the road from the store.

The Snopes wagon is here piled high with their shabby belongings: a battered stove, broken beds and chairs, a clock inlaid with mother-of-pearl. Sarty's two sisters, twins but not identical, in their Sunday dresses, and his mother and aunt in calico and wearing sun bonnets, are in the wagon.

Close shot. The Mother.
She is crying.
The angle widens.
The mother sees Sarty and she draws her sleeve across her face and starts out of the wagon. Snopes sees her.

Snopes (*to his wife*): Get back in the wagon.
Mother: He's hurt. I've got to get some water.
Snopes (*to his wife*): Get back in the wagon.

He gets a willow switch and gets in the front of the wagon and takes the reins. The older brother gets up beside him. The boy climbs onto the wagon over the tailgate. Snopes hits the mules two savage blows with the willow switch but without heat, and they start on.

Lena: Glad to be getting out of this place.
Sarty's Point of view.
He watches the store disappear as the wagon turns a corner.
Lena (OC): I was counting the other day how many times we moved.
Donna Mae (OC): I counted, too. I got seven.
Lena (OC): I got nine.
Aunt (OC): Sh...
Lena (OC): Sh, yourself...
Back to Sarty in Wagon
Sarty (*to himself*): Maybe he's satisfied now, now that he has...
The angle widens.
As the Mother turns to him.
Mother: Did you say something, Sarty?

The American Short Story Through Film

Sarty doesn't answer her. His mother reaches out and touches him.
Mother: Does that hurt?
Sarty: Naw. It don't hurt. Lemme be.
Mother: Can't you wipe some of the blood off before it dries?
Sarty: I'll wash tonight. Lemme be, I tell you.

Moving shot.

As the wagon continues on through the desolate Mississippi countryside. The two sisters hum quietly to themselves. The Aunt closes her eyes as if trying to doze. Sarty looks over at his father beside his older brother, then he turns away and watches the fields and the houses that they pass.

Exterior. A grove of oaks and beeches. Late afternoon.

The Snopes wagon comes to a halt. The family begin to pile out and unload what they need to cook their supper and sleep on in the night.

Snopes: Sarty, git one of them fences rails and cut it up for firewood.

Sarty goes to the fence rail and pulls one of the rails loose. He brings it back to the wagon, gets a small axe out of the wagon, and then chops it up. When it's done, he goes to get another railing.

Snopes: That's enough.

Lena: What kind of fire is that going to make?

The father doesn't answer her and begins to assemble the wood in a small, neat, almost niggardly pile.

Close shot. Snopes's face.
As he builds the fire.
Angle. Sarty.
As he watches his father.

Exterior. Night.

The Snopes are around the small fire. The mother dishing out food into their iron plates.
Donna Mae: I'm cold. That ain't no fire at all.
No one answers her. She begins to eat her food.

Exterior. A grove of oaks and beeches. Late same night.

Sarty is sitting beside the small campfire, half asleep, still holding his iron plate.
Snopes (OC): Sarty...
The boy turns around and sees his father back in the shadows and follows him away from the campfire.
Sarty's POV.

Unit Five   Tone and Style
Chapter 10   Barn Burning

He can see his father against the stars but without depth, a shape black, flat, and bloodless, a face as though cut from tin or the iron folds of his frock coat which has not been made for him. The voice, when he speaks, harsh...like tin and without heat like tin.

Moving shot.

As the boy follows his father up a slope out into the star-lit road.

Snopes: You were fixing to tell them. (*Silence. The boy looks at him, but doesn't answer.*) You would have told them. (*Again the boy doesn't answer. He strikes Sarty with the flat of his hand on the side of his head, hard but without heat.*) You're getting to be a man. You've got to learn. You've got to learn to stick to your own blood or you ain't going to have any blood to stick to you. Do you think either of them, any man there this morning would? Don't you know all they wanted was a chance to get at me, because they knew I had them beat? Eh? (*The boy doesn't answer. He just stands there.*) Answer me.

Sarty (*whispering*): Yes.

His father turns.

Snopes: Get on to bed. We'll be there tomorrow.

Sarty starts back for the wagon.

Discussion Questions:

1. By what values does the boy's father live? Does the boy renounce all of them in the end? Is there a sense in which the boy is being true to his father by betraying him?
2. How is the principal conflict related to the "peace and joy" the boy feels at the sight of Major de Spain's house?
3. How is the language related to the point of view? Is it always appropriate to the experience being related or undergone by the point of view character?
4. Discuss concepts of justice that emerge from the story. What does the story say about the evolution of justice from its primitive to its more civilized forms?
5. How do the shifts of scene and setting serve to express the meaning of the unfolding action?
6. Is the tone of the story essentially optimistic or pessimistic?

Further Reading and Watching:

A Rose for Emily

Unit Six

Symbol

Chapter 11

Almos' a Man

Richard Wright

Author Introduction:

Richard Wright (1908—1960) was born at Rucker's Plantation near Natchez, Mississippi, the grandson of slaves, the son of a mill worker and a schoolteacher. Deserted by his father at an early age, he spent most of his childhood traveling through the South as his mother looked for work as a cook or maid. The family soon dissolved after her death, and Richard was forced into a series of orphanages and foster homes. After the ninth grade, he struck out on his own, living briefly in Memphis. In 1927 he turned up in Chicago, where he joined the Communist party and began to write. In 1937, Wright moved to New York, and he gained national attention for the collection of four short
stories entitled *Uncle Tom's Children* (1938). A growing reputation as a short story writer was solidified with the publication of his first novel, *Native Son* (1940), a pathetic and gory narrative of a young black man hurled blindly into crime. Wright moved to Paris in 1946, and became a permanent American expatriate. He died in Paris of a heart attack at the age of 52, though his daughter Julia claimed that her father was murdered. Much of Wright's literature concerns racial themes, especially those involving the plight of African Americans during the late 19th to mid-20th centuries. *Black Boy* (1945), a vivid personal narrative, was followed by the novel *The Outsider* (1953) and *Black Power* (1954), an extensive report on the African Gold Coast countries. Many of his stories are collected in *Uncle Tom's Children* (1938) and *Eight Men* (1961).

Story Summary:

Dave is a black teenage farm worker in the late 1930s. Misunderstood by his family, patronized by his elders, taken for granted by the man he works for, he is at the stage in

The American Short Story Through Film

his life when he is no longer a boy and not yet a man. With a second-hand gun that he persuades his mother to let him buy—"I'm almos' a man," he argues—he accidentally shoots a mule and opens himself anew to misunderstanding and ridicule. In a final act of resolve, he retrieves the gun he buried in panic—the very object that symbolizes his adulthood—and hops a passing freight train, to be borne off to somewhere he could "be a man," free at last from the bonds of family and place.

Key Terms:
Adolescence, Powerlessness, Adulthood, Responsibility, Identity

Almos' a Man[①]

Dave struck out across the fields, looking homeward through parting light. Whut's the usa talkin wid em niggers in the field? Anyhow, his mother was putting supper on the table. Them niggers can't understan nothing. One of these days he was going to get a gun and practice shooting, then they couldn't talk to him as though he were a little boy. He slowed, looking at the ground. Shucks, Ah ain scareda them even ef they are biggern me! Aw, Ah know whut Ahma do. Ahm going by ol Joe's sto n git that Sears Roebuck catlog n look at them guns. Mebbe Ma will lemme buy one when she gits mah pay from ol man Hawkins. Ahma beg her t gimme some money. Ahm ol enough to hava gun. Ahm seventeen. Almos a man. He strode, feeling his long loose-jointed limbs. Shucks, a man oughta hava little gun aftah he done worked hard all day.

He came in sight of Joe's store. A yellow lantern glowed on the front porch. He mounted steps and went through the screen door, hearing it bang behind him. There was a strong smell of coal oil and mackerel fish. He felt very confident until he saw fat Joe walk in through the rear door, then his courage began to ooze.

"Howdy, Dave! Whutcha want?"

"How yuh, Mistah Joe? Aw, Ah don wanna buy nothing. Ah jus wanted t see ef yuhd lemme look at tha catlog erwhile."

"Sure! You wanna see it here?"

"Nawsuh. Ah wans t take it home wid me. Ah'll bring it back termorrow when Ah come in from the fiels."

"You plannin on buying something?"

"Yessuh."

"Your ma lettin you have your own money now?"

"Shucks. Mistah Joe, Ahm gittin t be a man like anybody else!"

[①] The story first appeared in *Harper's Bazaar* in 1940 under the title "Almos' a Man." The final version of "The Man Who Was Almost a Man" was not published until 1960—the year of Wright's death—in a collection of short stories entitled *Eight Men*.

Unit Six Symbol
Chapter 11 Almos' a Man

Joe laughed and wiped his greasy white face with a red bandanna①.

"Whut you plannin on buyin?"

Dave looked at the floor, scratched his head, scratched his thigh, and smiled. Then he looked up shyly.

"Ah'll tell yuh, Mistah Joe, ef yuh promise yuh won't tell."

"I promise."

"Waal, Ahma buy a gun."

"A gun? Whut you want with a gun?"

"Ah wanna keep it."

"You ain't nothing but a boy. You don't need a gun."

"Aw, lemme have the catlog, Mistah Joe. Ah'll bring it back."

Joe walked through the rear door. Dave was elated. He looked around at barrels of sugar and flour. He heard Joe coming back. He craned his neck to see if he were bringing the book. Yeah, he's got it. Gawddog, he's got it!

"Here, but be sure you bring it back. It's the only one I got."

"Sho, Mistah Joe."

"Say, if you wanna buy a gun, why don't you buy one from me? I gotta gun to sell."

"Will it shoot?"

"Sure it'll shoot."

"Whut kind is it?"

"Oh, it's kinda old.... a left-hand Wheeler. A pistol. A big one."

"Is it got bullets in it?"

"It's loaded."

"Kin Ah see it?"

"Where's your money?"

"Whut yuh wan fer it?"

"I'll let you have it for two dollars."

"Just two dollahs? Shucks, Ah could buy tha when Ah git mah pay."

"I'll have it here when you want it."

"Awright, suh. Ah be in fer it."

He went through the door, hearing it slam again behind him. Ahma git some money from Ma n buy me a gun! Only two dollahs! He tucked the thick catalogue under his arm and hurried.

"Where yuh been, boy?" His mother held a steaming dish of black-eyed peas.

"Aw, Ma, Ah jus stopped down the road t talk wid the boys."

"Yuh know bettah t keep suppah waitin."

He sat down, resting the catalogue on the edge of the table.

---

① A large handkerchief usually figured and brightly colored.

The American Short Story Through Film

"Yuh git up from there and git to the well n wash yosef! Ah ain feedin no hogs in mah house!"

She grabbed his shoulder and pushed him. He stumbled out of the room, then came back to get the catalogue.

"Whut this?"

"Aw, Ma, it's jusa catlog."

"Who yuh git it from?"

"From Joe, down at the sto."

"Waal, thas good. We kin use it in the outhouse[①]."

"Naw, Ma." He grabbed for it. "Gimme ma catlog, Ma."

She held onto it and glared at him.

"Quit hollerin at me! Whut's wrong wid yuh? Yuh crazy?"

"But Ma, please. It ain mine! It's Joe's! He tol me t bring it back t im termorrow."

She gave up the book. He stumbled down the back steps, hugging the thick book under his arm. When he had splashed water on his face and hands, he groped back to the kitchen and fumbled in a corner for the towel. He bumped into a chair; it clattered to the floor. The catalogue sprawled at his feet. When he had dried his eyes he snatched up the book and held it again under his arm. His mother stood watching him.

"Now, ef yuh gonna act a fool over that ol book, Ah'll take it n burn it up."

"Naw, Ma, please."

"Waal, set down n be still!"

He sat down and drew the oil lamp close. He thumbed page after page, unaware of the food his mother set on the table. His father came in. Then his small brother.

"Whutcha got there, Dave?" his father asked.

"Jusa catlog," he answered, not looking up.

"Yeah, here they is!" His eyes glowed at blue-and-black revolvers[②]. He glanced up, feeling sudden guilt. His father was watching him. He eased the book under the table and rested it on his knees. After the blessing was asked, he ate. He scooped up peas and swallowed fat meat without chewing. Buttermilk helped to wash it down. He did not want to mention money before his father. He would do much better by cornering his mother when she was alone. He looked at his father uneasily out of the edge of his eye.

"Boy, how come yuh don quit foolin wid tha book n eat yo suppah?"

"Yessuh."

"How you n ol man Hawkins gittin erlong?"

"Suh?"

"Can't yuh hear? Why don yuh lissen? Ah ast yu how wuz yuh n ol man Hawkins gittin

---

① An outdoor toilet.
② A pistol having a revolving cylinder with several cartridge chambers that may be fired in succession.

Unit Six Symbol
Chapter 11 Almos' a Man

erlong?"

"Oh, swell, Pa. Ah plows mo lan than anybody over there."

"Waal, yuh oughta keep yo mind on whut yuh doin."

"Yessuh."

He poured his plate full of molasses and sopped it up slowly with a chunk of cornbread. When his father and brother had left the kitchen, he still sat and looked again at the guns in the catalogue, longing to muster courage enough to present his case to his mother. Lawd, ef Ah only had tha pretty one! He could almost feel the slickness of the weapon with his fingers. If he had a gun like that he would polish it and keep it shining so it would never rust. N Ah'd keep it loaded, by Gawd!

"Ma?" His voice was hesitant.

"Hunh?"

"Ol man Hawkins give yuh mah money yit?"

"Yeah, but ain no usa yuh thinking bout throwin nona it erway. Ahm keepin tha money sos yuh kin have cloes t go to school this winter."

He rose and went to her side with the open catalogue in his palms. She was washing dishes, her head bent low over a pan. Shyly he raised the book. When he spoke, his voice was husky, faint.

"Ma, Gawd knows Ah wans one of these."

"One of whut?" she asked, not raising her eyes.

"One of these," he said again, not daring even to point. She glanced up at the page, then at him with wide eyes.

"Nigger, is yuh gone plumb crazy?"

"Aw, Ma—"

"Git outta here! Don yuh talk t me bout no gun! Yuh a fool!"

"Ma, Ah kin buy one fer two dollahs."

"Not ef Ah knows it, yuh ain!"

"But yuh promised me one—"

"Ah don care whut Ah promised! Yuh ain nothing but a boy yit!"

"Ma, ef yuh lemme buy one Ah'll *never* ast yuh fer nothing no mo."

"Ah tol yuh t git outta here! Yuh ain gonna toucha penny of tha money fer no gun! Thas how come Ah has Mistah Hawkins t pay yo wages t me, cause Ah knows yuh ain got no sense."

"But, Ma, we needa gun. Pa ain got no gun. We needa gun in the house. Yuh kin never tell whut might happen."

"Now don yuh try to maka fool outta me, boy! Ef we did hava gun, yuh wouldn't have it!"

He laid the catalogue down and slipped his arm around her waist.

"Aw, Ma, Ah done worked hard alla summer n ain ast yuh fer nothin, is Ah, now?"

"Thas whut yuh spose t do!"

"But Ma, Ah wans a gun. Yuh kin lemme have two dollahs outta mah money. Please, Ma. I kin give it to Pa ... Please, Ma! Ah loves yuh, Ma."

When she spoke her voice came soft and low.

"Whut yu wan wida gun, Dave? Yuh don need no gun. Yuh'll git in trouble. N ef yo pa jus *thought* Ah let yuh have money t buy a gun he'd hava fit."

"Ah'll hide it, Ma. It ain but two dollahs."

"Lawd, chil, whut's wrong wid yuh?"

"Ain nothin wrong, Ma. Ahm almos a man now. Ah wans a gun."

"Who gonna sell yuh a gun?"

"Ol Joe at the sto."

"N it don cos but two dollahs?"

"Thas all, Ma. Jus two dollahs. Please, Ma."

She was stacking the plates away; her hands moved slowly, reflectively. Dave kept an anxious silence. Finally, she turned to him.

"Ah'll let yuh git tha gun ef yuh promise me one thing."

"Whut's tha, Ma?"

"Yuh bring it straight back t me, yuh hear? It be fer Pa."

"Yessum! Lemme go now, Ma."

She stooped, turned slightly to one side, raised the hem of her dress, rolled down the top of her stocking, and came up with a slender wad[1] of bills.

"Here," she said. "Lawd knows yuh don need no gun. But yer pa does. Yuh bring it right back t me, yuh hear? Ahma put it up. Now ef yuh don, Ahma have yuh pa lick yuh so hard yuh won fergit it."

"Yessum."

He took the money, ran down the steps, and across the yard.

"Dave! Yuuuuuh Daaaaave!"

He heard, but he was not going to stop now. "Naw, Lawd!"

The first movement he made the following morning was to reach under his pillow for the gun. In the gray light of dawn he held it loosely, feeling a sense of power. Could kill a man with a gun like this. Kill anybody, black or white. And if he were holding his gun in his hand, nobody could run over him; they would have to respect him. It was a big gun, with a long barrel[2] and a heavy handle. He raised and lowered it in his hand, marveling at its weight.

He had not come straight home with it as his mother had asked; instead he had stayed out in the fields, holding the weapon in his hand, aiming it now and then at some imaginary foe. But he had not fired it; he had been afraid that his father might hear. Also he was not sure he knew how

---

[1] A sizable roll of paper money.
[2] The metal, cylindrical part of a firearm through which the bullet travels.

Unit Six Symbol
Chapter 11 Almos' a Man

to fire it.

To avoid surrendering the pistol he had not come into the house until he knew that they were all asleep. When his mother had tiptoed to his bedside late that night and demanded the gun, he had first played possum;① then he had told her that the gun was hidden outdoors, that he would bring it to her in the morning. Now he lay turning it slowly in his hands. He broke it, took out the cartridges②, felt them, and then put them back.

He slid out of bed, got a long strip of old flannel from a trunk, wrapped the gun in it, and tied it to his naked thigh while it was still loaded. He did not go in to breakfast. Even though it was not yet daylight, he started for Jim Hawkins' plantation. Just as the sun was rising he reached the barns where the mules and plows were kept.

"Hey! That you, Dave?"

He turned. Jim Hawkins stood eying him suspiciously.

"What're yuh doing here so early?"

"Ah didn't know Ah wuz gittin up so early, Mistah Hawkins. Ah wuz fixin t hitch up ol Jenny n take her t the fiels."

"Good. Since you're so early, how about plowing that stretch down by the woods?"

"Suits me, Mistah Hawkins."

"O.K. Go to it!"

He hitched Jenny to a plow and started across the fields. Hot dog! This was just what he wanted. If he could get down by the woods, he could shoot his gun and nobody would hear. He walked behind the plow, hearing the traces creaking, feeling the gun tied tight to his thigh.

When he reached the woods, he plowed two whole rows before he decided to take out the gun. Finally, he stopped, looked in all directions, then untied the gun and held it in his hand. He turned to the mule and smiled.

"Know whut this is, Jenny? Naw, yuh wouldn know! Yuhs jusa ol mule! Anyhow, this is a gun, n it kin shoot, by Gawd!"

He held the gun at arm's length. Whut t hell, Ahma shoot this thing! He looked at Jenny again.

"Lissen here, Jenny! When Ah pull this ol trigger, Ah don wan yuh t run n acka fool now!"

Jenny stood with head down, her short ears pricked straight. Dave walked off about twenty feet, held the gun far out from him at arm's length, and turned his head. Hell, he told himself, Ah ain afraid. The gun felt loose in his fingers; he waved it wildly for a moment. Then he shut his eyes and tightened his forefinger. *Bloom!* A report③ half deafened him and he thought his right hand was torn from his arm. He heard Jenny whinnying and galloping over the field, and he found himself on his knees, squeezing his fingers hard between his legs. His hand was numb; he

---

① To pretend to be sleeping or dead.
② Bullets.
③ An explosive noise.

jammed it into his mouth, trying to warm it, trying to stop the pain. The gun lay at his feet. He did not quite know what had happened. He stood up and stared at the gun as though it were a living thing. He gritted his teeth and kicked the gun. Yuh almos broke mah arm! He turned to look for Jenny; she was far over the fields, tossing her head and kicking wildly.

"Hol on there, ol mule!"

When he caught up with her she stood trembling, walling her big white eyes at him. The plow was far away; the traces had broken. Then Dave stopped short, looking, not believing. Jenny was bleeding. Her left side was red and wet with blood. He went closer. Lawd, have mercy! Wondah did Ah shoot this mule? He grabbed for Jenny's mane[①]. She flinched, snorted, whirled, tossing her head.

"Hol on now! Hol on."

Then he saw the hole in Jenny's side, right between the ribs. It was round, wet, red. A crimson stream streaked down the front leg, flowing fast. Good Gawd! Ah wuzn't shootin at tha mule. He felt panic. He knew he had to stop that blood, or Jenny would bleed to death. He had never seen so much blood in all his life. He chased the mule for half a mile, trying to catch her. Finally she stopped, breathing hard, stumpy tail half arched. He caught her mane and led her back to where the plow and gun lay. Then he stooped and grabbed handfuls of damp black earth and tried to plug the bullet hole. Jenny shuddered, whinnied, and broke from him.

"Hol on! Hol on now!"

He tried to plug it again, but blood came anyhow. His fingers were hot and sticky. He rubbed dirt into his palms, trying to dry them. Then again he attempted to plug the bullet hole, but Jenny shied away, kicking her heels high. He stood helpless. He had to do something. He ran at Jenny; she dodged him. He watched a red stream of blood flow down Jenny's leg and form a bright pool at her feet.

"Jenny ... Jenny," he called weakly.

His lips trembled. She's bleeding to death! He looked in the direction of home, wanting to go back, wanting to get help. But he saw the pistol lying in the damp black clay. He had a queer feeling that if he only did something, this would not be; Jenny would not be there bleeding to death.

When he went to her this time, she did not move. She stood with sleepy, dreamy eyes; and when he touched her she gave a low-pitched whinny and knelt to the ground, her front knees slopping in blood. "Jenny ... Jenny ..." he whispered.

For a long time she held her neck erect; then her head sank, slowly. Her ribs swelled with a mighty heave and she went over.

Dave's stomach felt empty, very empty. He picked up the gun and held it gingerly between his thumb and forefinger. He buried it at the foot of a tree. He took a stick and tried to cover the

---

① The long hair along the top and sides of the neck of a horse.

pool of blood with dirt—but what was the use? There was Jenny lying with her mouth open and her eyes walled and glassy. He could not tell Jim Hawkins he had shot his mule. But he had to tell something. Yeah, Ah'll tell em Jenny started gittin wil n fell on the joint of the plow... But that would hardly happen to a mule. He walked across the field slowly, head down.

It was sunset. Two of Jim Hawkins' men were over near the edge of the woods digging a hole in which to bury Jenny. Dave was surrounded by a knot of people, all of whom were looking down at the dead mule.

"I don't see how in the world it happened," said Jim Hawkins for the tenth time.

The crowd parted and Dave's mother, father, and small brother pushed into the center.

"Where Dave?" his mother called.

"There he is," said Jim Hawkins.

His mother grabbed him.

"Whut happened, Dave? Whut yuh done?"

"Nothin."

"C mon, boy, talk," his father said.

Dave took a deep breath and told the story he knew nobody believed.

"Waal," he drawled. "Ah brung ol Jenny down here sos Ah could do mah plowin. Ah plowed bout two rows, just like yuh see." He stopped and pointed at the long rows of upturned earth. "Then somethin musta been wrong wid ol Jenny. She wouldn ack right a-tall. She started snortin n kickin her heels. Ah tried t hol her, but she pulled erway, rearin n goin on. Then when the point of the plow was stickin up in the air, she swung erroun n twisted herself back on it ... She stuck herself n started t bleed. N fo Ah could do anything, she wuz dead."

"Did you ever hear of anything like that in all your life?" asked Jim Hawkins.

There were white and black standing in the crowd. They murmured. Dave's mother came close to him and looked hard into his face. "Tell the truth, Dave," she said.

"Looks like a bullet hole to me," said one man.

"Dave, whut yuh do wid the gun?" his mother asked.

The crowd surged in, looking at him. He jammed his hands into his pockets, shook his head slowly from left to right, and backed away. His eyes were wide and painful.

"Did he hava gun?" asked Jim Hawkins.

"By Gawd, Ah tol yuh tha wuz a gun wound," said a man, slapping his thigh. His father caught his shoulders and shook him till his teeth rattled.

"Tell whut happened, yuh rascal! Tell whut ..."

Dave looked at Jenny's stiff legs and began to cry.

"Whut yuh do wid tha gun?" his mother asked.

"Whut wuz he doin wida gun?" his father asked.

"Come on and tell the truth," said Hawkins. "Ain't nobody going to hurt you ..."

His mother crowded close to him.

"Did yuh shoot tha mule, Dave?"

Dave cried, seeing blurred white and black faces.

"Ahh ddinn gggo tt sshooot hher... Ah ssswear ffo Gawd Ahh ddin... Ah wuz a-tryin t sssee ef the old gggun would sshoot—"

"Where yuh git the gun from?" his father asked.

"Ah got it from Joe, at the sto."

"Where yuh git the money?"

"Ma give it t me."

"He kept worryin me, Bob. Ah had t. Ah tol im t bring the gun right back t me ... It was fer yuh, the gun."

"But how yuh happen to shoot that mule?" asked Jim Hawkins.

"Ah wuzn shootin at the mule, Mistah Hawkins. The gun jumped when Ah pulled the trigger ... N fo Ah knowed anythin Jenny was there a-bleedin."

Somebody in the crowd laughed. Jim Hawkins walked close to Dave and looked into his face.

"Well, looks like you have bought you a mule, Dave."

"Ah swear fo Gawd, Ah didn go t kill the mule, Mistah Hawkins!"

"But you killed her!"

All the crowd was laughing now. They stood on tiptoe and poked heads over one another's shoulders.

"Well, boy, looks like yuh done bought a dead mule! Hahaha!"

"Ain tha ershame."

"Hohohohoho."

Dave stood, head down, twisting his feet in the dirt.

"Well, you needn't worry about it, Bob," said Jim Hawkins to Dave's father. "Just let the boy keep on working and pay me two dollars a month."

"Whut yuh wan fer yo mule, Mistah Hawkins?"

Jim Hawkins screwed up his eyes.

"Fifty dollars."

"Whut yuh do wid tha gun?" Dave's father demanded.

Dave said nothing.

"Yuh wan me t take a tree n beat yuh till yuh talk!"

"Nawsuh!"

"Whut yuh do wid it?"

"Ah throwed it erway."

"Where?"

"Ah ... Ah throwed it in the creek."

Unit Six Symbol
Chapter 11 Almos' a Man

"Waal, c mon home. N firs thing in the mawnin git to tha creek n fin tha gun."

"Yessuh."

"Whut yuh pay fer it?"

"Two dollahs."

"Take tha gun n git yo money back n carry it t Mistah Hawkins, yuh hear? N don fergit Ahma lam you black bottom good fer this! Now march yosef on home, suh!"

Dave turned and walked slowly. He heard people laughing. Dave glared, his eyes welling with tears. Hot anger bubbled in him. Then he swallowed and stumbled on.

That night Dave did not sleep. He was glad that he had gotten out of killing the mule so easily, but he was hurt. Something hot seemed to turn over inside him each time he remembered how they had laughed. He tossed on his bed, feeling his hard pillow. *N Pa says he's gonna beat me...* He remembered other beatings, and his back quivered. *Naw, naw, Ah sho don wan im t beat me tha way no mo. Dam em all! Nobody ever gave him anything. All he did was work. They treat me like a mule, n then they beat me.* He gritted his teeth. *N Ma had t tell on*① *me.*

Well, if he had to, he would take old man Hawkins that two dollars. But that meant selling the gun. And he wanted to keep that gun. Fifty dollars for a dead mule.

He turned over, thinking how he had fired the gun. He had an itch to fire it again. *Ef other men kin shoota gun, by Gawd, Ah kin!* He was still, listening. *Mebbe they all sleepin now.* The house was still. He heard the soft breathing of his brother. *Yes, now!* He would go down and get that gun and see if he could fire it! He eased out of bed and slipped into overalls.

The moon was bright. He ran almost all the way to the edge of the woods. He stumbled over the ground, looking for the spot where he had buried the gun. *Yeah, here it is.* Like a hungry dog scratching for a bone, he pawed it up. He puffed his black cheeks and blew dirt from the trigger and barrel. He broke it and found four cartridges unshot. He looked around; the fields were filled with silence and moonlight. He clutched the gun stiff and hard in his fingers. But, as soon as he wanted to pull the trigger, he shut his eyes and turned his head. *Naw, Ah can't shoot wid mah eyes closed n mah head turned.* With effort he held his eyes open; then he squeezed. *Blooooom!* He was stiff, not breathing. The gun was still in his hands. *Dammit, he'd done it!* He fired again. *Blooooom!* He smiled. *Blooooom! Blooooom! Click, click.* There! It was empty. If anybody could shoot a gun, he could. He put the gun into his hip pocket and started across the fields.

When he reached the top of a ridge he stood straight and proud in the moonlight, looking at Jim Hawkins' big white house, feeling the gun sagging in his pocket. *Lawd, ef Ah had jus one mo bullet Ah'd taka shot at tha house. Ah'd like t scare ol man Hawkins jusa little... Jusa enough t let im know Dave Saunders is a man.*

---

① Reveal the secret.

The American Short Story Through Film

To his left the road curved, running to the tracks of the Illinois Central. He jerked his head, listening. From far off came a faint *hoooof-hoooof; hoooof-hoooof; hoooof-hoooof...* He stood rigid. Two dollahs a mont. Les see now... Tha means it'll take bout two years. Shucks! Ah'll be dam!

He started down the road, toward the tracks. Yeah, here she comes! He stood beside the track and held himself stiffly. Here she comes, erroun the ben... C mon, yuh slow poke! C mon! He had his hand on his gun; something quivered in his stomach. Then the train thundered past, the gray and brown box cars rumbling and clinking. He gripped the gun tightly; then he jerked his hand out of his pocket. Ah betcha[①] Bill wouldn't do it! Ah betcha... The cars slid past, steel grinding upon steel. Ahm ridin yuh ternight, so hep me Gawd! He was hot all over. He hesitated just a moment; then he grabbed, pulled atop of a car, and lay flat. He felt his pocket; the gun was still there. Ahead the long rails were glinting in the moonlight, stretching away, away to somewhere, somewhere where he could be a man ....

Film Comment:

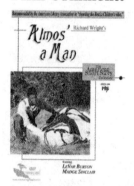

Richard Wright's *Almos' a Man*: 39 minutes, color
Starring: LeVar Burton & Madge Sinclair
Screenplay by: Leslie Lee
Directed by: Stan Lathan

Although Dave (LeVar Burton) and his family are poor sharecroppers in the Deep South in the 1930s, this 15 year-olds problem is shared by teenagers today: he stands with one foot in adulthood and the other in childhood. "Almos' a Man," yet still treated like a child, he struggles for an identity. There's one thing, one symbol of manhood, Dave thinks, that could guarantee him instant respect—a gun.

Dave finds a way to buy a pistol and at last, is ready to pull the trigger for the first time, never again will they call him a boy... But, he trembles, the gun overpowers the boy's body and he loses control—his young life forever changed.

Film Scenes:

Scene 1: to be a man
Scene 2: I want a gun
Scene 3: pump up!
Scene 4: the accident
Scene 5: running away

---

① Colloquial: bet you.

Unit Six Symbol
Chapter 11 Almos' a Man

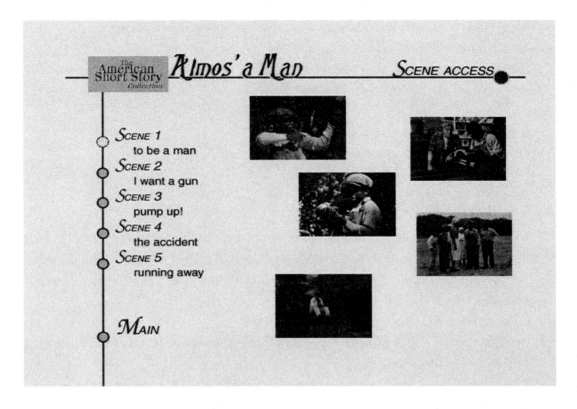

Script Excerpts:

Pushing a plow behind a mule, fifteen-year-old David Glover hears gunshots, as his white employer, Mr. Hawkins, goes hunting. When David daydreams about owning a gun of his own, his fellow field hands ridicule him. But the daydreams lead him to a general store where Mr. Joe, the owner, loans him a mail-order catalogue containing pictures of guns and offers to sell him a used handgun for two dollars. David returns home to eat supper with his mother Essie, his father Bob, and his younger brother. After supper, the following scene begins.

Interior. Kitchen. A little later that evening.

Medium shot of the kitchen. Essie is washing Dave's hair. The kitchen is empty with the exception of the two of them. Dave kneels over a large tub filled with water, as Essie hovers above him, kneading his hair. The whistle of a train can be heard in the distance. The scene conveys a quiet intimacy. Essie's scolding ways are but her means of loving Dave.

Dave: Momma, did—did Mr. Hawkins give you my pay yet?

Essie: Hold still, will you. He give it to me. Why you asking?

Dave: Nothing...I was just asking, that's all. (*Pause.*) Momma, can I show you something a minute?

Essie: I ain't through yet, David. Now you hold still.

Dave: Momma, just look at something a minute, will you? Just a minute—all right?

The American Short Story Through Film

Essie: David—all right. Wipe the soap from your face so's you don't burn your eyes. What is it I'm supposed to be looking at?

Dave (*wiping soap away with a towel and hurrying to the table, where the catalogue sits. He returns to her*): You see that one, Momma? That's the one—That's what I want to have. I really...

Essie: Boy, has you lost your mind?

Dave: Two dollars, Momma, that's what I can get it for—

Essie: Over my dead body you will.

Dave: Momma, you backing down on me now. You promised me I could have one some day.

Essie: I know what I told you, and the one thing you ain't is a man yet, so ...

Dave: I'm almos'! I sure wish everybody stop saying that! It's all right when I do something wrong. You and Poppa—"Young man this, and young man that." How come I'm a man then and not now—

Essie: You're not too big for me to spank now, David.

Dave: (*taking a precautionary step backward*): Momma, I mean it. If you let me, I promise I won't never ask you for nothing else...

Essie: Not one bit—you understand me? Why you think I told Mr. Hawkins to give me your pay, huh? 'Cause I know your foolishness, that's why. The money he give me is for your clothes for the winter, and ain't none of it's going for no nonsense, as hard as it is to make ends meet around here. Two dollars is a whole lot of money. (*He starts to protest.*) I don't want to hear another word, else I'm going to get your father to tan your hide. Now you get on back to the tub and let me finish what I was doing. Come on now!

Cut to

(*Close shot of Dave's face, the disappointment, the frustration.*)

Cut to

(*Medium shot of the kitchen. Dave hesitates and then goes to the tub, kneeling. Essie resumes washing, rubbing his head tenderly, starting to speak but stopping.*)

Dave: Momma, I—I ain't asked you for nothing all summer, has I? I done my work good...

Essie: That's what you're supposed to do, ain't it?

Dave: Yeah, Momma...Momma, I just want two dollars. I'll make it up real easy. All I has to do is work a little bit overtime. Mr. Hawkins—

Essie: Don't make me tired now, David. And hold your head still now.

Dave (*pause*): You know we needs a gun. Daddy ought to have one, the way folks is thieving around here. Remember last year when them men escaped from the state pen? You thought we needed one then! Come on, Momma, I get the gun and give it to Daddy—all right?

(*He pulls his head away from her hands and looks up at her, reaching simultaneously and stroking her arm. She starts to protest but pushes him again into a kneeling position and begins*

Unit Six Symbol
Chapter 11 Almos' a Man

massaging his hair.)

Essie (*smiling lightly at him*): You so restless. Ain't never seen nobody so restless...like some kind of jackrabbit. Restless!...Always been that way...(*pause.*) Your father'll have a fit if he knew I let you have some money for one of them things. Who's gonna sell it to you?

Dave: Mr. Joe said he would.

Essie: He did, huh?—the rascal! (*Pause, thinking.*) Folks work hard around here for two dollars. It just don't grow on no trees, David.

Dave: Momma, I told you I'd—

(*She shushes him, and is silent, sighing heavily. Dave turns away from her grasp and reaches up, rubbing her arm.*)

Cut to

(*A close shot of her face—thoughtful, deciding.*)

Cut to

(*A close shot of Dave's face—hopeful.*)

Cut to

(*A medium shot of both, Dave staring hopefully up at her. She responds after a moment by pushing his head toward the tub and beginning to rinse his hair.*)

Essie: All right, I'll let you get it, but—

Dave (*rising happily, kissing her cheek*): Oh, man! Oh, man, Momma, thanks!

Essie (*pushing him away*): Hold your horses now—just hold it, and sit right down here and let me finish.

(*He sits happily. She continues to rinse his hair and then begins drying him off with a towel.*)

Essie: I'll let you, but you has to promise me one thing. You get that gun and you bring it straight back here, you hear? (*He nods eagerly.*) We're getting it for your father, and I don't want no misunderstanding. You listening to me, boy?

Dave: Yes, ma'am. I'll go on up there tomorrow, soon as I finish my plowing—right after.

(*He rises quickly, taking the towel from her, and begins to dry his hair himself.*)

Dave: You...you gonna give it to me now—the money?

Essie: Don't you get so rambunctious now. Just take your time.

(*She rises slowly, as if still trying to be sure her decision. She stands, thinking, and then sighs, the decision made. Dave dries his hair vigorously, his eyes anxiously on her. She turns away and raises the hem of her dress, rolling down her stockings, pulling out the wad of bills, slowly peeling off two of them, and then puts the rolled-up wad back into her stocking.*)

Essie (*turning to him*): All right—for your father. So no whining, no lip, no nothing. And you get it and bring it straight back here and put it in my hand—tomorrow—right here! And I'll give it to him myself. You understand now?

The American Short Story Through Film

Dave (*eagerly*): Yes, ma'am. (*Dropping the towel on a chair.*)

Essie: All right...here...You got your money.

(*She hands it to him. He takes it in disbelief—two dollars! He grins, moving quickly toward her, kissing her, and then stares incredulously, happily, at the two dollars before jamming them into his pants pocket.*)

Dave: Thanks, Momma.

Essie: Yes, well...come here now. Sit yourself down and let me finish drying your head. You certainly ain't done it right. Come on, David, I ain't got time to fool.

(*He sits, happily, dreamily. She takes the towel and begins rubbing his head with it, making him wince slightly.*)

Essie (*sighing heavily. Off camera, over next shot*): Like a jackrabbit...just like a jackrabbit...

Time lapse cut

Exterior: Next day.

Dave running up road toward Mr. Joe's store.

Soft cut to

Dave running down steps of store with newly purchased gun in hand.

Discussion Questions:

1. What is the importance of the social setting in shaping Dave's motives and course of action?
2. How do the dialogue and limited point of view help reveal the meaning of local social pressures?
3. To what extent is the accidental shooting of the mule crucial to Dave's departure from home? Does it merely hasten him on a course he would in any case have followed?
4. What sort of future for Dave is implied by the last paragraphs?
5. Discuss the role of the minor characters in shaping Dave's character and in determining his actions.

Further Reading and Watching:

Eight Men

Chapter 12

The Sky Is Gray

Ernest Gaines

Author Introduction:

Ernest Gaines (1933—) was born in Pointe Coupee Parish, Louisiana, among the fifth generation of his sharecropper family. Although born generations after the end of slavery, Gaines grew up impoverished, living in old slave quarters on a plantation. When he was 15 years old, Gaines moved to Vallejo, California, to join his mother and stepfather, who had left Louisiana during the Second World War. After serving in the U.S. Army, he enrolled in San Francisco State College and graduated in 1957. He then won a creative writing fellowship to Stanford University. Gaines's boyhood experiences growing up in Louisiana provide the setting for many of his novels, and though none of his works is strictly autobiographical, his writing bears the distinctive stamp of the rural folk culture amid which he was raised. Although Gaines lived much of his life in San Francisco, he maintained close contact with Louisiana, the place and the people. As of November 2013, Gaines lives on Louisiana Highway 1 in Oscar, Louisiana, where he and his wife built a home on part of the old plantation where he grew up. Gaines has created an array of characters, conflicts, and themes as rich in their variety and in their universality as any in American literature. His main works are *Of Love and Dust* (1967), *Bloodline* (1968), *The Autobiography of Miss Jane Pittman* (1971), *A Long Day in November* (1971), *In My Father's House* (1978), *A Gathering of Old Men* (1984) and *A Lesson Before Dying* (1993).

Story Summary:

James is an eight-year-old black boy in rural Louisiana in the early 1940s. He valiantly tries to ignore a raging toothache. His mother has taught him not to complain, look for sympathy or squander money. After both aspirin and prayer fail to quell the toothache, his mother takes James to town to have it pulled. In the dentist's office they hear a preacher and a student quarrel about the troubles of black people. The dentist closes for lunch before getting to James. The boy and his mother must walk around hungry in the cold sleet until the office reopens, because they must save their money for bus fare home. The child hero in this odyssey begins to realize the world is complicated and neither black nor white.

Key Terms:

Personal Responsibility, Moral Behavior, Racial Injustice, Community Defined Values, Rite of Passage, Civil Rights Era

The Sky Is Gray[①] (Excerpts)

I

Go'n be coming in a few minutes. Coming round that bend down there full speed. And I'm go'n get out my handkerchief and wave it down, and we go'n get on it and go.

I keep on looking for it, but Mama don't look that way no more. She's looking down the road where we just come from. It's a long old road, and far 's you can see you don't see nothing but gravel. You got dry weeds on both sides, and you got trees on both sides, and fences on both sides, too. And you got cows in the pastures and they standing close together. And when we was coming out here to catch the bus I seen the smoke coming out of the cows's noses.

I look at my mama and I know what she's thinking. I been with Mama so much, just me and her, I know what she's thinking all the time. Right now it's home—Auntie and them. She's thinking if they got enough wood—if she left enough there to keep them warm till we get back. She's thinking if it go'n rain and if any of them go'n have to go out in the rain. She's thinking 'bout the hog—if he go'n get out, and if Ty and Val be able to get him back in. She always worry like that when she leaves the house. She don't worry too much if she leave me there with the smaller ones, 'cause she know I'm go'n look after them and look after Auntie and everything else. I'm the oldest and she say I'm the man.

I look at my mama and I love my mama. She's wearing that black coat and that black hat and she's looking sad. I love my mama and I want put my arm round her and tell her. But I'm not supposed to do that. She say that's weakness and that's crybaby[②] stuff, and she don't want no crybaby round her. She don't want you to be scared, either. 'Cause Ty's scared of ghosts and she's always whipping him. I'm scared of the dark, too, but I make 'tend I ain't. I make 'tend I ain't 'cause I'm the oldest, and I got to set a good sample for the rest. I can't ever be scared and I can't ever cry. And that's why I never said nothing 'bout my teeth. It's been hurting me

---

① First published in *Bloodline* (1963).
② A person who cries or complains frequently with little cause.

Unit Six Symbol
Chapter 12 The Sky Is Gray

and hurting me close to a month now, but I never said it. I didn't say it 'cause I didn't want act like a crybaby, and 'cause I know we didn't have enough money to go have it pulled. But, Lord, it been hurting me. And look like it wouldn't start till at night when you was trying to get yourself little sleep. Then soon 's you shut your eyes—ummmummm, Lord, look like it go right down to your heartstring.

"Hurting, hanh?" Ty'd say.

I'd shake my head, but I wouldn't open my mouth for nothing. You open your mouth and let that wind in, and it almost kill you.

I'd just lay there and listen to them snore. Ty there, right 'side me, and Auntie and Val over by the fireplace. Val younger than me and Ty, and he sleeps with Auntie. Mama sleeps round the other side with Louis and Walker.

I'd just lay there and listen to them, and listen to that wind out there, and listen to that fire in the fireplace. Sometimes it'd stop long enough to let me get little rest. Sometimes it just hurt, hurt, hurt. Lord, have mercy.

II

Auntie knowed it was hurting me. I didn't tell nobody but Ty, 'cause we buddies and he ain't go'n tell nobody. But some kind of way Auntie found out. When she asked me, I told her no, nothing was wrong. But she knowed it all the time. She told me to mash up a piece of aspirin and wrap it in some cotton and jugg it down in that hole. I did it, but it didn't do no good. It stopped for a little while, and started right back again. Auntie wanted to tell Mama, but I told her, "Uh-uh." 'Cause I knowed we didn't have any money, and it just was go'n make her mad again. So Auntie told Monsieur① Bayonne, and Monsieur Bayonne came over to the house and told me to kneel down 'side him on the fireplace. He put his finger in his mouth and made the Sign of the Cross on my jaw. The tip of Monsieur Bayonne's finger is some hard, 'cause he's always playing on that guitar. If we sit outside at night we can always hear Monsieur Bayonne playing on his guitar. Sometimes we leave him out there playing on the guitar.

Monsieur Bayonne made the Sign of the Cross over and over on my jaw, but that didn't do no good. Even when he prayed and told me to pray some, too, that tooth still hurt me.

"How you feeling?" he say.

"Same," I say.

He kept on praying and making the Sign of the Cross and I kept on praying, too.

"Still hurting?" he say.

"Yes, sir."

Monsieur Bayonne mashed harder and harder on my jaw. He mashed so hard he almost pushed me over on Ty. But then he stopped.

---

① Used as a form of polite address for a man in a French-speaking area.

"What kind of prayers you praying, boy?" he say.

"Baptist," I say.

"Well, I'll be—no wonder that tooth still killing him. I'm going one way and he pulling the other. Boy, don't you know any Catholic prayers?"

"I know 'Hail Mary,'[①]" I say.

"Then you better start saying it."

"Yes, sir."

He started mashing on my jaw again, and I could hear him praying at the same time. And, sure enough, after while it stopped hurting me.

Me and Ty went outside where Monsieur Bayonne's two hounds was and we started playing with them. "Let's go hunting," Ty say. "All right," I say; and we went on back in the pasture. Soon the hounds got on a trail, and me and Ty followed them all 'cross the pasture and then back in the woods, too. And then they cornered this little old rabbit and killed him, and me and Ty made them get back, and picked up the rabbit and started on back home. But my tooth had started hurting me again. It was hurting me plenty now, but I wouldn't tell Monsieur Bayonne. That night I didn't sleep a bit, and first thing in the morning Auntie told me to go back and let Monsieur Bayonne pray over me some more. Monsieur Bayonne was in his kitchen making coffee when I got there. Soon 's he seen me he knowed what was wrong.

"All right, kneel down there 'side that stove," he say. "And this time make sure you pray Catholic. I don't know nothing 'bout that Baptist, and I don't want know nothing 'bout him."

III

Last night Mama say, "Tomorrow we going to town."

"It ain't hurting me no more," I say. "I can eat anything on it."

"Tomorrow we going to town," she say.

And after she finished eating, she got up and went to bed. She always go to bed early now. 'Fore Daddy went in the Army, she used to stay up late. All of us sitting out on the gallery or round the fire. But now, look like soon 's she finish eating she go to bed.

This morning when I woke up, her and Auntie was standing 'fore the fireplace. She say: "Enough to get there and get back. Dollar and a half to have it pulled. Twenty-five for me to go, twenty-five for him. Twenty-five for me to come back, twenty-five for him. Fifty cents left. Guess I get little piece of salt meat with that."

"Sure can use it," Auntie say. "White beans and no salt meat ain't white beans."

"I do the best I can," Mama say.

They was quiet after that, and I made 'tend I was still asleep.

"James, hit the floor," Auntie say.

---

① A prayer based on the greetings of Gabriel and Saint Elizabeth to Virgin Mary.

Unit Six Symbol
Chapter 12 The Sky Is Gray

I still made 'tend I was asleep. I didn't want them to know I was listening.

"All right," Auntie say, shaking me by the shoulder. "Come on. Today's the day."

I pushed the cover down to get out, and Ty grabbed it and pulled it back.

"You, too, Ty," Auntie say.

"I ain't getting no teef pulled," Ty say.

"Don't mean it ain't time to get up," Auntie say. "Hit it, Ty."

Ty got up grumbling.

"James, you hurry up and get in your clothes and eat your food," Auntie say. "What time y'all coming back?" she say to Mama.

"That 'leven o'clock bus," Mama say. "Got to get back in that field this evening."

"Get a move on you, James," Auntie say.

I went in the kitchen and washed my face, then I ate my breakfast. I was having bread and syrup. The bread was warm and hard and tasted good. And I tried to make it last a long time.

Ty came back there grumbling and mad at me.

"Got to get up," he say. "I ain't having no teefes pulled. What I got to be getting up for?"

Ty poured some syrup in his pan and got a piece of bread. He didn't wash his hands, neither his face, and I could see that white stuff in his eyes.

"You the one getting your teef pulled," he say. "What I got to get up for. I bet if I was getting a teef pulled, you wouldn't be getting up. Shucks[1]; syrup again. I'm getting tired of this old syrup. Syrup, syrup, syrup. I'm go'n take with the sugar diabetes[2]. I want me some bacon sometime."

"Go out in the field and work and you can have your bacon," Auntie say. She stood in the middle door looking at Ty. "You better be glad you got syrup. Some people ain't got that—hard's time is."

"Shucks," Ty say. "How can I be strong."

"I don't know too much 'bout your strength," Auntie say; "but I know where you go'n be hot at, you keep that grumbling up. James, get a move on you; your mama waiting."

I ate my last piece of bread and went in the front room. Mama was standing 'fore the fireplace warming her hands. I put on my coat and my cap, and we left the house.

IV

I look down there again, but it still ain't coming. I almost say, "It ain't coming yet," but I keep my mouth shut. 'Cause that's something else she don't like. She don't like for you to say something just for nothing. She can see it ain't coming, I can see it ain't coming, so why say it ain't coming. I don't say it, I turn and look at the river that's back of us. It's so cold the smoke's just raising up from the water. I see a bunch of pool-doos not too far out—just on the other side

---

[1] Used to express mild disappointment, disgust, or annoyance.
[2] An informal or dialect word for diabetes mellitus.

The American Short Story Through Film

the lilies. I'm wondering if you can eat pool-doos. I ain't too sure, 'cause I ain't never ate none. But I done ate owls and blackbirds, and I done ate redbirds, too. I didn't want kill the redbirds, but she made me kill them. They had two of them back there. One in my trap, one in Ty's trap. Me and Ty was go'n play with them and let them go, but she made me kill them 'cause we needed the food.

"I can't," I say. "I can't."

"Here," she say. "Take it."

"I can't," I say. "I can't. I can't kill him, Mama, please."

"Here," she say. "Take this fork, James."

"Please, Mama, I can't kill him," I say.

I could tell she was go'n hit me. I jerked back, but I didn't jerk back soon enough.

"Take it," she say.

I took it and reached in for him, but he kept on hopping to the back.

"I can't, Mama," I say. The water just kept on running down my face. "I can't," I say.

"Get him out of there," she say.

I reached in for him and he kept on hopping to the back. Then I reached in farther, and he pecked me on the hand.

"I can't, Mama," I say.

She slapped me again.

I reached in again, but he kept on hopping out my way. Then he hopped to one side and I reached there. The fork got him on the leg and I heard his leg pop. I pulled my hand out 'cause I had hurt him.

"Give it here," she say, and jerked the fork out my hand.

She reached in and got the little bird right in the neck. I heard the fork go in his neck, and I heard it go in the ground. She brought him out and helt him right in front of me.

"That's one," she say. She shook him off and gived me the fork. "Get the other one."

"I can't, Mama," I say. "I'll do anything, but don't make me do that."

She went to the corner of the fence and broke the biggest switch over there she could find. I knelt 'side the trap, crying.

"Get him out of there," she say.

"I can't, Mama."

She started hitting me 'cross the back. I went down on the ground, crying.

"Get him," she say.

"Octavia?" Auntie say.

'Cause she had come out of the house and she was standing by the tree looking at us.

"Get him out of there," Mama say.

"Octavia," Auntie say, "explain to him. Explain to him. Just don't beat him. Explain to him."

Unit Six Symbol
Chapter 12 The Sky Is Gray

But she hit me and hit me and hit me.

I'm still young—I ain't no more than eight; but I know now; I know why I had to do it. (They was so little, though. They was so little. I 'member how I picked the feathers off them and cleaned them and helt them over the fire. Then we all ate them. Ain't had but a little bitty piece each, but we all had a little bitty piece, and everybody just looked at me 'cause they was so proud.) Suppose she had to go away? That's why I had to do it. Suppose she had to go away like Daddy went away? Then who was go'n look after us? They had to be somebody left to carry on. I didn't know it then, but I know it now. Auntie and Monsieur Bayonne talked to me and made me see.

Film Comment:

Ernest Gaines's *The Sky Is Gray*: 47 minutes, color
Starring: Olivia Cole & James Bond III
Screenplay by: Charles Fuller
Directed by: Stan Lathan

From Ernest J. Gaines, author of *The Autobiography of Miss Jane Pittman*, comes a deceptively simple, yet emotionally complex tale of a young boy's discovery of what it's like to be black in Louisiana during the 1940s.

James, the boy in question, has a raging toothache that necessitates a trip to the dentist. His mother (Olivia Cole, Emmy Award Winner), accompanies James to town on an eye opening odyssey where the boy gains valuable insights into poverty, racism—and his own sense of pride.

With an exciting musical score by Webster Lewis, this multi-award winning film explores a child's discovery that the world is a complicated place...where things are never truly black or white...only shades of gray.

Film Scenes:

Scene 1: the tooth ache
Scene 2: killing a bird
Scene 3: going to town
Scene 4: the dentist visit
Scene 5: the dance
Scene 6: the benefactor

The American Short Story Through Film

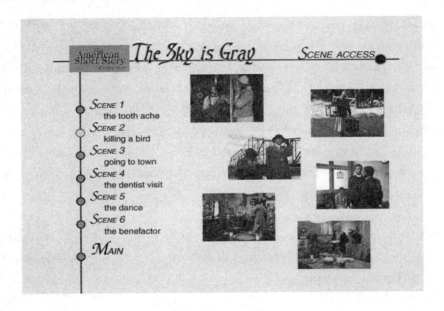

Script Excerpts:

Set in Louisiana in the early 1940's, the script opens by showing ten-year-old James's difficulty in working beside his mother, Octavia, because of a toothache he is hiding from his family. The next morning his aunt, Rosemary, overhears a conversation between James and Ty, his brother, which reveals his toothache—immediately prior to the following scenes.

Interior. Kitchen. Rosemary, James, and Ty. Bright morning.

Rosemary is cleaning up the kitchen after the morning breakfast. By their beds Ty and James put on their coats.

Rosemary: Hit it, James! Your Mama'll be finished cutting everything by the time you git out there! You too, Ty! (*Ty buttons up and starts out.*) Where's your hat? (*Ty stops, whirls around, grabs a hat from the foot of the bed, and darts out.*) James, how long your tooth been hurting you? (*James is shocked.*)

James: I ain't got no toothache!

Rosemary: Whose jaw was you holdin' last night? (*James reacts as though caught.*) Go git some aspirin and jugg it down in there! Wrap it in some cotton!

James nods and starts toward a chest of drawers.

Cut to: Rosemary and James

James's mouth is wide open and Rosemary reaches into it, placing cotton and aspirin on his tooth. She sits back.

Rosemary: Take your finger and press it in there! (*Rosemary rises as the boy does it.*) I'ma tell your Mama about it.

Unit Six Symbol
Chapter 12 The Sky Is Gray

James (*shakes his head*): Uh-uh! (*With difficulty.*) We ain't got no money, Auntie!

The statement surprises Rosemary, but she nods in acceptance.

Rosemary: Go on out to work, James.

James starts out. Rosemary looking after him thoughtfully, returning to her work.

Cut to: Exterior. Sharecropper's shack and farm. Same afternoon.

Camera opens on the front yard of the shack. In the foreground is a hog pen, where hogs are eating at a trough. Beyond it is the shack, a structure of wood and tarpaper, with a front porch and three rockers on it. Behind the shack is the road, on both sides of which are cane fields. To the left of the shack is a small vegetable garden and a wood pile. Chickens run about. The weather is cold. James walks into the frame carrying a bucket of slop for the hogs. He is pouring it into the trough when Rosemary appears at the door of the shack.

Rosemary: James! (*James reacts.*) Monsieur Bayonne is here! Come on in! (*James sets the bucket down and runs back toward the house.*)

Cut to: Interior. Kitchen. Monsieur Bayonne, Rosemary, Val, and James.

Monsieur Etienne Bayonne is a baldhead black man in a derby, coveralls, and waistcoat and boots. He wears wire-rimmed glasses and sports a wide mustache. He is well built and is pressing James to his knees by gently pushing on his shoulders in front of the stove. The almost ritualistic nature of the act has captured the attention of Val and Rosemary. They both watch a little awestruck. Bayonne ceremoniously makes the sign of the cross on James's jaw. James is a little frightened himself as Bayonne mumbles a prayer.

Bayonne (*repeating*): Through my fault, through my fault, through my most grievous fault.... (*He presses James's jaw and makes the sign of the cross again.*) How you feeling?

James: Same.

Bayonne (*bending forward praying and pressing James's jaw*): Through the power of the Holy Ghost—through him, with him, in the name of the Father, and the Son....(*He squeezes.*) Still hurting?

James: Yes, sir. (*Bayonne presses harder and James pulls away in pain.*)

Bayonne: What kind of prayers you praying, boy?

James: Baptist!

Bayonne: No wonder that tooth's still killing him! I'm going one way and he pulling another! Boy, don't you know any Catholic prayers?

James: I know "Hail Mary"!

Bayonne: Then you better start sayin' it!

James: Yes, sir! (*Starts mumbling the "Hail Mary," which is difficult with Bayonne's fingers pressing on his jaw.*) Hail Mary, full of grace...

Bayonne (*joining in*): ...the Lord is with thee! Blessed art thou! (*Presses harder.*) among woman. And blessed is the fruit (*Presses.*) of thy womb, Jesus! (*He lets go.*) How's that?

James (*astounded*): It stopped! (*Laughs. Everyone is pleased.*) It don't hurt! I'ma go out and play! (*Stands.*)

Octavia (OS, *outside, excited*): James! Come out here! You done caught a couple birds in your traps.

James (*elated*): I did?

He smiles, pleased, and hurries out.

Cut to: Exterior. Front yard. Octavia and James.

Octavia stands in the front yard holding two wooden cages. In each is a small excited bird. She is smiling as James runs out to greet her, followed by the family.

James: Can I keep them? (*Octavia sets them down and James bends over them examining the birds.*) Me and Ty could train 'em! (*Octavia ignores him.*) I could raise 'em, Mama!

Octavia (*suddenly*): Rosemary, get me a fork!

James is shocked and silent. He rises slowly as Rosemary gestures to Val to get the fork. James stares at his mother as Bayonne looks down at them.

Bayonne: They'll make a fine meal, Octavia.

Cut to: Another angle.

From inside the shack Val yells.

Val: I got it! (*In another moment she appears at the door and runs toward Octavia.*) I got it, Auntie! (*She hands the fork to Octavia, who turns to James.*)

James: I can't! (*Octavia hands it to him.*) I can't!

Octavia: Here. Take this fork, James.

James: Please, Mama, I can't kill him!

Octavia (*firmly*): Take this fork, James.

James has started crying and slowly, reluctantly, reaches for the fork. He takes it, bending over just as slowly above the cage. But for a moment he is frozen.

James: I can't Mama! (*He turns to her, appealing, then to everyone else. But there is no help.*) I can't!

Octavia: Get him out of there!

He continues to cry, but reluctantly reaches for the cage.

Cut to: James and cage.

James slowly unties the latch of the cage and cautiously slips his hand with fork under the lid. The bird is more excited. James jabs at it once, closing his eyes as he jabs. He jabs at it several times and misses each time.

Octavia (OS): Give it here!

Unit Six Symbol
Chapter 12 The Sky Is Gray

Cut to: Yard.

Octavia grabs James by the shoulders and yanks the fork from him, holds it up in a quick gesture of demonstration. She looks down at the cage for a moment, studying the bird's moments for a few seconds. Then with a sudden deathly swiftness jabs into the cage.

Cut to: Cage.

The bird is dead. The fork stuck into its bloody body.

Cut to: James and Octavia.

James is horrified. Octavia opens the cage, lifts the bird out on the end of the fork, and shows it to James. Then sits it on top of the cage and removes the fork.

Octavia: That's one. (*She hands the fork to James, demonstrating the manner in which he is to hold it.*) Get the other one.

James: I can't, Mama. I'll do anything, but don't make me do that!

Octavia: James, you get him out of there! (*James shakes his head no and Octavia slaps him on the rear of his head.*) Get him out of there! (*She slaps him again.*) Get him! (*She rears back to hit him again.*)

Rosemary: (*stopping Octavia*): Octavia! Explain to the child! Just don't beat him! Explain to him!

Octavia (*as if she hadn't heard*): James! Get him out!

She does not hit him but her tone is final. For a moment the boy is motionless, then, quickly, haphazardly, he begins to stab into the other cage, trying not to look but increasing his pace. Jabbing. Again, and again, and again.

Cut to: Interior. Kitchen. Family and Bayonne. Evening.

Everyone is seated around the table, where the small remains of the two birds sit on a plate in the center. Everyone has eaten and seems happy. Everyone except James. He sits looking forlorn, staring at the remains. The food on his own plate touched only slightly. His tooth seems to have started hurting again. His mouth is closed tightly. Rosemary jabs Bayonne, who is startled.

Bayonne: What? (*Rosemary looks at him, irritated.*) Sh. (*To James.*) You did a good job, James.

Ty: Yep. A pretty good job... I needed meat! (*Everyone laughs. James can't so he nods a little. Smiles.*)

Rosemary (*overlapping*): How you feel? (*James shrugs, then looks to Octavia. His mother looks at him for a long moment.*)

Octavia: James, tomorrow, we goin' to town.

James (*with difficulty*): It ain't hurting me no more...see? (*He smiles broadly.*) I can eat anything on it! (*He picks up a piece of meat and is about to demonstrate.*)

Octavia (*stopping him, calmly*): Tomorrow we goin' to town. (*James sets the meat down and shakes his head. Octavia rises.*) I'm tired. Goin' to bed. Good night. You and Ty don't be too far behind me, James.

She starts away. James looks after her, then back at the others.

Discussion Questions

1. What takes James to town?
2. What can we learn from the quarrel between the preacher and the student? What do you think of the argument between the old lady and the student in the dentist's office?
3. How do you read the walking of the mother and son back and forth of the street?
4. What does James learn from this eye-opening trip?
5. What do you think of the color image in the story, such as black, green, pink, white, red, and gray? What is the color of the sky?

Further Reading and Watching:

A Long Day in November

Appendix

I. A Brief Chronology of the American Short Story
1819—Washington Irving's "Rip Van Winkle" and "The Legend of Sleepy Hollow"
1821—*The Saturday Evening Post* established

Romantic Period: 1828—1865
1837—Nathaniel Hawthorne's *Twice-Told Tales*
1840—Edgar Allan Poe's *Tales of the Grotesque and Arabesque*
1843—*The Prose Romances of Edgar Allan Poe*
1846—Hawthorne's *Mosses from an Old Manse*
1850—Herman Melville's "Hawthorne and His Mosses"
1857—*Atlantic Monthly* established

Realistic Period: 1865—1900
1865—Mark Twain's "The Celebrated Jumping Frog of Calaveras County"
1868—Bret Harte's "The Luck of Roaring Camp"
1892—*The Yale Review* established
1893—Henry James's *The Real Thing and Other Tales*
1898—Stephen Crane's *The Open Boat and Other Tales of Adventure*

Naturalistic Period: 1900—1914
1900—Mark Twain's *The Man That Corrupted Hadleyburg and Other Stories*
1901—Edith Wharton's *Crucial Instances*
1905—Willa Cather's *The Troll Garden*
1906—O. Henry's *The Four Million*
1907—Jack London's *Love of Life*

Period of Modernism: 1914—1945
1922—F. Scott Fitzgerald's *Tales of the Jazz Age*
1925—*The New Yorker* established

1927—Ernest Hemingway's *Men without Women*
1933—Sherwood Anderson's *Death in the Woods and Other Stories*
1935—Katherine Anne Porter's *Flowering Judas and Other Stories*
1938—Richard Wright's *Uncle Tom's Children*
1942—William Faulkner's *Go Down, Moses*
      James Thurber's *My Life and Welcome to It*

Postwar Period: 1945—1963
1949—Shirley Jackson's *The Lottery*
1950—William Faulkner's *Collected Stories*
1953—J. D. Salinger's *Nine Stories*
1955—Flannery O'Connor's *A Good Man Is Hard to Find*
1962—John Updike's *Pigeon Feathers and Other Stories*

"Confessional" Period: 1963—1980
1963—Frank O'Connor's *The Lonely Voice*
1969—*The Collected Stories of Jean Stafford*, winning Pulitzer Prize
1971—Flannery O'Connor's *The Complete Stories*
1972—Ernest Hemingway's *The Nick Adams Stories*
1978—Isaac B. Singer winning the Nobel Prize for his life's work in the short story genre

Postmodern Period: 1980—
1980—*The Collected Stories of Eudora Welty*
1983—John Gardner's *The Art of Fiction*
1985—Bob Shacochis' *Easy in the Islands,* winning the American Book Award
1990—Stuart Dybek's *The Coast of Chicago*
1997—Annie Proulx's "Brokeback Mountain"

II. A Brief Glossary of Literary Terms

Antagonist—a character in a story that deceives, frustrates, or works against the main character, or protagonist, in some way. The antagonist doesn't necessarily have to be a person. It could be death, the devil, an illness, or any challenge that prevents the main character from living "happily ever after."

Character—a person who is responsible for the thoughts and actions within a story. Characters are extremely important because they are the medium through which a reader interacts with a piece of literature. Every character has his or her own personality, which a creative author uses to assist in forming the plot of a story or creating a mood.

Genre—a type of literature. We say a poem, novel, story, or other literary work belongs to a particular genre if it shares at least a few conventions, or standard characteristics, with other works in that genre.

Irony—a literary term referring to how a person, situation, statement, or circumstance is not as it would actually seem. Many times it is the exact opposite of what it appears to be. There are many types of irony, the three most common being verbal irony, dramatic irony, and cosmic irony.

Narrative—a collection of events that tells a story, which may be true or not, placed in a particular order and recounted through either telling or writing.

Narrator—one who tells a story, the speaker or the "voice" of an oral or written work. Although it can be, the narrator is not usually the author. The narrator is one of three types of characters: 1) participant (protagonist or participant in any action that may take place in the story); 2) observer (someone who is indirectly involved in the action of a story); or 3) non participant (one who is not at all involved in any action of the story).

Plot—the plot in a dramatic or narrative work is constituted by its events and actions, as these are rendered and ordered toward achieving particular emotional and artistic effects.

Point of View—a way the events of a story are conveyed to the reader, it is the "vantage point" from which the narrative is passed from author to the reader. The point of view can vary from work to work.

Protagonist—a protagonist is considered to be the main character or lead figure in a novel, play, story, or poem. It may also be referred to as the "hero" of a work.

Setting—the time, place, physical details, and circumstances in which a situation occurs. Settings include the background, atmosphere or environment in which characters live and move, and usually include physical characteristics of the surroundings.

Symbol—a word or object that stands for another word or object. The object or word can be seen with the eye or not visible.

Theme—a common thread or repeated idea that is incorporated throughout a literary work. A theme is a thought or idea the author presents to the reader that may be deep, difficult to understand, or even moralistic.

(The literary terms here are excerpted from M. H. Abrams' *A Glossary of Literary Terms*.)

III. A Brief Glossary of Film Terms

Types of Shots

Long Shot—(a relative term) a shot taken from a sufficient distance to show a landscape, a building or a large crowd.

Medium Shot—(also relative) a shot between a long shot and a close-up that might show two people in full figure or several people from the waist up.

Close-up—a shot of one face or object that fills the screen completely.

Extreme Close-up—a shot of a small object or part of a face that fills the screen.

Camera Angles

High Angle—the camera looks down at what is being photographed.

"Eye Level"—a shot that approximates human vision—a camera presents an object so that the line between camera and object is parallel to the ground.

Low Angle—the camera looks up at what is being photographed.

Camera Movement

Pan—the camera moves horizontally on a fixed base.

Tilt—the camera points up or down from a fixed base.

Tracking (Dolly) Shot—the camera moves through space on a wheeled truck (or dolly), but stays in the same plane.

Boom—the camera moves up or down through space.

Zoom—not a camera movement, but a shift in the focal length of the camera lens to give the impression that the camera is getting closer to or farther from an object.

Duration of Shots

Shots also vary in time from subliminal (a few frames) to quick (less than a second) to "average" (more than a second but less than a minute) to lengthy (more than a minute).

Editing

Cut—the most common type of transition in which one scene ends and a new one immediately begins.

Fade-out/Fade-in—one scene gradually goes dark and the new one gradually emerges from the darkness.

Dissolve—a gradual transition in which the end of one scene is superimposed over the beginning of a new one.

Wipe—an optical effect in which one shot appears to "wipe" the preceding one from the screen. Special wipes include flip wipes, iris wipes, star wipes, etc.

Sources of Sound in Film

Voice—over narration, dialogue, sound effects, and soundtrack music (underscoring).

(The film terms here are excerpted from Teasley & Wilder's *Reel Conversations: Reading Films with Young Adults*.)

IV. The American Short Story Collection

1. *Almos' a Man*—Richard Wright
2. *Barn Burning*—William Faulkner

Appendix

3. *Bernice Bobs Her Hair*—F. Scott Fitzgerald
4. *Blue Hotel, The*—Stephen Crane
5. *Displaced Person, The*—Flannery O'Connor
6. *Golden Honeymoon, The*—Ring Lardner
7. *Greatest Man in the World, The*—James Thurber
8. *Hollow Boy, The*—Hortense Calisher
9. *I'm a Fool*—Sherwood Anderson
10. *Jilting of Granny Weatherall, The*—Katherine Anne Porter
11. *Jolly Corner, The*—Henry James
12. *Love and Other Sorrows*—Harold Brodkey
13. *Man that Corrupted Hadleyburg, The*—Mark Twain
14. *Music School, The*—John Updike
15. *Parker Adderson, Philosopher*—Ambrose Bierce
16. *Paul's Case*—Willa Cather
17. *Pigeon Feathers*—John Updike
18. *Rappaccini's Daughter*—Nathaniel Hawthorne
19. *Revolt of Mother, The*—Mary E. Wilkins Freeman
20. *Sky Is Gray, The*—Ernest J. Gaines
21. *Soldier's Home*—Ernest Hemingway

References

Primary Sources

Anderson, Sherwood. "I'm a Fool" in *Horses and Men*. B.W. Huebsch, 1923.

Cather, Willa. "Paul's Case" in *The Troll Garden*. McClure, Phillips & Co., 1905.

Crane, Stephen. "The Blue Hotel" in *The Monster and Other Stories*. Harper & Brothers Publishers, 1899.

Faulkner, William. "Barn Burning" in *Collected Stories of William Faulkner*. Random House, Inc., 1950.

Fitzgerald, F. Scott. "Bernice Bobs Her Hair" in *Flappers and Philosophers*. Curtis Publishing Co, 1921.

Gaines, Ernest J. "The Sky Is Gray" in *Bloodline*. The Dial Press, 1963.

Hawthorne, Nathaniel. "Rappaccini's Daughter" in *Mosses from an Old Manse*. Houghton, Mifflin and Company, 1883.

Hemingway, Ernest. "Soldier's Home" in *In Our Time*. Charles Scribner's Sons, 1925.

Lardner, Ring. "The Golden Honeymoon" in *Round Up*. Charles Scribner's Sons, 1950.

Porter, Katherine Anne. "The Jilting of Granny Weatherall" in *Flowering Judas and Other Stories*. Harcourt Brace Jovanovich, Inc., 1930.

Thurber, James. "The Greatest Man in the World" in *The Middle-Aged Man on the Flying Trapeze*. Harper & Row, Publishers, Inc., 1935.

Wright, Richard. "Almos' a Man" in *Eight Men*. World Publishing Company, 1960.

Secondary Sources

Abrams, M. H. *A Glossary of Literary Terms* (10th edition). Boston: Wadsworth, Cengage Learning, 2012.

Beaty, Jerome, ed. *The Norton Introduction to Fiction* (6th edition). New York: Norton, 1995.

Bendixen, Alfred & James Nagel, eds. *A Companion to the American Short Story*. Hoboken: Wiley-Blackwell, 2010.

Bordwell, David & Kristin Thompson. *Film Art: An Introduction* (7th edition). New York: McGraw-Hill, 2004.

Cartmell, Deborah & Imelda Whelehan, eds. *The Cambridge Companion to Literature on*

Screen. Cambridge: Cambridge University Press, 2007.

Cassill, R. V., ed. *The Norton Anthology of Short Fiction* (7th edition). New York: Norton, 2006.

Charters, Ann. *The Story and Its Writer: An Introduction to Short Fiction* (7th edition). Boston: Bedford/St. Martin's, 2007.

Chatman, Seymour. *Story and Discourse: Narrative Structure in Fiction and Film*. Ithaca: Cornell University Press, 1980.

Corrigan, Timothy, ed. *Film and Literature: An Introduction and Reader* (2nd edition). London: Routledge, 2012.

Desmond, John M. & Peter Hawkes. *Adaptation: Studying Film and Literature*. New York: McGraw-Hill, 2006.

Emmens, Carol A. *Short Stories on Film and Video* (2nd edition). Littleton: Libraries Unlimited, 1985.

Gelfant, Blanche H., ed. *The Columbia Companion to the Twentieth-Century American Short Story*. New York: Columbia University Press, 2000.

Gordon, Jane Bachman & Karen Kuehher. *Fiction: An Introduction to the Short Story*. Lincolnwood: NTC/Contemporary Publishing Group, 1999.

Harrison, Stephanie, ed. *Adaptations: From Short Story to Big Screen*. New York: Three Rivers Press, 2005.

Hayward, Susan. *Cinema Studies: The Key Concepts* (3rd edition). London: Routledge, 2006.

Hitchcock, Bert & Virginia M. Kouidis. *American Short Stories* (8th edition). New York: Pearson Longman, 2007.

Kennedy, X. J. & Dana Gioia. *An Introduction to Fiction* (9th edition). New York: Pearson Longman, 2005.

Lothe, Jakob. *Narrative in Fiction and Film: An Introduction*. Oxford: Oxford University Press, 2000.

McFarlane, Brian. *Novel to Film: An Introduction to the Theory of Adaptation*. Oxford: Claredon Press, 1996.

Palmer, R. Barton, ed. *Nineteenth-Century American Fiction on Screen*. Cambridge: Cambridge University Press, 2007.

Palmer, R. Barton, ed. *Twentieth-Century American Fiction on Screen*. Cambridge: Cambridge University Press, 2007.

Pickering, James H., ed. *Fiction 100: An Anthology of Short Stories* (10th edition). Upper Saddle River: Prentice-Hall, 2003.

Sage, Howard. *Incorporating Literature in ESL Instruction*. Upper Saddle River: Prentice-Hall, 1987.

Scofield, Martin. *The Cambridge Introduction to the American Short Story*. Cambridge: Cambridge University Press, 2006.

Semali, Ladislaus M. *Literacy in Multimedia America: Integrating Media Education across the*

Curriculum. New York: Falmer Press, 2000.

Skaggs, Calvin, ed. *The American Short Story.* New York: Dell Publishing, 1980.

Stam, Robert & Alessandra Raengo, eds. *A Companion to Literature and Film.* Malden: Blackwell Publishing, 2004.

Stam, Robert & Alessandra Raengo, eds. *Literature and Film: A Guide to the Theory and Practice of Film Adaptation.* Malden: Blackwell Publishing, 2005.

Stevick, Philip. *The American Short Story 1900—1945: A Critical History.* Boston: Twayne Publishers, 1984.

Teasley, Alan B. & Ann Wilder. *Reel Conversations: Reading Films with Young Adults.* Portsmouth: Boynton/Cook Publishers, 1997.

Weaver, Gordon. *The American Short Story 1945—1980: A Critical History.* Boston: Twayne Publishers, 1984.